Study Guide

to accompany

Tavris • Wade

Psychology in Perspective
Second Edition

Nancy J. Gussett
Baldwin-Wallace College

 LONGMAN

An imprint of Addison Wesley Longman, Inc.

New York • Reading, Massachusetts • Menlo Park, California • Harlow, England
Don Mills, Ontario • Sydney • Mexico City • Madrid • Amsterdam

Study Guide
to accompany
Tavris/Wade, Psychology in Perspective, Second Edition

ISBN: 0-673-98420-6

97 98 99 00 01 9 8 7 6 5 4 3 2 1

TABLE OF CONTENTS

INTRODUCTION

Part I.   **Invitation to Psychology**

Chapter 1.   Explaining Human Behavior
Chapter 2.   Studying Human Behavior

Part II.   **The Biological Perspective**

Chapter 3.   The Genetics of Behavior
Chapter 4.   Neurons, Hormones, and Neurotransmitters
Chapter 5.   Evaluating the Biological Perspective

Part III.   **The Learning Perspective**

Chapter 6.   Behavioral Learning
Chapter 7.   Social and Cognitive Learning
Chapter 8.   Evaluating the Learning Perspective

Part IV.   **The Cognitive Perspective**

Chapter 9.   Thinking and Reasoning
Chapter 10.   Memory
Chapter 11.   Evaluating the Cognitive Perspective

Part V.   **The Sociocultural Perspective**

Chapter 12.   The Social Context
Chapter 13.   The Cultural Context
Chapter 14.   Evaluating the Sociocultural Perspective

Part VI.   **The Psychodynamic Perspective**

Chapter 15.   The Inner Life
Chapter 16.   Evaluating the Psychodynamic Perspective

Part VII.   **Putting the Perspectives Together**

Chapter 17.   The Whole Elephant

INTRODUCTION

The purpose of this study guide is to assist the student in effectively studying and learning the concepts, principles, and terminology presented in Psychology in Perspective, 2E by Carol Tavris and Carol Wade. The textbook and study guide are organized according to the five major perspectives that psychologists use to study human beings: 1. biological, 2. learning, 3. cognitive, 4. sociocultural, and 5. psychodynamic. Several textbook and chapters and study guide sections may correspond to each perspective.

One of the biggest advantages to learning about psychology is that it can help you in all your coursework. As you learn the psychological principles involved in learning, critical thinking, and memory, you can apply these principles and thereby develop and enhance your personal methods for academic success.

This introduction presents many ideas and suggestions for learning, studying, note-taking, time management, developing study groups, test-taking, motivating yourself, and managing test anxiety. (If you want a more detailed explanation of any of these skills, consult one of the excellent books listed under Suggested Readings at the end of this section.)

THE ORGANIZATION OF THIS STUDY GUIDE

Each chapter in this study guide corresponds to a chapter in your textbook. After reading and studying the material in the text and your class notes, you are ready to structure further studying and to check your understanding of the material by reviewing the relevant chapter in this manual.

You will note that there is a good deal of repetition in this manual; for each chapter, the Chapter Outline and the Chapter Summary follow the text material, and the sample test questions review the same material again. This is fully intentional; repetition improves learning and retention of the material. In particular, various types of exercises are used to help you to elaborate on and test your understanding of the material. By the time you read and re-read the chapter, attend class, review your notes, and complete the activities in this manual, you will have reviewed the same information five times or more, and you should know it very well.

Each chapter in this study guide contains:

Learning Objectives - You should begin by reading each of these carefully. The learning objectives describe the skills and the body of knowledge that are the outcome of your studying. After you finish studying, turn back to the learning objectives and evaluate yourself on each one.

Chapter Outline - This is a structured summary of the chapter material. It is written in full sentences or contains key phrases so that it will make sense by itself. If there is something in the outline you do not remember or understand, go back and review the relevant sections of your textbook.

Chapter Summary - This is a more detailed synopsis of the chapter with numbered blanks for you to fill in. The answers can be found in a separate section in the back of the manual. If you answer items incorrectly, review the relevant sections of your textbook. Occasionally, you might provide an equivalent term to the one found in the answer key. For instance, you could answer with a term like "reward" and find the term "positive reinforcement" in the answer key. These terms are roughly synonymous, so your answer is different but correct in this case. If you think your term is equivalent, it is still a good idea to check it by going back to the textbook.

Multiple Choice Self-test - These sample test items will help you further evaluate your retention of the textbook material. Each of these items has four alternatives, only one of which is the best answer. Some of these items can also be found in your instructor's test item file. Many of these items require you to apply concepts to novel situations. Therefore, you will be able to assess not only your learning of the concepts, but your understanding as well. Read and answer each item carefully. The answers can be found in the back of the manual. If you do not understand why you got an item wrong (or right, for that matter), review your textbook or see your instructor or teaching assistant. For each chapter a sample multiple choice item is provided with a rationale or solution explaining the reason for the best answer (and why the other alternatives are incorrect).

True-false Self-test - These sample test items will allow you to review the material and test your understanding in a different testing format. Follow the same procedure as with the other testing sections. The answers to these tests can also be found in the back of the manual. For each chapter a sample true-false item is provided with a rationale explaining why a particular item is true or false.

Key Terms - These are the same terms and definitions found in footnoted sections of your textbook. Read them carefully and make sure that you understand each term. You can use this section as a reference while you are working on other sections.

Suggested Research Projects - If you want to go beyond textbook learning into the application of psychological principles in the real world, you will find some suggestions here. You may want to see your instructor or teaching assistant for help in designing your research projects.

Suggested Readings - These books provide a more in-depth investigation of relevant topics of interest.

Audiovisual suggestions - These videos or movies provide an entertaining way of learning more about relevant topics of interest. Your instructor may show some of these in class.

The following sections provide many suggestions for success in this course. Feel free to tailor techniques to fit your own talents, learning style, and situation. If you want more detail, consult the books listed under Suggested Readings at the end of this section.

IN-CLASS

1. <u>Attend class regularly.</u> This seems like such a simple suggestion that it should go without saying, but it is amazing how often students miss class. If you miss class, you are likely to fall behind and you will have to guess at what the instructor is emphasizing. Students also tend to do something enjoyable when they skip class, like sleeping or relaxing. Behaviors followed by pleasant consequences tend to recur. If you do something pleasant when you skip class, you strengthen the habit of skipping class.

2. <u>Learn the style of your professor.</u> Talk to other students about your professor's style of teaching and testing. Also, talk directly to your professor. Some professors lecture. Others use experiential exercises in addition to lectures. Some require papers, some don't. Some professors follow the textbook faithfully in their lectures. Other professors expect you to learn the text on your own and provide supplementary material in class. Some professors give all multiple choice tests; others prefer a mixture of essay and multiple choice or even all essay. Learning the style of your professor can increase the likelihood of success in his/her class.

3. <u>Prepare for class.</u> Read or skim the material ahead of time. Outline the material before you come to class. You may even want to type an outline of a chapter and then you can fill in the details of the outline during the professor's lecture.

4. <u>Engage in active listening.</u> Listening is an underrated skill and is typically not formally taught. However, we learn as much as half of our information by listening, not only in the classroom, but by watching television or listening to the radio. Active listening requires that you:

➢ resist distractions.
➢ carefully pay attention to what the speaker is saying.
➢ anticipate forthcoming information.
➢ NOT evaluate until you have heard ALL of the message.
➢ silently paraphrase to increase understanding and repeat key information.

5. Takes notes effectively. Students tend to write down too little or too much. Students who write too much tend to be "stenographers", writing down everything the professor says without thinking. Other students fail to take notes on important information. Note taking should be an active process. Active note taking requires that you:

➢ Think about what to write before you write it down.
➢ Search for connections between ideas and themes in your notes.
➢ Review your notes after class so that you can note the weaknesses in your understanding of the lecture.
➢ Rephrase in your own words the notes you have taken.

6. Become aware of your learning style. People learn in different ways. Some people are auditory learners, some are visual. Some prefer lecture, others prefer hands-on experience. Learn how use other learning styles more effectively. You can't always control how information is presented. Learn your strengths and weaknesses. Your college or university may have personnel or resources available to help you learn more about your individual learning style and how to improve areas of weakness.

STUDYING

Many students find that they can perform effectively on tests by studying alone. Other students find they prefer to work in groups. However, students who work in groups not only tend to improve their class performance, but also learn other valuable skills. This section will discuss both individual and group study strategies.

INDIVIDUAL STUDY STRATEGIES

Structure the Environment

An important part of studying is setting up an effective study environment.

This includes:

1. A quiet study area. Some students prefer to study in their dorm rooms rather than the library. For some students this is effective. However, dorm rooms are notorious for being distracting environments. Dorms are wonderful places to watch television, meet new people, talk with friends, or relax. However, studying is better accomplished in a quiet environment where there are few interruptions. Commuter or non-traditional students may also find that an environment outside the home is less distracting, such as a public library or coffee shop.

2. <u>The correct tools</u>. Good lighting, pens, highlighters, and a comfortable chair or desk are essential. (If the chair you are using is TOO comfortable, you might fall asleep! For the same reason you probably shouldn't study in bed.) A personal computer can also be helpful for outlining the textbook or typing up and organizing class notes.

3. <u>The right time</u>. Many students may find that much of their studying may have to be accomplished at night. This is particularly true for students who work at part-time (or full-time) jobs or are involved in athletics or other student organizations. If possible, try to schedule your classes so that you have large blocks of time during the day to study before or after class. While some night studying is probably unavoidable, utilize time wisely during the day, if possible. For instance, non-traditional students may find that even an hour of studying at a lunch break at work, when they are more alert, can be very helpful rather than waiting to do all studying at night when they get home (after making dinner and helping children with homework!).

Studying

Each individual has his/her own style. What works for one person, may not be effective for another. Tailor your studying to your own individual preferences. If your strategy is not effective, you should consider modifying it.

A rough rule of thumb is to spend approximately two hours out-of-class for every hour in class. The amount of time spent studying will vary depending on the number of reading assignments and the complexity of the material. Studying includes not only reading the material but also reviewing it, understanding it, pondering it and memorizing it.

Reading the Textbook

1. <u>Plan to read approximately two chapters per week</u>. Stay "ahead of the game." Allow yourself at least one week prior to each exam just to concentrate on studying, NOT reading. All reading and re-reading should be accomplished well before the exam to allow time for understanding, integration, and memorization.

2. <u>Read the book at least 2-3 times</u>. Many students perform poorly on tests, mainly because they did not read the book more than once. In addition, students may "read" the book, but do not comprehend or understand what they read. Repetition helps with memorization. If you are not comprehending or understanding what you read, you may want to speak to your instructor. In addition, many colleges and universities have services that may help you improve your reading comprehension.

3. <u>Skim the chapter briefly</u>. Get an overview of what you are about to read.

4. <u>Read the chapter the first time carefully in a quiet place.</u> Many students prefer to highlight important concepts during the first reading. Some prefer to highlight later. Try to determine what is best for you. Enjoy your reading. Read as if you were reading any book.

5. <u>Re-read the chapter again.</u> At this point there should be some familiarity with the material. Re-read the chapters again approximately one week before each exam.

6. <u>Don't cram.</u> Read a fairly large chunk of material, but don't try to read too much at once. Read enough so that you remember several main points, but not too much that you become overly fatigued. If you are too tired when you are reading you probably won't remember very much of what you have read.

7. <u>Follow the SQ3R method.</u>

   1. Survey (S)
   2. Question (Q)
   3. Read (1R)
   4. Recite (2R)
   5. Review (3R)

This is a well-documented, effective technique for learning reading material by making the reader more active. SQ3R is shorthand for the five steps of the method, which are followed in sequence.

Survey: Skim the chapter and pay particular attention to major headings, pictures, graphs, captions, tables, and terms in boldface print or italics. Get a general idea of what you will be studying, how the chapter is organized, and how the topics are related to each other. Some people find it helpful to do this again for each new section they study.

Question: Before you read each section, ask yourself some questions about what will be covered and what you should learn. Also, during your reading of each section, ask yourself questions about what you are reading. For example, when you get to the section on "psychobabble" in the first chapter, you might wonder, "How can someone distinguish between a 'psychobabble' self-help book and one that contains more reliable information?" You might also want to apply the concept of "psychobabble" to experiences you have already had. For instance you might ask: "What are some examples of psychobabble that I've heard while watching talk shows, or have read about in popular magazines or self-help books?" You might also want to write down questions to discuss with other students or your instructor. Questioning helps you become active and involved in learning the material.

Read: Think actively about the material as you read. Try to find answers to your questions and think about the connections between topics not only <u>within</u> the chapter, but <u>between</u> chapters. Material you may have learned previously relates to material you may be currently learning and vice versa. Check the definitions of key terms highlighted in the textbook.

Recite: When you finish each section, recite its major points in your own words. You can structure this step by referring to relevant learning objectives. You can also write down the main points or definitions of key terms. This will help you to practice for examinations.

Review: Go back over all the material when you reach the end of the chapter. Try to see the "big picture" of the chapter by again focusing on its overall organization. If you can grasp the chapter's larger framework, the details will be easier to retain because they will fit into a specific place in this framework.

However, remember what helps some students to learn more effectively is not necessarily what may work for you. Find out what is an effective studying technique for you.

Understanding What You Have Read

1.   <u>Do a "reality check."</u> See if your understanding of the concept is consistent with other students or the instructor. If the instructor has an e-mail address and allows you to send him/her messages, ask the instructor to clarify your questions. It's fun and many instructors enjoy responding via e-mail and find it more convenient.

2.   <u>Use available resources.</u> Utilize psychology tutors or other resources available at your university or college.

3.   <u>Self-test.</u> Use the exercises in this book to test yourself to see whether or not you are understanding major concepts and terms. Study BEFORE you test yourself.

Memorization

Note: These memory strategies are also discussed in more detail in Chapter 8.

1.   <u>Give yourself enough time to memorize.</u> Distributed practice is better than massed practice. An important and well-established axiom of memory is that studying gradually over a longer period of time is typically more effective than "cramming" the night before.

2. <u>Effective memorization is a learned skill</u>. Effective memorization of complex material is NOT likely to involve rote memory or "cramming." Psychologists have found that **maintenance rehearsal**, or maintaining something for a very short time in your "working memory" by repeating it over and over again, does not result in long-term retention. However, psychologists have found that **elaborative rehearsal** involves imposing meaning on the material by relating it to information that you already know. For example, you might study classical conditioning (Chapter 5) by comparing its various components to behavior you have observed in your cat, who salivates at the sound of the electric can opener.

Another useful strategy for some types of material (particularly lists) involves the use of **mnemonics**. You probably remember ROYGBIV from grade school when you learned the colors of the rainbow.

You can also use **visualization** to help you remember material. For instance, remembering that a steel pole went through the <u>front</u> of Phineas Gage's skull (Chapter 4) will help you remember the structure, location, and function of the frontal lobe. You will read the tragic and highly memorable story of Phineas Gage. Visualizing this story as a movie in your head will help you remember.

GROUP STUDYING

Students often have a more positive educational experience when they collaborate with other students and actively discuss the material.   Not only do students learn the material better, but they also learn how to work with others more effectively as team members. However, there is the danger of what psychologists call **social loafing**, or failure to contribute to the group and reliance on others to do the work. A study group can be extremely helpful to group members, but only if group members are actively engaged in assisting each other. One way to reduce social loafing is to include making each member responsible and identifiable for reviewing, preparing and leading a discussion on a specific chapter or section of a chapter.   In addition, group skills are becoming increasingly important not only to be successful in college, but also in work environments.

BENEFITS OF GROUP WORK

Students benefit from group work because they:

- ➢ learn by teaching others.
- ➢ enhance interpersonal skills.
- ➢ debate and discuss concepts with other persons.
- ➢ may obtain better grades.

1. <u>Keep your study group small</u>. Effective groups generally consist of 3 - 5 persons. It is easier to find a common meeting time for a small group.

2.   <u>Set a regular meeting time and attend group meetings</u>. Agree on a time that is convenient for all persons in the group. Set up meetings in a quiet, comfortable location.

3.   <u>Write a brief group mission statement explaining group goals</u>. Goals should be reasonable, specific, high, yet attainable.

<u>Example:</u>

> "The mission of our study group is to learn and understand the material presented by the instructor and the textbook. We also want to learn how to apply psychology to our everyday life and increase our critical thinking abilities. One outcome of our efforts will be the attainment of at least a "B" grade in the class. Another outcome of our study group will be that we learn to increase our interpersonal communication and team skills."

A group mission statement provides an overall direction for the group.

4.   <u>Set sub-goals</u>. Clarify steps that are likely to be effective in reaching the group's overall goal. Set goals for each group meeting and document how well your group is meeting its goals.

5.   <u>Revise sub-goals</u>.

6.   <u>Clarify/assign group roles</u>. Typical group roles include a leader, a recorder (or secretary), and a facilitator. The leader is responsible for setting the agenda for the group meeting and for guiding the group's efforts. The recorder or secretary is responsible for taking notes, scheduling group meetings and distributing information to group members. The facilitator's role is to resolve group conflicts. Be flexible and rotate roles.

7.   <u>Conduct group process meetings</u>. Have meetings periodically to discuss and evaluate group process and clarify roles of group members. Group efforts may be stifled by group conflict, social loafing, or other behaviors. Some conflict is usually a natural part of working in a group. Discussion of how effectively the group is functioning and clarification of group roles can promote more effective learning and help the group attain its goals.

TYPES OF TEST QUESTIONS

Your tests may consist of a variety of types of questions, including multiple choice, true-false, short essay, or fill-in-the-blank. Your instructor may test only from the textbook or he or she may also test from supplementary information discussed in class.

Multiple Choice

Multiple choice questions usually consist of a stem and 3 - 5 alternatives, or a question that requires a response. The stem usually consists of a phrase that is to be completed by the alternatives. There is typically only one best answer to the question. While some "testwiseness" skills may help you to answer multiple choice questions better, testwiseness is usually no substitute for studying and learning the material. This is particularly true for well-written test items. Often testwiseness hints rely on the student finding flaws in item writing that may not exist. For example, while it is true that an alternative containing absolute terms, such as "always" or "never," is probably the wrong answer, it is also true that well-written multiple choice tests often do not contain such flaws. If you are unsure of an answer, narrow your choice to the two best alternatives and eliminate the ones that are obviously incorrect, if possible.

Most multiple choice questions test knowledge of terms, comprehension and understanding of important principles or concepts, and your ability to apply your knowledge of the subject to particular, concrete situations. For example, you might not only have to know that the operant conditioning technique of shaping involves reinforcing successive approximations to a target behavior, but also that you might be asked a question about how you would apply your knowledge of shaping to train your dog to sit up.

True-False

True-false questions consist of a short statement, which you are to evaluate and indicate whether or not it is true or false. Try to determine why you are evaluating a statement as true or false and you are more likely to be correct.

Essays

Essays usually consist of a single question or a question with several parts. Make sure you answer the essay in the manner directed by the question. For example, if a question asks you to compare and contrast behaviorism with cognitive psychology, you should make sure that in your answer you do just that.

<u>Fill-in-the blank</u>

Fill-in-the blank items consist of a sentence that is to be completed with the correct word or phrase. Make sure the word or phrase you select makes sense within the context of the sentence.

TAKING TESTS

1. <u>Learn to handle your anxiety</u>. Preparation tends to reduce anxiety. If you have prepared well for a test you will be less likely to be anxious. Some students (even well-prepared ones) tend to find that they still have an unreasonable degree of anxiety over tests. Many colleges and universities have counseling services to help students overcome test anxiety.

2. <u>Get sleep before the test</u>. If you are too tired to think clearly your exam performance will be affected. You will be able to get sufficient rest before a test if you avoid cramming. Learning a little at one time aids retention and also helps you avoid having to try to learn everything at the last minute.

MOTIVATION AND TIME MANAGEMENT

1. <u>Think about studying in positive terms</u>. When you tell yourself, "I have to study," you may feel resentful and deprived. The truth is, you really don't have to study if you don't want to. You want to study because it will benefit you. This doesn't mean you have to always enjoy studying, but it does mean you have control over your behavior. Learning new information enriches your life, especially if you learn the connection between it and your own life. Chapter 6 explains how interpretations of events have important implications for emotion and behavior.

2. <u>Prioritize your time</u>. Get a planner or organizer and carry it with you. Schedule your class times, work times, meal times, activities, and study time as appointments. Get a pocket electronic personal organizer if a planner is too bulky. Schedule time for fun activities as well as work and studying.

3. <u>Put it in perspective</u>. How do the classes you are taking relate to what you will be doing when you graduate from college? Relate the material to your workplace, to your career goals, and to your personal development. If something is personally meaningful it tends to be more likely to motivate your behavior.

SUGGESTED READINGS

Ellis, A.E., & Knaus, W.J. (1977). *Overcoming Procrastination*. New York: Signet. A description of thinking styles and behaviors that perpetuatue procrastination, along with strategies for dealing with the problem.

Flemming, L.E., & Leet, J. (1994). *Becoming a Successful Student*. New York: HarperCollins. A collection of strategies for maximizing your potential as a student.

Greenberg, J.S. (1994). *Comprehensive Stress Management* (3rd ed.). Dubuque, IA: Brown and Benchmark. A textbook on the effects of stress and a large variety of strategies for dealing with stress.

Lakein, A. (1973). *How to Get Control of Your Time and Your Life*. New York: Signet. A time management self-help guide.

Mealy, M. (1995). *Studying for Psychology*. New York: HarperCollins. A description of study skills for specific application to psychology.

Schmitt, D.E. (1992). *The Winning Edge: Maximizing success in college*. New York: HarperCollins. A guide for making the most of your academic potential.

PART I

INVITATION TO PSYCHOLOGY

CHAPTER 1

EXPLAINING HUMAN BEHAVIOR

LEARNING OBJECTIVES

After reading and studying this chapter, you should be able to:

1. Explain the difference between scientific psychology and pseudoscience.

2. Identify the characteristics of psychobabble.

3. Critically evaluate some examples of popular pseudosciences (e.g., astrology, psychics).

4. Explain the characteristics of critical thinking.

5. Demonstrate critical thinking in approaching some problem or question.

6. Describe the origins of psychology as a formal science.

7. Explain the difference between a Ph.D. and a Psy.D.

8. Explain the difference between a psychologist, psychiatrist, psychoanalyst, and a psychotherapist.

9. Compare and contrast the five major perspectives in psychology.

10. Explain humanistic psychology.

11. Explain feminist psychology.

CHAPTER OUTLINE

I. Introduction
   A. **Psychology** is the scientific study of behavior and mental processes and how they are affected by an organism's physical state, mental state, and external environment.
      1. The methods of psychology distinguish it from other fields that study behavior, such as literature, philosophy, or history.
      2. The methods of psychology distinguish it from popular, nonscientific explanations for behavior.

II. Pseudoscience and Psychobabble
   A. **Psychobabble** - language or terminology that appears to be psychological on the surface but is pseudoscientific and vague.
   B. **Pseudoscience** - "pseudo" means false; hence, "false science."
   C. Characteristics of psychobabble/pseudoscience:
      1. Promise quick fixes for emotional problems.
      2. Use vague and scientific-sounding language.
      3. Often exploit trust and belief in technology.
      4. Research evidence doesn't support claims.
      5. Provide simplistic answers.
      6. Confirm existing beliefs and prejudices rather than challenging them.
      7. Often make predictions after the fact, rather than in advance of the predicted event.
   D. The distinction between pseudoscience (or popular opinion) and psychology is important because major decisions are often based on psychological information.
   E. People often rely only on confirming cases as evidence for their beliefs (e.g., cases of abused children who become abusive adults as evidence that all or a majority of abused children will be abusers).

III. **Critical thinking** is the ability and willingness to assess claims and make objective judgments on the basis of well-supported reasons. (This will also be called **reflective judgment** in Chapter 9.)
   A. Characteristics of critical thinking:
      1. Involves ability to look for flaws in arguments; follows rules of logic.
      2. Involves ability to resist claims that have no supporting evidence.
      3. Is not merely negative thinking (thinks of alternatives as well criticizes).
      4. Fosters ability to be creative and constructive.
      5. Takes effort and practice to develop skills.
      6. All opinions are NOT created equal (must provide **empirical** evidence).

7. Formulates questions so that they do NOT presuppose the existence of what is being studied.
8. Involves a continuing process rather than a once-and-for-all accomplishment.

B. Critical thinking is especially relevant to psychology because psychology:
1. includes the study of reasoning, problem-solving, and creativity.
2. includes the study of <u>barriers</u> to critical thinking.
3. generates many competing findings on topics of personal/social relevance.

C. There are eight essential guidelines for critical thinking:
1. Ask questions; be willing to wonder.
2. Define the problem.
3. Examine the empirical evidence (**Empirical evidence** - evidence gathered by careful observation, experimentation, and measurement).
4. Analyze assumptions and biases.
5. Avoid emotional reasoning.
6. Don't oversimplify or argue by anecdote (**Arguing by anecdote** - generalizing from a personal experience or a few examples to everyone).
7. Consider other interpretations and utilize Occam's Razor (**Occam's Razor** - the explanation that requires the fewest assumptions is the best).
8. Tolerate uncertainty.

IV. Psychology Past and Present
A. Forerunners of modern psychology were philosophy, natural science, and medicine. Early investigators did not always rely on empirical evidence.
B. Psychology as a formal science began in 1879 in Germany with **Wilhelm Wundt**, who established the first psychological laboratory.
1. Wundt's method of **trained introspection** - observation and analysis of one's own mental experience under controlled conditions - was rejected as too subjective.
2. **Functionalism** emphasized the purpose of behavior - how behavior helped adaptation. The American **William James** was an early leader. Functionalism was inspired in part by **Charles Darwin's theory of evolution**.
C. Psychology as a method of psychotherapy began in Austria around 1900 with **Sigmund Freud**.
D. Despite the stereotype of the psychologist as a psychotherapist, psychology is a highly diverse field. Most professional activity falls into one of three categories:
1. **Teaching and research** in colleges and universities.
2. Providing health or mental health services referred to as **professional practice**.

3. Conducting and using **applied research** - relating psychological findings to nonacademic settings. Psychologists who conduct applied research or consult may work in hospitals, mental-health clinics, industry, law, and other settings. Many psychologists move flexibly across these three areas.

E. Research falls into two categories:
    1. Basic or "pure" research attempts to gain knowledge about a problem.
    2. Applied research is concerned with the practical uses of knowledge.

F. Psychologist Practitioners - goal is to understand and improve physical and mental health.
    1. **Counseling psychologists** - help people with problems of everyday life.
    2. **School psychologists** - work with parents and students to improve students' performance and resolve emotional difficulties.
    3. **Clinical psychologists** - diagnose, treat, and study mental or emotional problems and disabilities, including those highly disturbed.
    4. License to practice clinical psychology generally requires a Ph.D. Some practitioners have an Ed.D. or Psy.D.
    5. Psy.D. programs focus on professional practice and do not require a dissertation (a scholarly research project) like the Ph.D. Ph.D.s are trained as scientists and practitioners.

G. **Psychiatry** is the medical specialty concerned with mental and emotional disorders (M.D.s). Compared to psychologists, psychiatrists are:
    1. more likely to treat severe mental disorders.
    2. more medically oriented.
    3. able to prescribe medicine.
    4. often NOT trained in theories and methods of modern psychology.
    5. often likely to look for physical rather than psychological or social origins of mental disorders.

H. **Psychoanalyst** - person who practices one highly specific form of therapy: psychoanalysis.

I. **Psychotherapist** - a generic term for anyone who does any kind of therapy. The label typically is not regulated by law.

V. The Five Psychological Perspectives
A. There are five leading approaches to studying and explaining mental processes and behavior. Each has its own questions, assumptions, and explanations.
    1. **Biological perspective** - the study of the influence of biological events on psychological processes; the study of the interactions between body and mind.

a. In Germany in the 1920s and 1930s there was a group of researchers who founded **Gestalt psychology** - Gestalt means "pattern" or "configuration"; it studied how people interpret sensory information as patterns in order to acquire knowledge.

b. Today **Biological psychologists** are also called **behavioral neuroscientists, neuropsychologists, or psychobiologists.**

c. A new field of **evolutionary psychology** is the study of how our species' evolutionary past may explain some of our present behaviors and psychological traits.

d. **Psychoneuroimmunology (PNI)** - the study of how bodily processes can affect one's moods and emotions and vice versa.

e. Major controversy in biological research is relative contribution of "nature" and "nurture."

2. **Learning perspective** - the study of how behavior is acquired through interactions with the environment; responsible for many practical applications of psychology.

a. **John B. Watson** - earliest American behaviorist; rejected the concept of mind, focused on observable behavior.

b. **Ivan Pavlov** - Russian physiologist; showed many involuntary behaviors were learned responses to stimuli.

c. **B.F. Skinner** - focused on voluntary behavior; demonstrated behavior is a function of its consequences; **behaviorism** became predominant school of experimental psychology until the early 1960s.

d. **Albert Bandura (social learning theory)** - demonstrated that people learn by observation and that behavior is self-regulated, rather than only determined by external influences.

3. **Cognitive perspective** - (**cognitive** - from the Latin, "to know"); the study of the origins and consequences of thoughts, memories, beliefs, perceptions, explanations, and other mental processes; the " "cognitive revolution" has inspired much contemporary research on the human mind.

4. **Sociocultural perspective** - the study of how social and cultural values and contexts influence behavior and other psychological processes.

a. **culture** - a program of shared rules that governs the behavior of members of a community or society, and a set of values, beliefs, and attitudes shared by most members of the community.

5. **Psychodynamic perspective** - The study of unconscious energy dynamics within the individual; some research psychologists believe that this perspective belongs in philosophy and literature, rather than science; psychotherapists are more likely to utilize this perspective. Term psychodynamic derives from:

a. **intrapsychic** - refers to internal, hidden mechanisms of the "psyche" or mind.
b. **dynamic** - term from physics that refers to balance of systems under action of internal or external forces.
c. Perspective strives to understand how people protect themselves from threatening information and how rational behavior can be distorted by hidden aggressive or sexual impulses.

B. Other approaches:
1. **Humanistic psychology** - the study of the influence of human spirit and free will on people's lives; also called the "third force"; belief in free will and human potential.
2. **Feminist psychology** - the study of the effects of gender on behavior and psychological processes; the analysis of masculine bias in much of mainstream psychology.

VI. About This Book
A. The five perspectives represent qualitatively different approaches to the study of psychology.
B. No single perspective is sufficient in isolation from the others.
C. Many psychologists acknowledge the importance of integrating the perspectives, but most psychologists are highly specialized.

CHAPTER 1 SUMMARY

➤ Instructions: Complete the sentence with the appropriate word or words.

Scientific psychology differs from the popular conception of psychology as a special body of knowledge that allows a person magically to transform his or her life. The aim of modern scientific psychology is to examine and explain how people and animals learn, remember, solve problems, perceive, feel, and interact with one another.

Modern psychology is the scientific study of: 1. _behaviorism_ and 2._mental processes_ and how they are affected by biology, mental states, and environments.

The popular marketplace contains a great deal of language or terminology termed 3._psychobabble_ which appears to be psychological on the surface but is pseudoscientific and vague. Examples of psychology's nonscientific competitors include fortunetellers, psychics, astrologers, and graphologists. Often, pseudoscientists promise quick fixes for emotional problems and exploit trust and belief in technology. Typically, however, research evidence does not support their claims. Pseudoscientific thinking often relies on confirming existing beliefs and prejudices rather than challenging them. Often, pseudoscientists make predictions after the fact, rather than 4._before_ the predicted event. Pseudoscientific claims often rely on overgeneralizing from cases that confirm theories. At the same time, disconfirming cases is often ignored.

The ability and willingness to assess claims and make objective judgments on the basis of well-supported facts is termed 5._____. It involves looking for flaws in arguments and resisting claims made on the basis of inadequate evidence. The critical thinker is a creative and constructive person who can generate a range of possible explanations for a single event, as well as understand the implications of research findings.

Critical thinking involves following several guidelines, including examining evidence, particularly a type of evidence that involves careful observation, experimentation, and measurement, called 6._____ evidence. Critical thinkers also do not generalize from personal experiences or a few examples to everyone, termed 7._____. They also consider other interpretations and utilize 8._____ ,which means that the explanation that requires the fewest assumptions is the best.

Forerunners of modern psychology were philosophy, natural science, and medicine, but early investigators did not always rely on empirical evidence. The first psychological laboratory was established in 1879 by 9._____. His favorite research method was 10._____, a method of analyzing one's own mental experiences. This method was abandoned because it was 11._____.

The early school of 12._____ emphasized the purpose of behavior and adaptation to the environment. It was strongly influenced by the evolutionary theories of 13._____. One of its leaders was an American, 14._____.

Around 1900 in Austria, psychology as a method of 15._____ was developed by 16._____, who theorized that mental disorders are caused by conflicts, memories, and traumas that occurred in early childhood. These ideas evolved into a broad theory of personality and a specific method for treating people with emotional problems, called 17._____.

Psychology has grown into a complex field consisting of differing perspectives, methods, and training. Most people think of psychologists as therapists, but many psychologists do not fit this stereotype. Most professional activity falls into one of three categories:
1. 18._____ and 19._____ in colleges and universities.
2. Providing health or mental health services, referred to as 20._____.
3. Conducting and using 21._____ research, relating psychological findings to nonacademic settings. Research that attempts to gain knowledge for its own sake, is 22._____ research.

There are several types of psychologist practitioners, whose goal is to understand and improve physical and mental health. 23._____ psychologists help people with problems of everyday life. 24._____ psychologists work with parents and student to improve students' performance and resolve emotional difficulties. 25._____ psychologists diagnose, treat, and study mental or emotional problems and disabilities, including those highly disturbed. A license to practice clinical psychology generally requires a 26._____. Some practitioners have an Ed.D., or practitioner-only degree, called a 27.____ .

Other professions are also involved in the treatment of mental disorders. The medical specialty concerned with mental and emotional disorders is 28.____ . Persons who work in this specialty are more likely to treat severe mental disorders and are able to prescribe medicine. A 29._____ is a person who practices one highly specialized form of psychotherapy, called psychoanalysis. A generic term for anyone who does any kind of therapy is a 30.____ . This label is not typically regulated by law.

There are five leading psychological approaches to studying and explaining mental processes and behavior. These perspectives all have their own questions, assumptions, and explanations.

The 31.____ perspective emphasizes that all psychological processes involve physiological events. Its focus is the study of the complex interactions between mind and body.
The 32.____ perspective emphasizes the acquisition of behavior through interactions with the environment. One of its American founders, 33.____ , advocated the abandonment of introspection in favor of studying observable and measurable behavior. Russian physiologist, 34.____ , studied the acquisition of involuntary behaviors. Later, 35.____ extended the behavioral approach to voluntary behaviors and demonstrated that behavior is a function of its consequences. Still later, an outgrowth of behaviorism known as 36.____ theory combined research on behaviorism with research on thinking and consciousness in an effort to understand self-regulated behavior better.

In the 1950s and 1960s, computer models of the mind gave rise to the 37.____ perspective, the study of people's thoughts, memories, beliefs, perceptions, explanations, and other mental processes. One of its most important contributions has been to demonstrate how a person's explanations and perceptions influence his or her behavior. This approach has inspired a great deal of current psychological research.

The 38.____ perspective attempts to move beyond the study of the individual into the study of the effects of cultural values and social contexts on everyday experience. Researchers from this perspective point out that a great deal of behavior is powerfully influenced by the social context in which it occurs. A full understanding of human behavior can only be achieved by appreciation of relationships, socialization, physical environments, social custom, and cultural ideology.

An emphasis on unconscious forces within the individual is provided by the 39._____ perspective. Freud's view was that an understanding of consciousness provides only surface explanations of human functioning. His followers believe that the most important regions of the mind lie outside of conscious awareness.

Other schools of psychology exist independently of these five major perspectives. For example, 40._____ psychology emphasizes free will and the spiritual aspects of the person. 41._____ psychology focuses on the influence of gender on behavior and thought. It has also pointed out that research and psychotherapy are social processes, and it emphasizes the importance of correcting biases.

Each of these perspectives has its strengths, weaknesses, and limitations. However, we can combine and integrate these perspectives with the goal of achieving a fuller understanding of human functioning in all its complexity.

MULTIPLE CHOICE SELF-TEST

Instructions: Circle or indicate the best alternative or answer.

EXAMPLE:

Which one of the following statements is the most likely to be made by a critical thinker?

    a.   "My professor said that in her opinion it is true, so it must be true."

    b.   "Well, I think it's just another example of bad or wrong thinking, and that's my reason."

    c.   Even though there's really no support for that idea, I think I might have a possible alternative solution."

    d.   "Well, after all, my opinion's as good as anyone else's opinion about the subject."

Rationale for best answer:

The best answer is c. Alternative a is incorrect because the speaker in the statement appeals to authority and does not look for evidence. Alternative b is incorrect because the speaker engages in negative thinking only and does not look for alternatives. Alternative c is correct because the speaker examines the evidence (there's really no support for that idea) and proposes alternatives. Alternative d is incorrect because critical thinking involves examining evidence for opinions. Note that the answer to this question depends on your understanding of critical thinking rather than on rote memory.

1. Gloria picks up a self-help book, which advertises how she can overcome her "perfectionism complex" by erasing parental messages "implanted" in childhood. The author of this book can be described as using

    a. medical jargon.
    b. literary language.
    c. scientific terminology.
    d. psychobabble.

2. Which one of the following statements is most likely to be made by a scientist discussing a new treatment for depression?

    a. "I've heard of a person who tried this therapy and she got better immediately."
    b. "The evidence demonstrates that a significant number of the subjects in this study were less depressed after this particular type of therapy."
    c. "This method for treating depression uses the latest technology. It's got to work!"
    d. "Everyone knows that depression is caused by childhood conflicts, and because this therapy is aimed at treating these conflicts, it should be effective."

3. Nadine is interested in scientifically studying the process by which people come to believe in astrology. Nadine is most likely a

    a. pseudoscientist.
    b. psychotherapist.
    c. psychologist.
    d. psychoanalyst.

4. Psychology differs most from other attempts to understand behavior because of

    a. the material it studies.
    b. its methods and approaches.
    c. its historical development.
    d. its philosophical tradition.

5. Quick cures for emotional problems

    a. are very rare or nonexistent.
    b. reflect psychology's state-of-the-art technology.
    c. can be obtained only from expert psychotherapists.
    d. reflect the new knowledge gained from research on dysfunctional families.

6.   Research studies on children who have been abused find that the majority of these children

      a.   do NOT abuse their own children when they become adults.
      b.   do NOT become parents because they fear abusing their own children.
      c.   need psychological help to avoid abusing their own children.
      d.   abuse their children.

7.   In a discussion of the merits of welfare, Barry says, "I get fed up when I think about how many millions of lazy people are sitting on their rear ends collecting welfare without contributing to society at all." This statement is best characterized as

      a.   empirical evidence in support of abolishing welfare.
      b.   evidence of critical thinking.
      c.   an evaluation of available evidence.
      d.   emotional reasoning.

8.   Towanda dreams of her classmate asking her out on a date. The next day, this actually happens. According to the principle of Occam's Razor, which is the best explanation for these events?

      a.   Dreams really do predict the future.
      b.   Towanda unconsciously communicated her availability to her classmate.
      c.   The dream and the date were coincidental events.
      d.   Towanda's unconscious mind helped her understand her classmate's subtle communications about dating her.

9.   In studying the formation of language, a functionalist would focus on how language

      a.   operates to allow the individual to adapt to the environment.
      b.   serves an emotionally expressive function.
      c.   changes as a function of thought.
      d.   can be impaired by brain injury.

10.   The term "empirical" refers to evidence gathered by

      a.   logic and reason.
      b.   experimentation and observation.
      c.   examining expert opinion on a subject.
      d.   analyzing personal anecdotes.

11. Arnold states, "I know at least three people who used 'WonderPump' bodybuilding formula and all of them won bodybuilding contests. WonderPump really works". Arnold is basing his argument on

    a. expert opinion.
    b. logical deduction.
    c. empirical evidence.
    d. personal anecdote.

12. Dr. Cruz works with adults who have schizophrenia, a serious mental disorder. She is most likely to be a _____ psychologist.

    a. school
    b. experimental
    c. clinical
    d. counseling

13. Dr. Taylor prescribes medicine to help people with mental disorders. Her professional specialty is

    a. psychiatry.
    b. social work.
    c. psychology.
    d. psychotherapy.

14. A professional psychologist who is trained to focus on professional practice rather than research is most likely to have a _____ degree.

    a. Ph.D.
    b. Ed.D.
    c. Psy.D.
    d. J.D.

15. A researcher investigates the relationship between psychological stress and the development of cancer. This researcher's perspective is

    a. biological.
    b. behaviorist.
    c. cognitive.
    d. sociocultural.

16. Dr. Jones does research on community programs to prevent teenage pregnancy. She is most likely to be a

      a. psychologist.
      b. psychotherapist.
      c. psychiatrist.
      d. psychoanalyst.

17. Marie is a highly ambitious person. The sociocultural perspective suggests that Marie probably

      a. unconsciously competes with her parents.
      b. has learned a strong value from her community.
      c. has been punished for failing to achieve.
      d. has a mental network of beliefs that support her behavior.

18. Which of the following statements is most likely to have been made by a humanistic psychologist about human accomplishment?

      a. "I believe that people can reach their potential if given the freedom to do so."
      b. "People are governed by societal norms and values that influence their attainment."
      c. "People are controlled by unconscious forces, which motivate their aggressive and sexual impulses into work and artistic accomplishment."
      d. "If we could better understand the neurological basis of motivation, we could better understand human achievement."

19. Ivan is a 50-year-old man who wants to quit smoking. A psychologist from the behaviorist perspective would recommend that Ivan quit by

      a. liberating his buried rage against his mother.
      b. controlling his biological urge for nicotine.
      c. having him think positive thoughts about quitting.
      d. modifying the environmental conditions that control his behavior.

20. Which psychologist was responsible for developing an influential method of psychotherapy, called psychoanalysis?

      a. Wilhelm Wundt
      b. Ivan Pavlov
      c. Sigmund Freud
      d. John B. Watson

21. Early psychologists who were interested in studying how people interpreted sensory information as patterns in order to acquire knowledge were the _____ psychologists.

    a. behaviorist
    b. gestalt
    c. psychodynamic
    d. functionalist

22. Which of the following research questions would most interest an applied psychologist?

    a. "How do children acquire language skills?"
    b. "How does anxiety affect hormone production?"
    c. "What educational programs can best prevent the spread of AIDS?"
    d. "How do adults adjust to the loss of a job?"

23. Which of the following research questions would most interest a psychologist who conducts basic research?

    a. "What intervention works best so that children learn to read?"
    b. "How can we get people to give more blood during the summer?"
    c. "How can parents best teach children to behave morally?"
    d. "How do people develop sexual orientation preferences?"

24. Historians of psychology recall that slaves who wanted to escape were once said to suffer from a psychological disorder called drapetomania. Persons from which of the following approaches would be most likely to point this out?

    a. behavioral
    b. feminist
    c. sociocultural
    d. cognitive

25. Behaviorists resist theorizing about the unconsious and mental states because these concepts

    a. are better left to psychoanalysts.
    b. have long been demonstrated not to exist.
    c. are too difficult to work with.
    d. are not directly observable.

26. Garth hits his younger brother while they are watching violent cartoons on television. The perspective that would explain Garth's behavior as a result of observational learning is

  a. sociocultural.
  b. social learning.
  c. psychodynamic.
  d. cognitive.

27. Lee is conducting research to investigate the perceptions of "feminity" and "masculinity" among college students. His choice of topics reveals the influence of

  a. the psychodynamic perspective.
  b. feminist psychology.
  c. humanistic psychology.
  d. the behaviorist perspective.

28. A humanistic psychologist is most likely to study

  a. paranormal events.
  b. the neurological basis of behavior.
  c. learning and memory.
  d. altruism and creativity.

29. Jenny is a 25-year-old recovering anorexia patient. A cognitive perspective would explain Jenny's anorexia as the result of

  a. negative body perceptions and beliefs about herself.
  b. cultural messages from the media to be thin.
  c. environmental conditions reinforcing her anorexia.
  d. sexist influences from her parents and society.

30. The claims of each of the five major theoretical perspectives in psychology

  a. compete with one another.
  b. are made about different topics.
  c. are accepted by all psychologists.
  d. reflect different views of the same phenomena.

TRUE FALSE SELF-TEST

(T) F 1. Psychologists write and publish self-help books that have a scientific basis.

T (F) 2. Psychology is all about psychotherapy and fixing yourself.

T (F) 3. Children of abusive parents almost always become abusive when they become parents.

(T) F 4. Psychology is the science of behavior and mental processes.

T (F) 5. A confirming case can prove a theory.

(T) F 6. A confirming case can support a theory.

T (F) 7. Anecdotal evidence is usually sufficient to support a theory.

T (F) 8. Critical thinking is negative thinking.

(T) F 9. Critical thinkers tolerate uncertainty.

(T) F 10. The simplest explanation that requires the fewest assumptions is usually the most useful.

(T) F 11. Empirical evidence is used to support scientific theories.

T (F) 12. Scientific predictions sometimes occur after the fact.

T (F) 13. Functionalists emphasized the observation and analysis of mental experience.

T (F) 14. Psychology as a method of psychotherapy began with B.F. Skinner in 1960.

T (F) 15. Basic research is concerned with the practical uses of knowledge.

(T) F 16. Wilhelm Wundt established psychology as a formal science.

(T) F 17. Charles Darwin's theory of evolution inspired the functionalists.

(T) F 18. Counseling psychologists help people with the problems of everyday life.

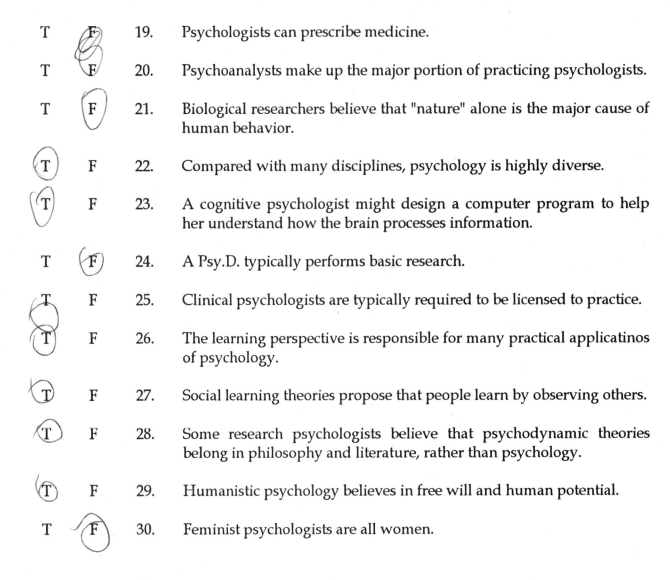

T F 19. Psychologists can prescribe medicine.

T F 20. Psychoanalysts make up the major portion of practicing psychologists.

T F 21. Biological researchers believe that "nature" alone is the major cause of human behavior.

T F 22. Compared with many disciplines, psychology is highly diverse.

T F 23. A cognitive psychologist might design a computer program to help her understand how the brain processes information.

T F 24. A Psy.D. typically performs basic research.

T F 25. Clinical psychologists are typically required to be licensed to practice.

T F 26. The learning perspective is responsible for many practical applicatinos of psychology.

T F 27. Social learning theories propose that people learn by observing others.

T F 28. Some research psychologists believe that psychodynamic theories belong in philosophy and literature, rather than psychology.

T F 29. Humanistic psychology believes in free will and human potential.

T F 30. Feminist psychologists are all women.

KEY TERMS

critical thinking - The ability and willingness to assess claims and make objective judgments on the basis of well-supported reasons; to resist claims that have no supporting evidence; and to be creative and constructive in explaining events.

psychology - The scientific study of behavior and mental processes and how they are affected by an organism's physical state, mental state, and external environment.

empirical - Relying on or derived from observation, experimentation, or measurement.

functionalism - An early psychological approach that stressed the function or purpose of behavior and consciousness.

basic psychology - The study of psychological issues in order to seek knowledge for its own sake rather than for its practical application.

applied psychology - The study of psychological issues that have direct practical significance and the application of psychological findings.

psychiatry - The medical specialty concerned with mental disorders, maladjustment, and abnormal behavior.

biological perspective - An approach to behavior that emphasizes bodily events and changes associated with actions, feelings, and thoughts.

behaviorism - An approach to psychology that emphasizes the study of objectively observable behavior and the role of the environment as a determinant of human and animal behavior.

social learning theory (or cognitive social learning theory) - The theory that behavior is learned and maintained through observation and imitation of others, positive consequences, and cognitive processes, such as plans and expectations.

cognitive perspective - An approach to behavior that emphasizes mental processes in perception, memory, language, problem solving, and other areas of behavior.

sociocultural perspective - An approach to behavior that emphasizes social and cultural influences on behavior.

psychodynamic perspective - Psychological approaches, originating with Freud's theory of psychoanalysis, that emphasize unconscious energy dynamics within the individual, such as inner forces, conflicts, or the movement of instinctual energy.

intrapsychic - Within the mind or self.

SUGGESTED RESEARCH PROJECTS

1. Watch popular talk shows in order to identify examples of psychobabble and pseudoscientific thinking. Identify which characteristics of psychobabble and/or pseudoscience are exhibited by speakers on these shows. Identify the credentials of speakers who claim to be therapists.

2. Newspaper editorial sections often contain speculations about the causes of behaviors like violence, risky sexual practices, politically corrupt actions, and the like. Read a few editorials or letters to the editor and try to discern each writer's assumptions, biases, and psychological perspective. Identify the writer's claim.

3. Browse through the popular psychology section of a local bookstore. What are the common themes of many of these books? Which books seem to be "psychobabble" and which ones seem to have a scientific basis? What percentage of popular psychology appears to be "psychobabble"?

SUGGESTED READINGS

Hothersall, D. (1990). *History of Psychology*. (2nd ed.). New York: McGraw-Hill, Inc. A lively and fascinating history of the science of psychology.

McBurney, D.H. (1996). *How to Think Like a Psychologist: Critical Thinking in Psychology*. Upper Saddle River, New Jersey: Prentice-Hall, Inc.

Tavris, C. (1992). *The Mismeasure of Woman*. New York: Simon and Schuster. A critique of popular theories of sex differences and traditional interpretations of findings on women.

SUGGESTED AUDIOVISUALS

Nova (PBS Video). "The Amazing Randi," who is a professional magician and skeptic, exhibits critical thinking and debunks a number of "psychic" and other bogus phenomena.

PSYCHOLOGY ON THE INTERNET

There any many resources on the Internet for psychologists and psychology students, both graduate and undergraduate. Some addresses that may be of interest include the following:

The Archives of Undergraduate Research
(http://www.wabash.edu)

This site contains an electronic journal that provides an outlet for undergraduates to publish original scholarship in psychology, including reports of original empirical research, theoretical papers, and review papers.

Psychology Web
(http://www.gasou.edu.psychweb.htm)

This site contains texts of books, discussion pages, topics relevant to college-level psychology courses, quizzes for introductory psychology students, information on careers in psychology, psychology journals, and many other links.

ANSWER KEY

CHAPTER 1

CHAPTER 1 SUMMARY ANSWERS

1.   behavior
2.   mental processes
3.   psychobabble
4.   before
5.   critical thinking
6.   empirical
7.   arguing by anecdote
8.   Occam's Razor
9.   Wilhelm Wundt
10.   trained introspection
11.   subjective
12.   functionalism
13.   Charles Darwin
14.   William James
15.   psychotherapy
16.   Sigmund Freud
17.   psychoanalysis
18.   Teaching
19.   research
20.   professional practice
21.   applied
22.   basic
23.   Counseling
24.   School
25.   Clinical
26.   Ph.D
27.   Psy. D.
28.   psychiatry
29.   psychoanalyst
30.   psychotherapist
31.   biological
32.   behaviorist
33.   John B. Watson
34.   Ivan Pavlov
35.   Skinner
36.   social learning
37.   cognitive
38.   cultural

39.   psychobabble
40.   humanistic
41.   feminist

MULTIPLE CHOICE SELF-TEST ANSWERS

1.   D
2.   B
3.   C
4.   B
5.   A
6.   A
7.   D
8.   C
9.   A
10.   B
11.   D
12.   C
13.   A
14.   C
15.   A
16.   A
17.   B
18.   A
19.   D
20.   C
21.   B
22.   C
23.   D
24.   C
25.   D
26.   B
27.   B
28.   D
29.   A
30.   D

TRUE FALSE SELF-TEST ANSWERS

1.   T
2.   F
3.   F
4.   T

5. F
6. T
7. F
8. F
9. T
10. T
11. T
12. F
13. F
14. F
15. F
16. T
17. T
18. T
19. F
20. F
21. F
22. T
23. T
24. F
25. T
26. T
27. T
28. T
29. T
30. F

CHAPTER 2

STUDYING HUMAN BEHAVIOR

LEARNING OBJECTIVES
After reading and studying this chapter, you should be able to:

1. Explain why nonscientists need to understand scientific methods.

2. Describe the attitudes and procedures that make research scientific.

3. Compare and contrast descriptive and experimental research.

4. Summarize the advantages and disadvantages of various research methods.

5. Understand the concepts of reliability and validity.

6. Distinguish between correlation and causation.

7. Design a simple experiment or other research study.

8. Describe some sources of bias in experiments and suggest ways to avoid or control for these biases.

9. Distinguish between an independent and dependent variable and identify them from examples of experimental studies.

10. Understand the purpose of random assignment.

11. Distinguish between experimental, control, and placebo control groups in an experiment.

12. Explain the function of statistics.

13. Distinguish between descriptive and inferential statistics.

14. Define statistical significance.

15. Distinguish between cross-sectional and longitudinal research.

16. Describe meta-analysis.

17. Understand the appropriate uses and misuses of psychological tests.

18. Understand the ethical concern for humans and animals in psychological research.

19. Discuss the controversy between traditional science and postmodern views.

CHAPTER OUTLINE

I. Introduction
    A. Scientific method helps sift conflicting views and correct false ideas; understanding of scientific method is important in evaluating conflicting claims.
    B. Testimonials on the effectiveness of "facilitated communication" to help autistic persons are insufficient as evidence; controlled experiments found that facilitated communication was really facilitator communication.
    C. College students erroneously tend to base responses to research on how well results confirm their own expectations.

II. What Makes Research Scientific?
    A. Precision
        1. **Hypothesis** - a statement that attempts to describe or explain behavior; stated very specifically before empirical evidence is gathered.
        2. **Theory** - an organized system of assumptions and principles that is useful in explaining certain phenomena and how they are related and that is consistent with many empirical findings.
        3. **Operational definition** - specify how behavior or situation is to be observed and measured. (Example: Anxiety = response to threat on an anxiety test).
    B. Skepticism - accepting conclusions with caution while at the same time being open to new ideas and evidence.
    C. Reliance on empirical evidence - evidence that is based on careful and systematic observation rather than an appeal to authority or anecdotes. (Example: belief that autism was caused by poor parenting based on weak case study analysis by Bruno Bettelheim, rather than being a neurological disorder).
    D. Willingness to adhere to **principle of falsifiability** - involves willingness to make risky predictions and to state hypotheses such that they are capable of being proven wrong. Any theory that purports to explain everything that could possibly happen is unscientific; no evidence could ever possibly count against the theory.
    E. Openness and willingness to share ideas, methods, and results with other scientists.
        1. Research results must be **replicated** or repeated by other scientists.
        2. **Peer review** - the scientific community must publicly scrutinize the evidence.

III. **Descriptive Research** - methods that allow a researcher to describe and predict behavior but not necessarily to choose one explanation over other, competing ones.
  A. **Case studies** (case history) - detailed description of a particular person.
    1. Characteristics:
        a. May be based on careful observation or psychological testing.
        b. Most commonly used by clinicians and sometimes academic researchers.
    2. Advantages:
        a. Valuable in investigation of new topic.
        b. Provide rich source of hypotheses for future research.
        c. Produce more detailed picture of an individual.
        d. Useful when ethical or practical considerations prevent gathering information.
    3. Disadvantages:
        a. Depend on possibly selective and inaccurate memory.
        b. Open to subjective interpretations.
        c. Each case is unique; thus, difficult to generalize about human behavior.
  B. Observational Studies - the researcher systematically observes and records behavior without interfering in any way with the people (or animals) being observed.
    1. Characteristics:
        a. Usually is the first step in a program of research.
        b. Purpose is to describe behavior of many individuals.
        c. Involves counting, rating, or measuring behavior systematically.
    2. Two types of observational studies:
        a. **Naturalistic observation** - Describes behavior as it occurs in the natural environment.
        b. **Laboratory observation** takes place in a more controlled situation.
    3. Advantages:
        a. Systematic measurement ensures reliability of observations.
        b. Minimizes tendency of observers to notice only what they expect to see.
        c. Behavior tends to be more natural.
    4. Disadvantages:
        a. Presence of researcher may change behavior; thus, researchers may conceal themselves so that people will behave more naturally.
        b. Does not illuminate causes of behavior; more useful for description rather than explanation.
  C. **Psychological Tests** - procedures used for measuring and evaluating personality traits, emotional states, aptitudes, interests, abilities, and values.
    1. Characteristics:
        a. Require oral or written responses.

b. Obtain a total numerical score that reveals something about the person.

c. Often generate information indirectly (rather than directly, as do surveys).

2. General types:

a. **Objective tests** (inventories) measure beliefs, feelings, or behaviors of which an individual is aware.

b. **Projective tests** reveal unconscious feelings or motives.

3. Advantages:

a. Many uses, including promotion of self-understanding, treatment evaluation, or research.

b. Well-constructed tests clarify individual differences.

4. Qualities of well-constructed tests:

a. Well-constructed tests are less biased evaluators of abilities and traits as compared to judgment (e.g., negative halo effect - see one negative trait in someone, assume presence of others as well).

b. Good tests are **standardized** - there are uniform procedures for giving and scoring it.

c. Scoring is performed in reference to **norms** or established standards of performance based on giving the test to a large group of people who resemble those for whom the test is intended.

d. Tests are **reliable** - produce consistent results from one time and place to the next. Various types of reliability:

1. **test-retest reliability** - give test twice to same group of people to determine if scores relate. Disadvantage: Practice effect - people tend to improve scores on same test taken again.

2. **alternate forms reliability** - give different versions (similar format, different content) of the same tests to the same group on two separate occasions. Performance may improve only due to familiarity with general test taking rather than same items.

e. **Validity** - a test measures what it is supposed to measure. Various types of validity:

1. **Content validity** - test is a representative sample of behavior or trait of interest.

2. **Criterion validity** - test is predictive or relates to (correlates with) other independent criteria of the behavior or trait of interest.

5. Criticism and reevaluation of psychological tests and measures keep psychological assessment scientifically rigorous.

6. Disadvantages:

a. Inappropriate use and interpretation of testing.

    b. Insufficient research base to justify use and interpretation of tests to make decisions about people (e.g., polygraph).

D. **Surveys** - generate information by asking people to respond directly to questions about their experiences, attitudes, or opinions.

  1. Advantages:
    a. Collect data about a large group of people, which may be representative of a population of interest if sampling is conducted appropriately.
    b. Collect data about sensitive topics and/or unusual behavior.

  2. **Sample** - a group of subjects selected for study from a larger population.

  3. **Representative sample** - a smaller group of people that is selected to be representative of a larger group that the researcher wishes to describe; in a good survey, researchers can generally draw conclusions about larger samples from smaller samples.

  4. Size is less critical than representativeness.

  5. Disadvantages:
    a. **Volunteer bias** - those who answer polls or call in responses voluntarily probably differ from those who stay silent.
    b. People may lie; probability of lying reduced if guarantee anonymity.
    c. People may not remember accurately.
    d. Phrasing of questions can influence responses or attitudes as well as measure them.
    e. People may respond in such a way so as not to appear abnormal or to tailor views to fit majority opinion.

E. Correlational Research - describes how two or more phenomena are related and, if so, how strongly they are related.

  1 **Correlation** is a numerical measure of the strength of a relationship between two sets of variables; data comes from many individuals who are measured on the two variables of interest.

  2. Variables can vary in quantifiable ways.

  3. Two aspects of correlation:
    a. size/magnitude - the actual number (a number between -1.0 and +1.0).
    b. sign/direction - positive or negative.

  4. **Correlation coefficient** - is the statistic used to express a correlation.

  5. **Positive correlation** means that high values on one variable are associated with high values of the other and vice versa.

  6. **Negative correlation** means that high values of one variable are associated with low values of the other.

  7. Uncorrelated - no relationship exists between the two variables.

  8. Correlations are rarely perfect (e.g., -1.0 or +1.0).

  9. Advantages:
    a. Allow researchers to make general predictions if they know variables are related.

          b.   Predictions about particular individuals may be inaccurate.
    10.   Disadvantages:
         a. Correlation does not show causation.
         b. Does not control for other variables that may influence the behavior of interest.

IV.   Experimental Research - an experiment allows the researcher to control the situation being studied and to draw conclusions about cause and effect.

    A.   A basic experimental design involves:
        1.   Subjects - persons being studied in the experiment.
        2.   An **independent variable** - aspect of an experimental situation that is manipulated or varied by the researcher.
        3.   **A dependent variable** - the reaction of the subjects; the behavior that the researcher is trying to predict.
    B.   Everything about the experimental situation is held constant except the independent variable. The outcome of the study depends on the independent variable.
    C.   There are typically at least two groups or conditions in an experiment, the control condition and the experimental group.
        1.   **Control condition** - comparison group that is treated exactly like those subjects in the experimental condition except that they are not exposed to the same treatment or manipulation of the independent variable.
        2.   Without control condition, cannot be sure behavior would have occurred anyway without manipulation.
        3.   **Experimental group** - group that receives the experimental manipulation.
        4.   **Random assignment** - procedure to ensure that subjects have an equal chance or probability of being placed into experimental or control groups; purpose is to balance individual differences in the two groups so that they are roughly equivalent before the experimental manipulation is conducted.
        5.   There may be several experimental or control groups. Different experimental groups may have different levels of an independent variable (e.g., levels: person smokes one versus two cigarettes).
    D.   An experiment may have several types of control groups.
        1.   **Control group** - no treatment at all.
        2.   **Placebo** - fake treatment; fake pills are frequently used in drug research; purpose is to determine if independent variable has an effect beyond mere belief in efficacy of treatment.
    E.   Expectations can influence the results of a study. **Experimenter effects** - expectancies of the experimenter can influence study outcomes (e.g., Rosenthal's study of "maze bright" versus "maze dull" rats found that college students' expectations about equally intelligent rats resulted in performance differences such that the rats thought to be more intelligent actually did

perform better). There are several designs that can help a researcher avoid such effects, including:

    1.   **Single-blind study** - subjects should not know whether they are in an experimental or control group.

    2.   **Double-blind study** - subjects and actual person having contact with the subjects do not know who is in experimental or control group. Double-blind more difficult to conduct.

F.   Disadvantages of the experiment:

    1.   Procedures used for convenience of researcher can alter results of study.

    2.   More control may result in less realism.

V.   Why Psychologists Use Statistics

A.   Statistics help researchers to:

    1.   describe data.

    2.   assess how reliable and meaningful data is.

    3.   explain results.

B.   **Descriptive statistics** summarize and organize data and often use graphs and charts to depict data.

    1.   the **arithmetic mean** - commonly used type of average calculated by adding up all the individual scores and dividing the result by the number of scores.

        a.   Advantage: Provides average for set of data.

        b.   Disadvantage: Results may not reflect the "typical" response.

    2.   the **range** - provides difference between lowest and highest scores in a distribution.

    3.   the **variance** - more informative than the range; tells how clustered or spread out the individual scores are around the mean; the more spread out they are, the less typical is the mean.

    4.   Descriptive statistics do not tell whether or not result is due to chance.

C.   **Inferential statistics** - purpose is to determine how significant the data is and permit a researcher to draw inferences or conclusions based on evidence about the findings.

    1.   They tell the researcher how likely it is that the result of the study occurred by chance.

    2.   **Statistically significant** - a result that is highly unlikely to have occurred by chance. Statistical significance does not always imply real-world importance.

    3.   Conventional level of significance: "Point oh five" (.05) level; means likelihood of result occurring by chance is less than 5 in 100.

D.   The last step in an experiment is interpreting the results.

    1.   Explanations of results must take many factors into account.

    2.   Rarely does one study prove anything.

    3.   The best interpretations of a finding often emerge after the hypothesis is tested in several different ways.

> a. **Cross-sectional** research involves studying groups of subjects of different ages at a given time.
>
> b. **Longitudinal** studies periodically reassess the same subjects over a period of time.
>
> c. **Meta-analysis** involves combining and analyzing data from many studies to determine how much of the variance can be accounted for by a particular variable.

VI. Evaluating Research Methods: Science Under Scrutiny

    A. Psychological tests are sometimes used for inappropriate purposes (Example: the polygraph).

    B. Psychologists are concerned about ethics in research, including:

        1. the use of deception.

        2. the use of animals in research.

            a. only used in 7-8 percent of research; 95% of animals used are rodents.

            b. use of animals has many practical benefits and most scientists oppose a ban on animal research.

    C. The APA has ethical guidelines for all psychological research.

    D. There is a conflict over what research can and cannot reveal.

        1. The traditional view is that knowledge is objective, value-free, and detached.

        2. **Postmodernism** views scientific conclusions as influenced by the scientist's values, judgments, and status.

        3. The postmodern view of **social constructionism** holds that knowledge is constructed more than it is discovered (Example: The concept of "race" is a social invention, is not scientifically defensible and can be defined in many ways). Textbook uses the term **ethnic group.**

        3. Critique of postmodernism by many scientists is that there is legitimate truth to be discovered using standard methods, while taking into account biases.

CHAPTER 2 SUMMARY

Psychological research methods allow researchers to separate truth from unfounded beliefs. Nonscientists need to understand these methods in order to be critical thinkers and more sophisticated consumers of psychological and other scientific findings. In evaluating the findings of a study or in evaluating a new technique or therapy, one must consider how the information was obtained. For example, in studying a new technique, called 1._____, which was thought to help autistic children by using controlled conditions, researchers found that the facilitator and not the autistic child was doing the actual communication.

Several attributes are characteristic of scientists. They begin by formulating a precise 2._____, or speculation about some phenomenon. It may be suggested by previous findings or observations, and/or it may be part of a more general 3._____, which is an organized set of assumptions that purports to explain phenomena.

The next step is to make explicit 4._____ about what will happen. This, process, known as the construction of 5._____ definitions, consists of taking vague terms and specifying how the behavior or situation is to be observed and measured.

Scientists do not accept ideas on faith. Rather, they employe a good deal of 6._____,which means they are cautious about accepting conclusions. In evaluating claims, scientists search for 7.____ evidence that is based on careful and systematic observation.

The principle of 8._____ states that an idea must be stated in a way that allows it to be refuted by counterevidence. In other words, a scientist must predict not only what will happen, but also what will not happen. Scientists must also be willing to share their methods and results with other scientists who may want to verify their findings by 9.____.

Psychologists may use several different methods in their research. A study that involves describing and predicting behavior, but not necessarily choosing one explanation over another, is termed a 10.____ study. These methods include 11._____,which are in-depth descriptions of individuals. They are commonly used by clinicians and sometimes academic researchers. These methods are especially useful in investigating a new topic, or when information cannot be gathered in other ways.

12._____ studies involve systematically watching and recording behaviors without interfering with the subjects being watched. One form of this method is called 13._____ observation, which is used to describe behavior as it occurs in the environment. When using these methods, it is important to count, rate, or measure behavior in reliable and consistent ways. Sometimes this involves the use of sophisticated equipment, in which case the psychologist must often use the method of 14.____ observation. In this case, however, the presence of the equipment and/or researchers may cause subjects to behave differently than they would otherwise. In addition, such studies may not illuminate the causes of behavior and may be more useful for description rather than explanation.

15.____ is the measurement and evaluation of personality traits, emotional states, aptitudes, interests, abilities, and values. This process helps to clarify differences among individuals. There are two general types of psychological tests, including 16._____, which measure beliefs, feelings and motives of which an individual is aware, and 17._____, which reveal unconscious feelings or motives.

Good psychological tests have several features. First, they are 18._____, which means that the same instructions and procedures are used every time. Second, they are scored according to established standards of performance, or 19._____. Third, test constructors have demonstrated that the tests produce similar results from one time and place to the next and have 20.____. Last, but not least, the tests are also demonstrated to be 21._____, that is, they actually measure what they set out to measure.

Reliability is evaluated by giving the test twice to the same group of people and then doing a statistical comparison of their scores. This is known as 22._____ reliability. A similar approach is to use two different versions of the same test in evaluating 23.____ reliability.

Validity is determined in several ways. 24.____ validity involves an analysis of test items to evaluate if they are representative of the trait in question. Tests are also judged by their ability to predict an independent measure of the same trait, a characteristic known as 25.____ validity.

Questionnaires and interviews, or 26.____, are direct ways of gathering information from people. In order to be done well, the group of subjects, known as the 27.____, must be 28.____ of the larger population that the researcher wishes to describe. Information from a survey can be distorted by volunteer bias, subjects' lying, or by biased questions. Sometimes surveys actually influence as well as reflect people's attitudes and opinions.

A measure of the degree of relationship between two variables is known as a 29.____. This relationship is computed from a 30.____ of variables, although the variables may come from one individual. This relationship can be 31.____, meaning that high values of one variable are associated with high values of the other, or 32.____, whereby high values of one variable are associated with low values of the other. When there is no relationship between variables, they are said to be 33.____. Statistically, the degree of relationship is expressed by a number called a 34.____, which ranges from the perfect positive correlation of 35.____ to the perfect negative correlation of 36.____. A 37.____ correlation means that the variables are unrelated. The correlation allows the researcher to make 38.____ about a group of persons if he or she knows the variables are related.

While correlations allow researchers to make general predictions about one variable from a second variable, they must be interpreted with caution. They cannot make precise predictions whether or not one variable is actually the 39.____ of the other.

The descriptive methods provide speculations about explanations of behaviors, but cause can only be established by 40.____ methods that allow the researcher to 41.____ the situation being studied.

This aspect of an experimental situation that the researcher manipulates or varies is known as the 42.____ variable. Ideally, everything else in the experiment is held 43.____. The behavior that the researcher tries to predict is the 44.____ variable.

Experiments usually require an experimental condition, in which subjects receive some "treatment" or a manipulation is conducted, and a 45.____ condition, in which subjects are treated exactly like the experimental subjects with the exception of the "treatment." In putting subjects in the two groups, researchers often use the procedure of 46.____ so that each subject has the same probability of being in the experimental or control group. Drug studies often include a 47.____ group in order to control for the influence of subjects' expectations about the effect of the drug on their behavior. When subjects are unaware of which group they are in, they are said to be taking part in a 48._____ study.

Researchers' expectations can also affect subjects' behavior, a phenomenon known as 49._____ effects. In order to avoid these effects, the person who administers the experiment also should not know which group the subjects are in. This is known as a 50._____ study.

Psychologists use 51._____ to describe, assess, and explain data. 52._____ statistics summarize data. The group average, or 53._____, is one commonly used statistic. While it describes the central point of a group's scores, it does not provide any information about the variation in scores. The 54._____, which gives the difference between the highest score and the lowest score in a distribution, provides some of this information. The 55._____ is a measure of how scores cluster or spread around the mean and provides even more information.

56._____ statistics permit a researcher to draw inferences or conclusions based on the data. They also tell a researcher how likely a result is to have occurred by chance. A result that is highly unlikely to have occurred by chance is said to be 57._____.

The last step in any study is interpreting the results. The best interpretation of a finding often emerges after the hypothesis is tested in several different ways. 58._____ research involves studying groups of subjects of different ages at a given time. 59._____ research periodically evaluates the same subjects over a period of time. 60._____ involves combining and quantitatively analyzing data from many studies to determine how much of the variance can be accounted for by a particular variable.

Another important issue in psychology is the ethics of research. Two such ethical concerns of psychologists are the use of 61._____ and the use of 62._____.

Scientists have traditionally considered themselves to be detached and objective. Recently, however, adherents of the viewpoint known as 63._____ have argued that the observer's values, judgments, world view, culture, and social status inevitably affect his or her approach to study and explanation. One of these theories, 64._____, holds that knowledge is not so much discovered as it is invented. Many scientists believe there is a legitimate truth to be discovered using standard methods, while taking into account biases.

MULTIPLE CHOICE SELF-TEST

1.   Bruno Bettleheim's misguided theory of the "refrigerator mother" was accepted largely on the basis of:

     a.   empirical support.
     b.   his status.
     c.   the popularity of the idea.
     d.   prejudice against mothers.

2.   A psychologist studying childhood aggression defines aggression as the number of times a child hits another child. The psychologist has developed a(n):

     a.   hypothesis.
     b.   theory.
     c.   operational definition.
     d.   prediction.

3.   A researcher reads and critically evaluates the quality of another researcher's study. This process is called:

     a.   replication.
     b.   experimentation.
     c.   falsification.
     d.   peer review.

4.   LaToya reads a study which states that depressed people tend to have more health problems than nondepressed people. She is skeptical about the findings, so she performs a similar study. This process is known as:

     a.   falsification.
     b.   scientific criticism.
     c.   replication.
     d.   operationalization.

5.   A psychic researcher performs many experiments, all of which are failures. He believes the reason that he can't find any evidence to support the existence of psychic powers is because there were "negative vibes" during the experiments. This researcher is violating the principle of:

     a.   replication.
     b.   falsification.
     c.   experimentation.
     d.   operationalization.

6. Dr. Marquinez performs an in-depth analysis of the multiple personalities of a woman named "Emily", by interviewing her and writing a description and interpretation of her life. Dr. Marquinez is using the _____ method.

    a. experimental
    b. naturalistic observation
    c. case study
    d. survey

7. An advantage of the case study is that it is

    a. the best way of determining cause and effect.
    b. useful when ethical considerations prevent gathering information.
    c. more objective than other methods.
    d. easier to make generalizations about human behavior.

8. Phineas Gage was a railroad foreman in Vermont who suffered a brain injury. His behavior was of interest to psychologists because brain injury in humans can only be ethically studied by using the _____ method.

    a. experimental
    b. longitudinal
    c. cross-sectional
    d. case study

9. A psychologist views the play behavior of children behind a one-way mirror and carefully records what she sees. This psychologist is using the method of:

    a. naturalistic observation.
    b. laboratory observation.
    c. experimentation.
    d. psychological testing.

10. Wendy is applying for a bank teller job and is asked by a psychologist to take a standardized written inventory, which asks about her attitudes and behaviors towards stealing and other forms of dishonest behavior. The psychologist then compares Wendy's responses to a norm group in order to decide if she should be hired. This psychologist is using the _____ method.

    a. psychological testing
    b. survey
    c. experimental
    d. laboratory observation

11. A researcher gives an intelligence test that has strict time limits. However, the researcher decides to give people as much time as they want to complete the test. This researcher has ignored the _____ of the test.

   a. norms
   b. test-retest reliability
   c. standardization
   d. alternate forms reliability

12. Dr. Mfume is a psychologist who is developing a test of political conservatism. She gives her test to 1,000 volunteers. Three weeks later, she gives the same test to the volunteers again in order to ensure that she obtains similar results. She is checking for

   a. reliability.
   b. standardization.
   c. validity.
   d. variability.

13. Dr. Bartow gives a mechanical ability test to one group of job applicants. The next week, another group of applicants is given a similar mechanical ability test that contains different test items but correlates highly with the first test. Dr. Bartow has ensured the test's

   a. validity.
   b. test-retest reliability.
   c. alternate forms reliability.
   d. standardization.

14. In order to investigate the validity of a job knowledge test for nuclear power plant operators, a psychologist ensures that the test is a representative sample of the knowledge required for the job. This study is examining the test's

   a. content validity.
   b. criterion-related validity.
   c. norms.
   d. standardization.

15. A psychologist finds that a test that purports to sample student scholastic abilities fails to predict actual grades in college. This test lacks:

    a. content validity.
    b. criterion-related validity.
    c. norms.
    d. reliability.

16. A magazine wants to survey how often sexually active college students actually use condoms to prevent AIDS. The magazine asks the students to complete the survey and send it in to the magazine in a postage-paid envelope. However, one should interpret the findings of the survey with caution, as the findings may be distorted by

    a. volunteer bias.
    b. unreliability.
    c. a lack of content validity.
    d. a negative halo effect.

17. A college student surveys friends and family about their attitudes towards political candidates. The sample in this survey is NOT likely to be

    a. honest.
    b. standardized.
    c. biased.
    d. representative.

18. If A is highly correlated with B, then:

    a. A causes B.
    b. B causes A.
    c. C causes both A and B.
    d. A and B are related.

19. Which correlation indicates the LOWEST degree of relationship?

    a. +.09
    b. -.16
    c. +.22
    d. -.37

20. A panel of judges rates the quality of wines. A researcher then correlates judgments of quality with the cost of the wine and finds as the quality of the wine increases so does the price. This relationship is very strong. Which correlation coefficient most likely expresses this relationship?

   a. +.30
   b. +.75
   c. -.40
   d. -.85

21. A study of several local school districts finds that as playground space increases, the number of accidents decreases. The action that the school should take based on this information is to:

   a. invest immediately in increasing playground space because smaller playgrounds cause more accidents to occur.
   b. study what other variables could possibly explain the relationship between the two variables.
   c. close all the larger playgrounds.
   d. place more playground monitors at the larger playgrounds.

22. Dr. Ivanisevich studies the effect of listening to country-western music on emotional depression as measured by a psychological test. The independent variable in this study is the

   a. music.
   b. anxiety measure.
   c. subject's prior history of depression.
   d. subject's motivation to participate.

23. A researcher ensures that the subjects in her study have an equal chance of being in an experimental group or a control group. This researcher is using the procedure of

   a. representative sampling.
   b. placebo control.
   c. random assignment.
   d. meta-analysis.

24. Sophia receives a fake pill as part of a study examining the effectiveness of a new drug. Sophia is probably in the _____ group of the study.

   a.   no treatment control
   b.   treatment
   c.   experimental
   d.   placebo control

25. In Rosenthal's classic study of equally intelligent rats who were labeled as "maze bright" and "maze dull," students' expectations about the rats resulted in performance differences such that the rats thought to be more intelligent actually did better on a maze learning task. The results of this study can be attributed to

   a.   lack of random assignment.
   b.   inappropriate operational definitions.
   c.   double-blind procedures.
   d.   experimenter effects.

26. A study in which subjects do not know if they are in an experimental or control group but the researcher does know is a _____ study.

   a.   double-blind
   b.   single-blind
   c.   case
   d.   naturalistic

27. The variance is a measure of the

   a.   spread of scores around the mean.
   b.   average score.
   c.   range of scores.
   d.   the degree of relationship between variables.

28. Psychologists Smith and Glass did an important study in which they combined data from hundreds of studies on the effectiveness of psychotherapy. This data-combining technique is known as

   a.   factor analysis.
   b.   descriptive statistics.
   c.   averaging.
   d.   meta-analysis.

29. Most animals used in psychological experiments are

   a.   cats.
   b.   monkeys and chimpanzees.
   c.   rodents.
   d.   dogs.

30. A psychologist criticizes a lack of good research on the role of men as "househusbands" because most researchers assume homemakers are women. Her view could best be described as

   a.   humanist.
   b.   psychodynamic.
   c.   postmodernist.
   d.   behaviorist.

TRUE FALSE SELF-TEST

T   F   1.   College students tend to base responses to research on how well results confirm their own expectations.

T   F   2.   Facilitated communication has been proven to be effective in treating autism.

T   F   3.   Hypotheses are usually stated very generally.

T   F   4.   Specifying that intelligence can be measured by a score on an intelligence test is an example of an operational definition.

T   F   5.   Skeptics are closed to new ideas and evidence.

T   F   6.   Autism is caused by poor parenting.

T   F   7.   Falsifiability in science means a willingness to be proven wrong.

T   F   8.   Scientists generally rely on one crucial study to prove their theories.

T   F   9.   Scientists publicly scrutinize the studies of other scientists.

T   F   10.   Replication means repeating the study again.

T   F   11.   Descriptive methods allow for judgments of cause and effect.

T   F   12.   Polygraph tests are a reliable and valid means of detecting deception.

53

T (F)   13.   The case study allows researchers to choose one explanation over another.

(T) F   14.   Case studies are advantageous in investigating unique, rare or unusual behavior.

(T) F   15.   Case studies are open to subjective interpretations.

T (F)   16.   Naturalistic observation takes place in a controlled situation.

(T) F   17.   A test can be reliable but not valid.

T (F)   18.   A test can be valid but not reliable.

(T) F   19.   Content validity involves the prediction of an independent criterion measuring the behavior of interest.

(T) F   20.   In a survey, a sample should be representative of the population the researcher wants to describe.

T (F)   21.   A correlation of .80 indicates the relationship is very small.

T (F)   22.   The number 1.50 could represent a correlation coefficient.

T (F)   23.   If television viewing and violent behavior are strongly positively correlated, then watching television must cause violent behavior.

T (F)   24.   The variable the researcher manipulates or varies is the dependent variable.

(T) F   25.   The purpose of random assignment is to ensure that each subject has an equal probability of being assigned to a control or experimental group.

(T) F   26.   A placebo is a fake treatment.

T (F)   27.   In a single-blind study the subject and the actual person having contact with the subject do not know who is in the experimental or control group.

T (F)   28.   The variance is a measure of the average score.

(T) F   29.   Meta-analysis involves statistically combining the results of several studies.

T ⒡ 30. The postmodern viewpoint views science as totally objective and free of bias and values.

KEY TERMS

hypothesis - A statement that attempts to predict or account for a set of phenomena. Scientific hypotheses specify relationships among events or variables and are supported or disconfirmed by empirical investigations.

theory - An organized system of assumptions and principles that purports to explain a specified set of phenomena and their interrelationships.

operational definition - A precise definition of a term in a hypothesis, which specifies the operations for observing and measuring the process or phenomenon being defined.

principle of falsifiability - The principle that a scientific theory must make predictions that are specific enough to expose the theory to the possibility of disconfirmation; that is, the theory must predict not only what will happen, but what will not happen.

descriptive methods - Methods that yield descriptions of behavior but not necessarily causal explanations.

case study - A detailed description of a particular individual under study or treatment.

observational study - A study in which the researcher carefully and systematically observes and records behavior without interfering with the behavior; it may involve either naturalistic observation or laboratory observation.

psychological tests - Procedures used to measure and evaluate personality traits, emotional states, aptitudes, interests, abilities, and values.

standardize - In test construction, to develop uniform procedures for giving and scoring a test.

norms - In test construction, established standards of performance.

reliability - In test construction, the consistency of scores derived from a test from one time and place to another.

validity - The ability of a test to measure what it was designed to measure.

surveys - Questionnaires and interviews that ask people directly about their experiences, attitudes, or opinions.

sample - A group of subjects selected from a population for study in order to estimate characteristics of the population.

representative sample - A sample that matches the population in question on important characteristics, such as age and sex.

volunteer bias - A shortcoming of findings derived from a sample of volunteers instead of a representative sample.

correlational study - A descriptive study that looks for a consistent relationship between two phenomena.

correlation - A measure of how strongly two variables are related to one another; it is expressed statistically by the coefficient of correlation.

variables - Characteristics of behavior or experience that can be measured or described by a numeric scale; variables are manipulated and assessed in scientific studies.

positive correlation - An association between increases in one variable and increases in another.

negative correlation - An association between increases in one variable and decreases in another.

experiment - A controlled test of a hypothesis in which the researcher manipulates one variable to discover its effect on another.

independent variable - A variable that an experimenter manipulates.

dependent variable - A variable that an experimenter predicts will be affected by manipulations of the independent variable.

control condition - In an experiment, a comparison condition in which subjects are not exposed to the same treatment or manipulation of the independent variable as in the experimental condition.

random assignment - A procedure for assigning people to experimental and control groups in which each individual has the same probability as any other of being assigned to a given group.

placebo - An inactive substance or fake treatment used as a control in an experiment or given by a medical practitioner to a patient.

single-blind study - An experiment in which subjects do not know whether they are in an experimental or control group.

experimenter effects - Unintended changes in subjects' behavior due to cues inadvertently given by the experimenter.

double-blind study - An experiment in which neither the subjects nor the researchers know which subjects are in the control group(s) and which are in the experimental group(s) until after the results are tallied.

descriptive statistics - Statistics that organize and summarize research data.

variance - A measure of the dispersion of scores around the mean.

inferential statistics - Statistical tests that allow researchers to assess how likely it is that their results occurred merely by chance.

statistically significant - A term used to refer to a result that is extremely unlikely to have occurred by chance.

cross-sectional study - A study in which subjects of different ages are compared at a different time.

longitudinal study - A study in which subjects are followed and periodically reassessed over a period of time.

meta-analysis - A statistical procedure for combining and analyzing data from many studies; it determines how much of the variance in scores across all studies can be explained by a particular variable.

social constructionism - The view that there are no universal truths about human nature because people construct reality differently, depending on their culture, the historical moment, and power arrangements within their society.

SUGGESTED RESEARCH PROJECTS

1.   Go to your academic library and flip through different types of psychological journals. Try to identify what type of study was conducted by the researcher. The "Abstract" (a short paragraph at the beginning of the article) will give you an overview of what the study was about. The "Methods" section will also help you to determine what type of study was conducted.

2.   Select a research problem of interest to you and list several different ways of approaching it. For example, if you were interested in the effects of politeness, you could perform a case study, a naturalistic observation, a laboratory observation, and an experiment. Describe your general approach using each of these methods. What practical and ethical problems might you have in conducting your research?

3.   Scan magazines, newspapers or articles found on the Internet that discuss the results of research studies. How did the researchers design their study and draw their conclusions? Are there any potential flaws in the research? For example, a study based on self-reported data on eating habits found a correlation between eating pasta and breast cancer. What could some flaws in this study be?

SUGGESTED READINGS

Agnes, N.M., & Pyke, S.W. (1991). *The Science Game* (5th ed.). Englewood Cliffs, NJ: Prentice Hall. A basic book on scientific reasoning and research, written in an entertaining style.

Brannigan, G.G., & Merrens, M.R. (1993). (Eds.) *The Undaunted Psychologist.* New York: McGraw-Hill, Inc. Provides profiles of many contemporary psychologists who describe in their own words how they became interested in their specialty of psychological research.

Hock, R.R. (1995). *Forty Studies that Changed Psychology: Explorations into the history of psychological research.* (2nd ed.). Englewood Cliffs, NJ: Prentice Hall. Provides excerpts from classic studies in psychology across many areas of psychology.

Stanovich, K.E. (1996). *How to Think Straight about Psychology.* (4th ed.). New York: HarperCollins. Reviews the concepts of falsifiability, operationism, experimental control, correlational versus experimental studies, and the importance of statistics in clear non-technical language. Provides many interesting examples to ill :strate concepts.

SUGGESTED AUDIO-VISUALS

Research Methods for the Social Sciences (1995). Insight Media. New York, New York. This video examines various standard methodologies including the experiment, clinical, correlational, and field methods. It also considers ethical issues.

CHAPTER 2

ANSWERS TO CHAPTER SUMMARY

1. facilitated communication
2. hypothesis
3. theory
4. predictions
5. operational
6. skepticism
7. empirical
8. falsifiability
9. replication
10. descriptive
11. case studies
12. Observational
13. naturalistic
14. laboratory
15. Psychological testing (assessment)
16. objective
17. projective
18. standardized
19. norms
20. reliability
21. valid
22. test-retest
23. alternate forms
24. Content
25. criterion
26. surveys
27. sample
28. representative
29. correlation
30. set
31. positive
32. negative
33. uncorrelated
34. correlation coefficient
35. +1.0
36. -1.0
37. 0.0
38. predictions
39. cause

40. experimental
41. control
42. independent
43. constant
44. dependent
45. control
46. random assignment
47. placebo
48. single-blind
49. experimenter
50. double-blind
51. statistics
52. Descriptive
53. mean
54. range
55. variance
56. Inferential
57. statistically significant
58. Cross-sectional
59. Longitudinal
60. Meta-analysis
61. deception
62. animals
63. postmodern
64. social constructionism

ANSWERS TO MULTIPLE CHOICE SELF-TEST

1. B
2. C
3. D
4. C
5. B
6. C
7. B
8. D
9. B
10. A
11. C
12. A
13. C
14. A
15. B
16. A
17. D

CHAPTER 2 CONT.

18.   D
19.   A
20.   B
21.   B
22.   A
23.   C
24.   D
25.   D
26.   B
27.   A
28.   D
29.   C
30.   C

ANSWERS TO TRUE FALSE SELF-TEST

1.   T
2.   F
3.   F
4.   T
5.   F
6.   F
7.   T
8.   F
9.   T
10.   T
11.   F
12.   F
13.   F
14.   T
15.   T
16.   F
17.   T
18.   F
19.   T
20.   T
21.   F
22.   F
23.   F
24.   F
25.   T
26.   T
27.   F
28.   F
29.   T
30.   F

CHAPTER 3

STUDYING HUMAN BEHAVIOR

LEARNING OBJECTIVES

After reading and studying this chapter, you should be able to:

1. Compare and contrast the nativist and empiricist position.

2. Describe some major research findings of the two related fields within the biological perspective: behavioral genetics and evolutionary psychology.

3. Explain the concept of the interaction of heredity and environment, using examples from research (example: obesity).

4. Describe the genetic basis of traits.

5. Explain the purpose of a linkage study.

6. Describe the process of evolution and its influence on human traits and tendencies.

7. Distinguish between sensation and perception.

8. Explain the concept of a critical period in terms of at least two examples or research studies from the text.

9. Describe the research findings on some universal behavioral tendencies, including emotional expression, sociability and attachment, and language acquisition.

10. Discuss the research problems involved in separating genetic from environmental influences on behavior.

11. Describe some research methods for studying heritability and some of the important findings from heritability studies of intelligence, temperament, personality.

12. Describe the "Big Five" personality factors.

13. Discuss the controversy over ethnic differences in IQ and the book <u>The Bell Curve</u>.

CHAPTER 3 OUTLINE

I.   Introduction
      A.   **Nativists** emphasize genes and inborn characteristics (nature).
      B.   **Empiricists** focus on learning and experience (nurture).
      C.   The modern view is that heredity and environment interact to produce psychological and even physical traits.
            1.   Biological factors place certain limits on how much a person can change, as illustrated by findings on weight and **setpoint** -- genetically programmed weight a person stays at when not consciously trying to gain or lose weight based on:
                  a.   basal metabolism rate, rate at which body burns calories for energy.
                  b.   fixed number of fat cells that store fat for energy.
                  c.   hormones.
            2.   Two related fields within the biological perspective:
                  a.   **evolutionary psychology,** emphasizes evolutionary mechanisms that explain commonalities in human psychology, including cognition, development, emotion, social practices; overlaps with but differs from **sociobiology** -- an interdisciplinary field that looks for evolutionary explanations of social behavior in animals and humans.
                  b.   **behavioral genetics,** examines the contribution of heredity to individual differences in many human characteristics.

II. What's in a Gene
      A.   **Genes** which contain instructions for the synthesis of proteins are the basic **units of heredity.**   They are located on **chromosomes,** which contain threadlike strands of **DNA** (deoxyribonucleic acid) found in all cells.
            1.   Human egg cells and sperm cells each contain 23 chromosomes.
            2.   At conception, the fertilized egg contains 46 chromosomes, as do all cells that develop from it (except sperm cells and ova); (23 pairs).
            3.   The father's sperm (X or Y chromosome) determines the sex of the offspring.
            4.   Each human chromosome contains thousands of different genes (XX = female; XY = male).
            5.   The **genome** is the full set of genes in each cell of an organism. The human genome consist of about 100,000 genes.
            6.   Genes can be **recessive** or **dominant.**
            7.   Most traits depend on more than one gene pair.

      B.   **Linkage studies** involve looking for genetic markers in large families that have a particular physical or mental condition in common (e.g., Huntington's disease).

C.   A given gene or set of genes does not always have the same outcome, even in the same environment; cross-over and genetic mutation are also factors.

III.   The Human Heritage
A.   **Evolution** is a change in gene frequencies within a population over many generations.
B.   According to the principle of **natural selection**, the fate of genetic variations depends on the environment. If a certain genetically influenced trait enhances survival and reproduction in a particular environment, the trait will become more common over generations. Some evolutionary biologists design empirical studies to verify cross-cultural evidence for specialized mental abilities or "modules" to handle specific survival problems.
C.   Because of the evolutionary history of some species, some qualities are universal among human beings. For example:
1.   certain reflexes -- simple, automatic responses to specific stimuli.
2.   attraction to novelty.
3.   certain perceptual capacities.
4.   a motive to explore and manipulate objects.
5.   some basic emotional expressions.
6.   a capacity for language.
7.   play - practice play is behavior later used for serious purposes by young animals and humans.

D.   Genetics of Similarity - The Origins of Perception
1.   **Sensation** is the detection or direct experience of physical energy in the external or internal environment due to stimulation of receptors in the sense organs.
2.   **Perception** is the process by which the brain organizes and interprets sensory information.
3.   The development of some perceptual abilities depends on certain experiences during **critical periods** of development (e.g., kittens visually exposed to only either vertical or horizontal lines remained unable to detect opposite type of line).
4.   Complex features of the visual world are processed by special feature detector cells.
5.   Depth perception in children is tested using the "visual cliff."
6.   Some perceptual and sensory abilities appear to be inborn, including:
a.   being startled by a loud noise.
b.   perceiving sound as localized in space.
c.   distinguishing a person's voice from other kinds of sound.
d.   discriminating among certain odors and tastes.
e.   some depth perception.
f.   sense of pain.
g.   detection and discrimination of edges and angles of objects.

        h.   perception of different sizes and colors.

7.   Differences in sensory and perceptual abilities among species reflect different survival needs.

E.   The Face of Emotion

    1.   Some emotional expressions are present from birth.

    2.   Universal facial expressions function in communication and have survival value.

F.   Attachment and Sociability

    1.   **Attachment** is the emotional tie that children and their caregivers feel toward each other.

        a.   Attachment requires touch, or **contact comfort**. Harry Harlow's monkey studies demonstrated the importance of contact comfort.

        b.   Infants deprived of contact comfort show retarded emotional and physical development.

        c.   Attachment serves two purposes:

            1.   a secure base from which to explore the environment -- develops cognitive skills.

            2.   a safe haven to which the child can return when afraid -- develops trust.

    2.   Infant development of sociability:

        a.   infants are primed to respond to human faces.

        b.   4-6 week old children smile regularly, especially in response to faces.

        c.   babies and their caregivers exchange signals in a rhythmic pattern and adjust their behavior (**synchrony**).

    3.   Mary Ainsworth used the **strange situation** to study a child's degree of attachment. Results showed babies can be:

        a.   securely attached; cry when parent leaves.

        b.   avoidant; don't care when parent leaves.

        c.   anxious/ambivalent; resist contact with parent.

    4.   Insecurely attached children are more likely to have later social, cognitive or behavioral problems.

G.   The Capacity for Language

    1.   **Language** is a system for combining meaningless elements into utterances that convey meaning.

        a.   Language development requires learning a large set of rules that make up the grammar of the language.

        b.   Children's vocabulary increases at a rapid rate.

    2.   Aspects of language include:

        a.   rules of syntax, regulations for combining elements (e.g., words or signs) in the particular language.

        b.   **surface structure,** the way the sentence is actually spoken.

        c.   **deep structure,** the meaning inferred by applying rules of syntax.

3. Children do not simply imitate adults. They are able to perceive deep structure. Noam Chomsky theorized that this is due to a biologically-based "universal grammar" due to the brain's language acquisition device. He and others cite several arguments in support:
   a. stages of linguistic development are similar across cultures.
   b. children combine words in ways that adults do not.
   c. adults do not always correct children's syntax.
   d. children who are profoundly retarded acquire language.
4. Experience also plays a role.
   a. Parents tend to recast children's ungrammatical sentences.
   b. Children imitate parents' accents, inflections, and tones.
5. There may be a critical period for language development; probably ages 1 to 5-6.
6. The brain organizes language acquisition, but language acquisition during the critical period may also organize the brain.
7. By puberty, the brain is normally **lateralized**; that is, the two sides of the cerebral cortex have become specialized. In most people, language processing occurs on the left side.

IV. The Genetics of Difference
   A. **Behavioral genetics** is an interdisciplinary field concerned with the genetic bases of behavior and personality.
   B. **Heritability** is a statistical estimate of the proportion of total variance in a trait that is attributable to genetic variation within a group. Heritability:
      1. applies only to traits that vary in a population; therefore heritability does not mean the same thing as "genetic" because some genetic traits do not vary at all.
      2. applies only to a particular group living in a particular environment.
      3. does not apply to individuals, only to variations within a group.
      4. does not mean that traits cannot be modified by the environment.
      5. is usually not dependent on a single gene; traits are usually influenced by many genes working in combination.
      6. means that even highly heritable traits can be modified.
      7. includes the fact that genes turn "on" and "off" over a lifetime.
   C. The Heritability Hunt
      1. Heritability is inferred by studying people whose degree of genetic similarity is known.
         a. Adopted children share half their genes, but not their environments, with their birth parents.
         b. Identical (**monozygotic**) twins share all of their genes.
         c. Fraternal (**dizygotic**) twins are only as genetically alike as any siblings.
         d. Identical twins raised apart from each other are of special interest to researchers because they have identical genes but have been raised in different environments.

2. Researchers compare correlations between children's traits and those of their biological and adoptive relatives, compare groups of same-sex fraternal twins with groups of identical twins, or examine correlations between traits for identical twins reared apart in order to estimate heritability.

D. Heritability and Intelligence

    1. The measure of intelligence is usually the IQ score.

        a. Historically, IQ meant "intelligence quotient" -- the child's **mental age** divided by his or her **chronological age** and multiplied by 100.

        b. Modern IQ measurements are derived differently but still compare a child with others in his or her age group or an adult with other adults.

        c. The concept of intelligence is controversial, and IQ scores do not reflect all aspects of mental performance.

    2. Variations in IQ test scores are partly heritable; in most studies, about half of the variance is explainable by genetic differences; studies of adults obtain higher estimates.

    3. Scores of identical twins are always more highly correlated than those of fraternal twins.

    4. Scores of adopted children are more highly correlated with those of birth parents than those of adoptive parents; however, on average, adopted children have IQs that are ten to twenty points higher than those of their birth parents.

    5. Environment can have a large impact even though heritability is fairly high.

    6. Ethnic differences in average IQ are controversial as evidenced by The Bell Curve.

        a. As a group, Asians score higher than whites, who score higher than African-Americans.

        b. Some theorists have confused the finding that IQ differences within groups are partly heritable, with speculation that IQ differences between groups are genetic; studies are often based on white samples.

        c. Minority children tend to have access to fewer educational and material resources.

        d. Black-white differences on achievement and aptitude tests have decreased as more opportunities have become available to African-Americans.

        e. The few studies that overcome methodological problems fail to support a genetic basis for black-white IQ differences.

E. Genes and Personality

    1. **Temperaments** are a characteristic style of responding to the environment and are influenced by heredity. Temperaments:

        a. appear in infancy.

        b.   tend to remain stable throughout childhood (Example: Jerome Kagan's research on "inhibited" versus "uninhibited" temperaments).

   2.   A **trait** is any characteristic that is assumed to describe a person across many situations.

        a.   Certain traits appear to be highly stable and highly heritable, with heritability estimates typically around .40 -.60.

        b.   Research using the statistical technique of **factor analysis** has identified clusters of correlated personality trait test items that seem to be measuring some common, underlying quality.

   3.   Researchers have identified five basic factors underlying the complexities of personality. These are:

        a.   introversion versus extroversion.

        b.   neuroticism.

        c.   agreeableness.

        d.   conscientiousness.

        e.   openness to experience.

   4.   Consistent finding is that shared environment and parental child-rearing practices seem to have no significant effect on adult personality traits.

F.   Interpretation and Critique of Behavioral Genetics Research

   1.   Interpreting behavioral genetics research requires sensitive measures of genetic and environment.

   2.   In studies of twins separated at birth the twins may still have grown up in fairly similar environments.

   3.   Even children at the extremes of a trait may change as they get older due to parental and other influences.

   4.   When environments are not highly variable, heritability estimates increase, but their meaningfulness decreases.

   5.   Some people tend to overlook the interactions between genetics and environments.

   6.   There is a tendency to confuse heritability with permanence.

G.   In Praise of Human Diversity

   1.   Heredity and environment always interact to produce the unique mixture of qualities in a person.

   2.   The survival of the species depends in part on diversity.

CHAPTER 3 SUMMARY

Psychologists have long been interested in the nature-nurture question. Historically, two positions tended to emerge: the 1._____ emphasized inborn characteristics, and the 2._____ focused on learning and experience. Most contemporary psychologists do not argue solely for one or the other position, but rather believe that heredity and environment 3._____ to produce traits. For example, research on weight has revealed that heaviness is not simply caused by overeating, but rather biological factors place certain limits on how much a person can weigh. Biological mechanisms regulating weight include basal metabolic rate, the number of fat cells, and hormones. These contribute to the 4._____, which is the genetically programmed weight a person stays at when not consciously trying to gain or lose weight.

There are two related fields within the biological perspective which contribute to our understanding of nature and nurture. These two fields are: 5._____ which emphasizes evolutionary mechanisms that explain commonalities in human psychology, including cognition, development, emotion, and social practices, and 6._____ which examines the contribution of heredity to individual differences in many human characteristics.

The basic units of heredity are 7._____. They are located on rod-shaped structures called 8._____, which consist of threadlike strands of a substance called 9._____. Each parent contributes 10._____ chromosomes to his or her offspring. The sex of the child is determined by the genetic contribution of the 11._____. Because there are thousands of genes that can be combined in thousands of ways, and because genes can spontaneously change or mutate, genetic diversity is great. The full set of genes in each cell of an organism is the 12._____.

Genetic research is difficult because most human traits depend on more than one gene pair. One method that is used to investigate genetics is the 13._____ study, in which scientists look for genetic markers in large families in which a particular condition is common.

14._____ is a change in gene frequency within a population over many generations. The environment determines which genes will survive through the process of 15._____. Because of our evolutionary history, some abilities, traits, and characteristics are universal among human beings, including reflexes, the attraction to novelty, and certain perceptual tendencies.

The detection or direct experience of physical energy in the external or internal environment due to stimulation of receptors in the sense organs is 16._____. The process by which the brain organizes and interprets sensory information is 17._____. The development of some perceptual abilities depends on certain experiences during 18._____ of development. Certain abilities may develop abnormally without certain experiences during this time.

There is a good deal of evidence that some perceptual and sensory abilities appear to be inborn, including the startle response, perceiving a sound as localized in space, distinguishing a person's voice from other kinds of sounds, discriminating odors and tastes, and the detecting of edges and angles of objects. Depth perception may also be present, and is tested in children using the 19._____.

In addition, certain emotional expressions are present at birth. There are seven universal facial expressions, including anger, happiness, fear, surprise, disgust, sadness, and contempt, that are recognized everywhere in the world and have evolved in order to help humans communicate with one another.

The emotional tie between children and caregivers is 20._____ and is initially based on 21._____. Children and animals who are deprived of being touched and held show retarded emotional and physical development. Attachment has two adaptive purposes. First, it provides a secure base from which to explore the environment. Second, it provides a safe haven to which the child can return when afraid. Mary Ainsworth demonstrated the importance of attachment in her studies using a 22._____ in which children where physically separated from their caregivers. Ainsworth found that insecurely attached children were more likely to have later social, cognitive, or behavioral problems.

Children are biologically primed to respond to human faces. They smile regularly at faces by the age of 4 to 6 weeks and engage in a rhythmic pattern of social exchange with their caregivers. Both the child and the caregiver adjust their behavior to coordinate with each other, a process known as 23._____.

24._____ is a system for combining meaningless elements into utterances that convey meaning. In order to learn this system, children must internalize a large set of grammatical rules. Children must also learn the 25._____, which is the way the sentence is actually spoken and the 26._____, the meaning inferred by applying rules of syntax.

Children do not simply imitate adults. According to Noam Chomsky, the capacity to develop language is biologically present in humans in the form of a 27._____. Chomsky and others have advanced several arguments in support of a biological basis of language. First of all, stages of linguistic development are similar across cultures. Second, children combine words in ways that adults do not. Third, adults do not always correct a child's syntax. Fourth, children who are profoundly retarded do acquire language.

Experience also plays a role. Parents tend to recast children's ungrammatical sentences, and children imitate parents' accents, inflections, and tones. There is also a 28._____ for language development probably between the ages of 1 to 5 or 6 during which language learning must occur or it may always be abnormal if learned later.

29._____ is an interdisciplinary field concerned with the genetic bases of behavior and personality. These scientists use a statistical estimate of 30._____, the proportion of the total variance in a trait that is attributable to genetic variation in a group to discern the relative contribution of heredity or environment to the development of human characteristics. There are many misconceptions about heritability. Although the terms "heritable" and "genetic" are sometimes used interchangeably, "heritable" only refers to traits that 31. _____ within a population. Also, heritability applies to a particular group living in a particular environment. It does not apply to individuals, but only to variations within a group. It does not mean that traits cannot be modified by the environment and is usually not dependent on a single gene. Genes may also turn "on" and "off" over a lifetime.

Scientists interested in heritability study people whose degree of genetic similarity is known. These studies often include comparisons of adopted children with their biological parents and adopted parents, as well as comparison of two kinds of twins, 32. _____ who share all of their genes, and 33. _____ who are only as genetically alike as any siblings. Of special interest is the study of identical twins raised apart.

One major area of heritability study is intelligence. Historically, the measure of intelligence was the 34. _____, which is the mental age divided by the chronological age times 100. Although modern measures of intelligence are computed differently, modern scores still reflect comparisons of a person with others in his or her age group. The concept of intelligence is controversial.

In most studies, about 35. _____ of the variance in IQ scores is explainable by genetic differences. 36. _____ twins always have more highly correlated scores than do 37. _____ twins, and IQ scores of adopted children correlate higher with those of their 38. _____ parents than with those of their 39. _____ parents. However, the environment can have a large impact on intelligence even when heritability is high.

The study of group differences in IQ scores has produced some controversy. Different ethnic groups have different average scores. Group average scores do not indicate anything about an individual person's score who belongs to a particular group. Some theorists have confused the finding that IQ differences within groups are partly heritable with the speculation that IQ differences 40. _____ groups are also heritable. Minority children also have less access to important resources, and there is evidence to suggest that ethnic differences in IQ decrease as this access is increased.

Personality is another major area for heritability studies. Infants seem to be born with different 41. _____, which are characteristic styles of responding to the environment. These tend to remain stable throughout childhood. A 42. _____ is any characteristic that is assumed to describe a person across many situations, and also appears to be highly heritable. Research using the statistical technique of 43. _____ has identified clusters of correlated personality trait test items that seem to be measuring some common, underlying quality. These qualities include the personality factors of introversion-extroversion, neuroticism, agreeableness, conscientiousness, and openness to experience.

One should be cautious in interpreting the results of heritability studies. To estimate heritability, one needs sensitive ways of measuring genes and environments. When environments are not highly variable, heritability estimates may increase, but their meaningfulness decreases. Some people tend to overlook the interactions between genetics and environment. Finally, there is a tendency to confuse heritability with permanence.

MULTIPLE CHOICE SELF-TEST

1. In the nature-nurture debate, those who emphasize learning and experience have been known as the:

    a. nativists.
    b. interactionists.
    c. nurturists.
    d. empiricists.

2. Loretta is frequently on a diet trying to lose weight. However, when she goes off her diet she always returns to her previous weight, probably because she:

    a. lacks willpower.
    b. overeats frequently.
    c. has emotional problems.
    d. has a stable setpoint.

3. Major depression is found disproportionalely among people in some Amish communities. Research on depression to identify the genetic marker of this disorder would be carried out in a(n) _____ study:

    a. meta-analytic.
    b. case
    c. linkage
    d. cross-sectional.

4. The interdisciplinary field that conducts heritability studies to examine individual differences in intelligence, personality and other variable traits is:

    a. evolutionary psychology.
    b. sociobiology.
    c. behavioral genetics.
    d. functionalism.

5. At conception, a fertilized egg contains _____ chromosomes.

    a. 23
    b. 32
    c. 46
    d. 48

6. Research on the role of leptin and obesity indicates that:

   a. leptin levels are lower than average in most obese people.
   b. obese people are less sensitive to leptin because of a genetic mutation.
   c. there is minimal evidence that leptin plays a role in obesity.
   d. leptin acts similarly in rats and humans.

7. The purpose of a linkage study is to:

   a. identify genes associated with physical or mental conditions through patterns of inheritence.
   b. determine the changes or mutations in gene frequencies within a population over many generations.
   c. determine similarities in genetic material between humans and primates.
   d. determine environmental factors influencing the development of a disease.

8. Virgil, the blind man who regained his sight, could identify the paw, nose, tail, and ears of a cat and yet could NOT recognize the fact that he was looking at a cat. Virgil's inability to identify a cat is the result of a failure of his:

   a. sensation abilities.
   b. depth perception deficit.
   c. feature detectors.
   d. perceptual abilities.

9. The study of kittens who were exposed to either only vertical or horizontal patterns indicates that:

   a. their vision will continue to be abnormal because of the lack of normal experience during a critical period.
   b. they have an inborn ability to perceive both vertical and horizontal lines and therefore experience has no effect on vision.
   c. kittens will develop normally once exposed to normal visual experiences.
   d. kittens recover much more readily from deficits in their visual environment than do adult cats.

10. Experiments with the visual cliff and infants indicate that:

    a. the world of a newborn is a "blooming, buzzing confusion."
    b. even at two months of age babies slow their heart rate to indicate they perceive depth.
    c. newborns perceive the world exactly as adults do.
    d. the ability to crawl is necessary to establish depth perception through experience.

11. Cross-cultural research on emotions indicates that:

    a. emotional expression is unique in different cultures.
    b. emotional expressions in infants do NOT resemble those of adults until 6 months of age.
    c. many basic emotional expressions are interpreted in the same way.
    d. emotions cannot be categorized.

12. The Harry Harlow study found that the source of a baby monkey's attachment to its mother was:

    a. protection from predators.
    b. touch or contact comfort.
    c. milk or other liquid nourishment.
    d. monkey chow.

13. Maria is playing with her newborn baby. She gazes at the baby, who gazes back. After a few seconds, the baby looks away and so does Maria. After another few seconds, the baby looks back at Maria and smiles. Maria smiles back. This exchange between mother and baby is characterized by:

    a. contact comfort.
    b. infant dominance.
    c. synchrony.
    d. therapeutic touch.

14. The purpose of infant attachment in humans is to:

    a. provide security to allow the development of cognitive skills and trust.
    b. ensure that the child receives adequate food and water.
    c. provide a child with an understanding of punishment and reward.
    d. instill moral values in the child from attachment to the mother.

15. In Mary Ainsworth's strange situation study, children who cried or protested when a parent left them with a stranger in an unfamiliar room were described as:

    a. securely attached.
    b. avoidant.
    c. anxious.
    d. ambivalent.

16. Children who do NOT develop an early, secure attachment to a caregiver tend to grow into adults who are:

    a. independent and more capable of handling challenges.
    b. anxious or avoidant in their own close relationships.
    c. less likely to have emotional problems.
    d. less likely to be neurotic.

17. One of the arguments in favor of Noam Chomsky's theory about language acquisition is that:

    a. children in different cultures go through similar stages of linguistic development.
    b. adults consistently correct their children's syntax.
    c. language learning is based on rewards and punishments.
    d. children imitate words and sentences exactly like adults.

18. Melanie, a five-year-old child, hears two different sentences: "The cat ate a mouse" and "A mouse was eaten by the cat". Melanie's ability to understand both sentences will be:

    a. limited because the sentences have the same surface structure.
    b. accomplished on her own because both sentences have the same deep structure.
    c. accomplished at that age if an adult can explain the meaning of the sentences.
    d. accomplished when she gets older.

19. "Genie" was abused, neglected, and was not exposed to language until she was discovered and released at age 13. The result of researchers' attempts to teach her language was that:

    a. she quickly overcame her early experiences and learned to speak normally.
    b. while Genie did learn some words, her grammar and pronunciation of words remained abnormal even after several years.
    c. for the rest of her life, Genie understood only the few words she had learned before her release.
    d. she regressed to an even more childish state and remained fearful of people.

20. One apparently <u>unique</u> aspect of human language is that it allows us to:

    a. communicate with others of our species.
    b. express emotions.
    c. affect the behavior of others of our species.
    d. express or comprehend novel utterances.

21. Intelligence is a trait that is moderately to highly heritable. This means that for this characteristic:

    a. environment can play very little role in influencing a particular individual's intelligence.
    b. most of the variation is genetic for all groups of people in the world.
    c. about half of the variation among individuals can be accounted for by genetic differences.
    d. the majority of an individual's personality is due to heredity.

22. Correlations of IQ scores are the highest for:

    a. identical twins reared apart.
    b. fraternal twins reared together.
    c. fraternal twins reared apart.
    d. parents and their children.

23. IQ scores of adopted children correlate most highly with the IQ scores of their:

    a. adoptive parents.
    b. birth parents.
    c. foster parents.
    d. siblings in the adoptive home.

24. On the average, the ethnic group that scores the highest on IQ tests is:

   a. Asians.
   b. whites.
   c. African-Americans.
   d. Native-Americans.

25. If we knew that hypnotizability was highly heritable in Americans of European descent, one can infer that heritability for this trait in Americans of Asian descent:

   a. is high for them, also.
   b. is low for them.
   c. may or may not be high.
   d. is culturally irrelevant for Asians.

26. Adam, a quiet baby, and Eve, a cranky baby differ in:

   a. neuroticism.
   b. sensation seeking.
   c. attachment level.
   d. temperament.

27. Edina is a compulsive shopper who likes to complain about how horrible her life is. She is best described as having the characteristic of:

   a. introversion.
   b. imagination
   c. extroversion.
   d. neuroticism.

28. Arnetta is a steady, persistent worker. A "Big Five" personality theorist would describe her as being:

   a. agreeable.
   b. open to experience.
   c. conscientious.
   d. introverted.

29. Heritability estimates for personality typically range from:

    a.   .00 to .10
    b.   .20 to .30
    c.   .40 to .60
    d.   .70 to .90

30. The personality of a shy baby is most likely to:

    a.   remain stable throughout childhood but can be modified.
    b.   be similar to other babies after the first year of life.
    c.   be determined from birth to ensure a shy adult.
    d.   be highly and easily modifiable so that the adult is outgoing.

TRUE FALSE SELF-TEST

T   F   1.   Most modern researchers are nativists.

T   F   2.   Most of us could attain the cultural body ideal if we worked at it hard enough.

T   F   3.   Psychology overlaps with biology.

T   F   4.   Obese people are more likely to be emotionally disturbed than normal weight people.

T   F   5.   Linkage studies help to identify patterns of genetic markers in large families in which a particular condition is common.

T   F   6.   Gene mutation adds to genetic diversity.

T   F   7.   At conception, the fertilized egg contains 23 chromosomes.

T   F   8.   Most traits depend on one gene pair.

T   F   9.   Perception is the detection and direct experience of physical energy due to stimulation of receptors in the sense organs.

T   F   10.   Most of depth perception is learned after the age of one.

T   F   11.   A baby can tell a human voice from another kind of sound.

T F 12. Perceptual abilities may develop abnormally if certain environmental experiences are absent during critical periods.

T F 13. Some emotional expressions are universal across cultures.

T F 14. Fulfillment of food needs rather than contact comfort or touch is the basis of attachment to a parent in animals and humans.

T F 15. Securely attached children cry when a parent leaves them with a stranger.

T F 16. Language develops in children mainly because correct words are rewarded and incorrect ones are punished by parents.

T F 17. Children everywhere go through similar stages of linguistic development.

T F 18. Modern formulations of IQ divide a child's mental age by his or her chronological age and multiply the result by 100.

T F 19. Variations in IQ test scores are highly heritable.

T F 20. IQ tests reflect all aspects of mental performance.

T F 21. When heritability is high, environment can have little impact on a trait.

T F 22. As a group, whites score higher than Asians.

T F 23. Black-white differences on achievement and aptitude tests have increased in recent years.

T F 24. IQ test scores of fraternal twins are always more highly correlated than those of identical twins.

T F 25. IQ test scores of adopted children are more highly correlated with adoptive parents than birth parents.

T F 26. "Heritable" is synonymous with "genetic".

T F 27. Temperament remains stable throughout childhood.

T F 28. Personality traits are highly heritable.

T F 29. Monozygotic twins share more genetic material than dizygotic twins.

T   F   30.   One of the five basic personality factors is conscientiousness.

KEY TERMS

behavioral genetics - An interdisciplinary field of study concerned with the genetic bases of behavior and personality.

evolutionary psychology - A field of psychology emphasizing evolutionary mechanisms that may help explain human commonalities in cognition, development, emotion, social practices, and other areas of behavior.

set point - According to one theory, the genetically influenced weight range for an individual, thought to be maintained by a biological mechanism that regulates food intake, fat reserves, and metabolism.

genes - The functional units of heredity; they are composed of DNA and specify the structure of proteins.

chromosomes - Rod-shaped structures within every body cell that carry the genes.

DNA (deoxyribonucleic acid) - The chromosomal molecule that transfers genetic characteristics by way of coded instructions for the structure of proteins.

genome - The full set of genes in each cell of an organism.

linkage studies - Studies that look for patterns of inheritance of genetic markers in large families in which a particular condition is common; the markers consist of DNA segments that vary considerably among individuals and that have known locations on the chromosomes.

evolution - A change in gene frequencies within a population over many generations; a mechanism by which genetically influenced characteristics of a population change.

natural selection - The evolutionary process in which individuals with genetically influenced traits that are adaptive in a particular environment tend to survive and to reproduce in greater numbers than other individuals; as a result, their traits become more common in the population over time.

sensation - The detection or direct experience of physical energy in the external or internal environment due to stimulation of receptors in the sense organs.

perception - The process by which the brain organizes and interprets sensory information.

language - A system that combines meaningless elements such as sounds or gestures into structured utterances that convey meaning.

heritability - A statistical estimate of the proportion of the total variance in some trait within a group that is attributable to genetic differences among individuals within the group.

identical (monozygotic) twins - Twins born when a fertilized egg divides into two parts that develop into separate embryos.

fraternal (dizygotic) twins - Twins that develop from two separate eggs fertilized by different sperm; they are not more alike genetically than any pair of siblings.

intelligence quotient (IQ) - A measure of intelligence originally computed by dividing a person's mental age by his or her chronological age and multiplying the result by 100; it is now derived from norms provided for standardized intelligence tests.

temperaments - Characteristic styles of responding to the environment that are present in infancy and are assumed to be innate.

trait - A descriptive characteristic of an individual, assumed to be stable across situations and time.

factor analysis - A statistical method for analyzing the intercorrelations among different measures or test scores. Clusters of measures or scores that are highly correlated are assumed to measure the same underlying trait or aptitude (factor).

Suggested Research Projects

1. Try to find a place (with permission) where you can observe the behavior of very young children. See if you can distinguish between temperaments. Perhaps your instructor could help you find a set of behavioral guidelines for observing temperamental styles. If the children are in a setting that allows them to interact, try to systematically observe whether or not children with similar temperamental styles tend to associate with each other. Develop some hypotheses as to why this is or is not so.

2. Interact or talk with young children who are learning language skills. Ask them questions about sentences which have a different surface structure, but the same deep structure to see if they infer the same meaning from the sentences.

Suggested Readings

Dunn, J., & Plomin, R. (1990). Separate Lives: Why Siblings are so Different. NY: BasicBooks. This book contributes to our understanding of heritability from the nurture viewpoint. The authors explain the concept of "nonshared environments" – environmental events that affect only certain individuals in a family and cause them to differ from others in the same family.

Ekman, P. (1992). Telling Lies: Clues to Deceit in the Marketplace, Politics, and Marriage. NY: Norton. This expert on nonverbal cues to emotion discuss lying and lie detection.

Kagan, J. (1994). Galen's prophecy: Temperament in Human Nature. NY: BasicBooks. A prominent developmental psychologist examines the evidence for inborn personality temperaments.

Plomin, R., Defries, J.C., & McClearn, G.E. (1980). Behavioral Genetics: A Primer. San Francisco: Freeman. A basic description of the behavior genetics field.

Suggested Audio-Visuals

PBS (1995). The Human Language Series. Includes 3 videos: Part One: Discovering the Human Language "Colorless Green Ideas"; Part Two: Acquiring the Human Language "Playing the Language Game" Part Three: The Human Language Evolves "With and Without Words" Explains human language in a visually entertaining manner. Discusses the nature versus nurture debate, the evolution of language, universal grammer, how children acquire language, and the universality of human facial expressions.

CHAPTER 3

ANSWERS TO CHAPTER 3 SUMMARY

1. nativists
2. empiricists
3. interact
4. setpoint
5. evolutionary psychology
6. behavioral genetics
7. genes
8. chromosomes
9. DNA (deoxyribonucleic acid)
10. 23
11. father
12. genome
13. linkage
14. evolution
15. natural selection
16. sensation
17. perception
18. critical periods
19. visual cliff
20. attachment
21. contact comfort
22. strange situation
23. synchrony
24. language
25. surface structure
26. deep structure
27. language acquisition device
28. critical period
29. behavioral genetics
30. heritability
31. vary
32. monozygotic (identical)
33. dizygotic (fraternal)
34. IQ score
35. half (50%)
36. identical (monozygotic)
37. fraternal (dizygotic)
38. birth
39. adoptive
40. between
41. temperaments

42. trait
43. factor analysis

ANSWERS TO MULTIPLE-CHOICE SELF-TEST

1. D
2. D
3. C
4. C
5. C
6. B
7. A
8. D
9. A
10. B
11. C
12. B
13. C
14. A
15. A
16. B
17. A
18. B
19. B
20. D
21. C
22. A
23. B
24. A
25. C
26. D
27. D
28. C
29. C
30. A

ANSWERS TO TRUE-FALSE SELF-TEST

1. F
2. F
3. T
4. F
5. T

6. T
7. F
8. F
9. F
10. F
11. T
12. T
13. T
14. F
15. T
16. F
17. T
18. F
19. T
20. F
21. F
22. F
23. F
24. F
25. F
26. F
27. T
28. T
29. T
30. T

CHAPTER 4

NEURONS, HORMONES, AND NEUROTRANSMITTERS

LEARNING OBJECTIVES

After reading and studying this chapter, you should be able to:

1.   Describe the area of study known as neuropsychology.

2.   Distinguish between the various aspects of the central nervous system and divisions of the peripheral nervous system.

3.   Describe the structure of a neuron.

4.   Explain how neurons receive and transmit information.

5.   Describe some major neurotransmitters and how they affect behavior.

6.   Describe some medical conditions that are linked to excesses or deficits of particular neurotransmitters.

7.   Describe the role of endorphins and hormones.

8.   Describe several methods for studying the brain.

9.   Discuss the locations and functions of various parts of the brain.

10.   Compare and contrast the functions of the left and right hemispheres.

11.   Summarize findings about the physiology of memory.

12.   Summarize findings about the physiology of sleep.

13.   Describe biological explanations of dreaming.

CHAPTER 4 OUTLINE

I. Introduction
    A. **Neuropsychology** is the study of the neural and biochemical basis of behavior and mental processes.

II. The Nervous System: A Basic Blueprint
    A. The nervous system functions to gather and process information, produce responses to stimuli, and coordinate the workings of different cells. It consists of two parts:
        1. The **central nervous system** (CNS) receives, processes, interprets, and stores incoming sensory information. It also sends out messages to muscles, glands, and body organs. It has two components:
            a. the brain.
            b. the spinal cord which:
                1. acts as a bridge between the brain and the parts of the body below the neck; is an extension of the brain.
                2. handles some reflexes.
                3. is protected by the spinal column.
        2. The **peripheral nervous system** (PNS) contains all portions of the nervous system outside the brain and spinal cord and handles the CNS's input and output. It includes:
            a. **sensory nerves**, which carry messages from skin, muscles, and other internal and external sense organs to the spinal cord.
            b. **motor nerves**, which carry messages from the central nervous system to muscles, glands, and internal organs.
        3. There are two divisions of the peripheral nervous system:
            a. **somatic nervous system** (bodily system), nerves connected to sensory receptors and to skeletal muscles.
            b. **autonomic nervous system** (self-governing system), regulates the functioning of blood vessels, glands, and internal organs; operates without conscious self-control.
        4. **biofeedback** can be used to help a person learn to control some autonomic responses. The autonomic nervous system is divided into two parts:
            a. **sympathetic nervous system**, mobilizes bodily resources and increases the output of energy during emotion and stress.
            b. **parasympathetic nervous system,** operates during relaxed states and conserves energy.

III. Communication in the Nervous System

A. **Neurons**, or nerve cells, are the basic units of the nervous system.
1. They are held in place by **glial cells**, which insulate them, provide them with nutrients, and remove cellular debris when neurons die (glial from Greek for "glue"); may also carry electric or chemical signals between parts of the nervous system.
2. Neurons transmit signals to, from, and within the central nervous system; they are the communication specialists.

B. The Structure of the Neuron
1. A neuron has three main parts:
   a. **dendrites**, which receive messages from other neurons and transmit these messages to the cell body (in Greek dendrite means "little tree"). Tiny projections on dendrites are called <u>spines</u> which increase in size and number as a result of maturation and experience.
   b. **cell body,** which contains the biochemical machinery to keep the cell alive and determines whether the neuron will fire (transmit a message).
   c. **axon,** which transmits messages away from the cell body to other neurons or to muscle and gland cells (from the Greek for "axle"). The end of an axon is often divided into branches called **axon terminals**.
   d. bundles of neuron fibers in the central nervous system are called <u>tracts</u>.
2. A **nerve** is a bundle of nerve fibers (axons and sometimes dendrites) in the peripheral nervous system.
   a. Most nerves enter or leave the spinal cord.
   b. The 12 **cranial nerves** are connected directly to the brain.
3. The **myelin sheath** is a layer of fatty insulating material that is found on many axons and derived from glial cells, especially on larger axons. It functions to:
   a. prevent signals from adjacent cells from interfering with one another.
   b. speed up the conduction of neural impulses by forcing them to "hop" from one break in the myelin to another rather than moving more slowly down the entire length of neuron.
4. New research indicates that it may be possible to stimulate regeneration or growth of neurons in the central nervous system.

C. How Neurons Communicate
1. The **synapse** is the site where transmission of a nerve impulse from one neuron to another occurs. It includes:
   a. the axon terminal of one axon.
   b. the **synaptic cleft** where the axon terminal of one neuron nearly touches a dendrite or cell body of another neuron.

c.   the membrane of the receiving dendrite or cell body.

2.   Certain synaptic pathways are more excitable when we store information for the long term through a process called **long-term potentiation**. Unused connections may die; this illustrates the brain's flexibility or **plasticity**.

3.   The process of neural transmission begins when a neural impulse, or **action potential**, travels down the transmitting axon; involves a change in electrical potential between the inside and outside of the cell causing a wave of electrical voltage.

4.   When the impulse reaches the **synaptic end bulb** (the tip of the axon terminal), **synaptic vesicles** (tiny sacs in the end bulb) open and release a **neurotransmitter** (a chemical substance that can alter the activity of receiving neurons).

5.   Neurotransmitters bind with **receptor sites**, special molecules in the membrane of the receiving neuron, briefly changing the membrane of the receiving cell in one of two ways:

   a.   a voltage shift in a positive direction is **excitatory**, making the cell more likely to fire.

   b.   a voltage shift in a negative direction is **inhibitory**, making the cell less likely to fire.

6.   Neural firing is an **all-or-none** event.

7.   New learning results in the establishment of new synaptic connections.

IV.   Chemical Messengers in the Nervous System

   A.   Neurotransmitters: Versatile Couriers

      1.   Neurotransmitters bind only to certain specific types of receptor sites. Some well-known neurotransmitters are:

         a.   **serotonin**, which is involved in sleep, appetite, sensory perception, temperature regulation, pain suppression, and mood.

         b.   **dopamine**, which is involved in voluntary movement, learning, memory, and emotion.

         c.   **acetylcholine**, which is involved in muscle action, cognition, memory, and emotion.

         d.   **norepinephrine**, which is involved in cognitive and emotional functions and bodily arousal.

         e.   **GABA**, which is the main inhibitory neurotransmitter in the brain.

         f.   **glutamate**, which is an important excitatory neurotransmitter involved in long-term potentiation of memory.

2. Harmful effects occur from excesses or deficits of particular neurotransmitters.
   a. In <u>Alzheimer's disease</u>, which leads to memory loss, personality changes, and disintegration of all physical and mental abilities in the elderly; brain cells responsible for producing acetylcholine have been destroyed.
   b. In <u>Parkinson's disease</u>, a condition characterized by tremors, muscular spasms, and muscular rigidity, there is degeneration of brain cells that produce and use dopamine.

B. Endorphins: The Brain's Neural Opiates
   1. **Endorphins** (<u>endogenous opioid peptides</u>) are internal, reduce pain and promote pleasure, similar to natural opiates. They act primarily as **neuromodulators**, which increase or decrease the activity of specific neurotransmitters. They operate when the person or animal is stressed.

C. Hormones: Long-Distance Messengers
   1. **Hormones** are chemical substances secreted by glands that affect other organs. **Endocrine glands** release hormones into the bloodstream. They are affected by nervous system impulses and can also affect the way the nervous system functions.
   2. The **neuroendocrine system** consists of the parts of the nervous and endocrine systems that interact.
   3. Hormones have many functions. For example:
      a. **adrenal hormones** are involved in emotion and stress responses and enhance memory; are produced by the adrenal glands perched above the kidneys. Each adrenal gland is composed of:
         1. an outer layer or cortex, which produces cortisol.
         2. an inner core or medulla, which produces:
            a. epinephrine, which causes glucose to rise in the bloodstream to enhance memory.
            b. norepinephrine which is involved in bodily arousal and cognitive and emotional functions.
      b. **melatonin** (secreted by the pineal body) regulates biological rhythms, which are regular fluctuations in various biological systems; **Circadian rhythms** recur every 24 hours; various biological clocks are linked together by a "super clock" in the **hypothalamus.**
      c. **sex hormones** regulate the development and functioning of reproductive and sex organs and stimulate the development of sexual characteristics. There are three main types:
         1. **estrogens** are feminizing hormones produced primarily in the ovaries but also in the testes and adrenal cortex.

2. **progesterone** is also produced primarily in the ovaries but also in the testes and adrenal cortex.
3. **androgens** (including **testosterone**) are masculinizing hormones produced mainly in the testes but also in the ovaries and adrenal cortex.

V. The Brain
   A. Mapping the Brain
      1. Several methods for studying the brain have been developed, including:
         a. studying patients who have had a part of the brain damaged or removed.
         b. **lesioning,** damaging or removing sections of the brain in animals.
         c. probing the brain with **electrodes** that detect the electrical activities of neurons. Electrical activity is translated into visual patterns called **brain waves** by a device called an **electroencephalogram** (EEG). Researchers use needle- or microelectrodes inserted into the brain.
         d. **PET scan (positron-emission-tomography)** - requires injection of a glucose-like radioactive substance which accumulates in highly active brain areas. Computer-processed radioactive signals are translated into colors on a monitor.
         e. **magnetic resonance imaging (MRI)** - magnetic vibrations in the nuclei of atoms are read and analyzed using computer technology.
   B. A Tour Through the Brain
      1. The **brain stem** is located at the base of the skull. It consists of:
         a. the **medulla,** which controls functions that do not have to be consciously willed, such as heart rate and breathing.
         b. the **pons,** which is involved in sleeping, waking, and dreaming.
      2. The **reticular activating system (RAS)** arouses the cortex and screens incoming information.
      3. The **cerebellum** ("lesser brain") is involved in balance and coordination.
      4. The **thalamus** relays sensory information to the cortex, except for the sense of smell, which is relayed by the **olfactory bulb.**
      5. The **hypothalamus** is involved in emotions and drives vital to survival (hunger, thirst, sex). It regulates the **pituitary gland** (the body's "master gland") and the autonomic nervous system; (*hypo* means "under").
      6. The **pituitary gland** secretes hormones that regulate other endocrine glands.

7. The **limbic system** is a group of structures involved in emotion and motivated behavior; (limbic is Latin for "border"). Olds and Milner's research reported the existence of a pleasure pathway in the limbic system. It includes:

   a. the **amygdala**, which is involved in evaluating the emotional importance of sensory information and mediating anxiety and depression.

   b. the **hippocampus**, which is involved in the storage of new information in memory (named after its seahorse shape) and the comparison of sensory messages with what the brain has learned to expect about the world. It is the "gateway to memory" and enables us to store <u>declarative memories</u>, memories of facts and events.

8. The **cerebrum** is the site of higher brain functions. It is divided into two separate halves, or **cerebral hemispheres**, which are connected by a bundle of nerve fibers called the **corpus callosum**.

   a. Generally, the right hemisphere controls the left side of the body and the left hemisphere controls the right side of the body.

   b. Each hemisphere is somewhat specialized, a phenomenon known as **lateralization**.

   c. The **cerebral cortex** is a collection of several thin layers of cells covering the cerebrum. Cell bodies in the cortex produce a grayish tissue, hence the term <u>grey matter</u>. It is divided into:

      1. **occipital lobes** (from the Latin for "in back of the head") in the back of the brain, which contain the **visual cortex** and have other functions.

      2. **parietal lobes** (from the Latin for "pertaining to walls") at the top of the brain, which contain the **somatosensory cortex**, which receives information about body pressure, pain, and temperature and provides information about body position.

      3. **temporal lobes** (from the Latin for "pertaining to the temples") at the sides of the head, which are involved in memory, perception, emotion, and language. They contain the **auditory cortex**, which processes sounds.

      4. **frontal lobes** at the front of the brain, which are involved in planning, taking initiative and thinking creatively; they contain the **motor cortex**, which controls voluntary movements. Damage to frontal lobes and forwardmost parts of the frontal lobes, the **prefrontal cortex,** may account for personality changes and criminally violent behavior.

93

5.   **association cortex** areas, which appear to be responsible for higher mental processes.

C.   Split Brains: A House Divided

    1.   Right and left hemisphere functions have been discovered partly through the study of **split-brain** patients, who have had their corpus callosum surgically severed.

    2.   Language is processed mainly in the left hemisphere.

        a.   **Broca's area**, in the left frontal lobe, is associated with speech production.

        b.   **Wernicke's area**, in the left temporal lobe, is associated with language meaning and comprehension.

    3.   Visual-spatial material is processed mainly in the right hemisphere.

    4.   In real-life activities, the two hemispheres cooperate naturally as partners, rather than distinct halves.

D.   In Search of Memory

    1.   Debate regarding whether or not memory is localized or distributed can be reconciled by recognizing that most memories consist of information gathered from many sources and senses.

VII.   The Biology of Sleep and Dreams

A.   Sleep puts an organism at risk, yet it is necessary.

B.   Why We Sleep

    1.   A likely function of sleep is to restore the body.

    2.   However, one night's sleep can eliminate all fatigue, even in a highly sleep-deprived person. Therefore, the sole purpose of sleep cannot be physiological restoration.

    3.   Many researchers believe that sleep is important for neurological restoration.

C.   Sleep occurs in regular cycles of REM (**rapid eye movement**) and **non-REM (NREM)** sleep. Each stage is characterized by certain brain wave patterns.

    1.   Relaxation prior to sleep - high **alpha-wave** (high amplitude, low frequency) activity.

    2.   **Stage 1** - small, irregular waves; low voltage and mixed frequencies.

    3.   **Stage 2** - short bursts of rapid, high-peaking waves called **sleep spindles**.

    4.   **Stage 3** - occasional slow, high-peaked **delta** waves; deeper sleep.

    5.   **Stage 4** - deep sleep, mostly delta waves.

    6.   Following this 30-45 minute sequence, stages occur in reverse order.

    7.   REM sleep occurs after stage 1. It is characterized by:

        a.   rapid, irregular waves.

        b.   increases in heart rate, blood pressure, and respiration.

        c.   changes in sex organs.

        d.   the most dreaming.

    8.   REM periods get longer and closer together as sleep goes on.

9.   Dreams occur in "real time" rather than in a "flash."

D. The Dreaming Brain

    1.   Psychological theories emphasize unconscious wishes or emotional concerns of everyday life.

    2.   The **activation-synthesis** theory holds that dreams are the result of neurons firing spontaneously in the lower part of the brain and being interpreted by the cortex.

    3.   Some theorists contend that dreaming is really a modification of what goes on while we are awake.

VIII.   The Oldest Question

    A.   The oldest question is: where is the mind?

        1.   Mind is matter.

        2.   The brain is an exceedingly complex mechanism with no identifiable center for the exercise of will.

        3.   The brain may be a loose confederation of independent "modules" all working in parallel.

CHAPTER 4 SUMMARY

1._____ are scientists who seek to understand the neural and biochemical bases of behavior. One major area of study is the 2._____ system, which gathers and processes information, produces responses to stimuli, and coordinates the workings of different cells.

The 3._____ nervous system receives, processes, interprets, and stores incoming sensory information. It also sends out messages to muscles, glands, and body organs. It has two components, the 4._____ and the 5._____, which handles reflexes and is protected by the spinal column.

The 6._____ nervous system contains all portions of the nervous system outside the brain and spinal cord and handles the central nervous system's input and output. It includes 7._____ nerves, which carry messages from the skin, muscles, and other internal and external sense organs to the spinal cord and 8._____ nerves, which carry messages from the central nervous system to muscles, glands, and internal organs.

There are two divisions of the peripheral nervous system including the 9._____ nervous system, which consists of nerves that are connected to sensory receptors and skeletal muscles, and the 10._____ nervous system, which regulates the functioning of blood vessels, glands, and internal organs. This system operates without conscious self-control. It is possible for people to control some autonomic responses through a process known as 11._____. The autonomic nervous system is divided into two parts including the 12._____ nervous system, which mobilizes bodily resources and increases the output of energy during emotion and stress, and the 13._____ nervous system, which operates during relaxed states and conserves energy.

14._____ or nerve cells are the basic units of the nervous system. They are held in place by 15._____ cells, which insulate them, provide them with nutrients, and remove cellular debris when neurons die. Neurons are the communication specialists that transmit signals to, from, and within the central nervous system. The neuron has three main parts including the 16._____, which receive messages from other neurons and transmit these messages to the cell body. Tiny projections from these structures are called 17._____, which increase in size and number as a result of maturation and experience. The neuron also has a 18._____, which contains the biochemical machinery to keep the cell alive and determines whether the neuron will fire. The 19._____ transmits messages away from the cell body to other neurons or to muscle and gland cells. The end of an axon is often divided into branches called 20._____.

A 21._____ is a bundle of nerve fibers in the peripheral nervous system. Most nerves enter or leave the spinal cord. In fact, the twelve 22._____ nerves are connected directly to the brain. The 23._____ is a layer of fatty insulating material that is found on many axons and derived from glial cells, especially on large axons. It functions to prevent signals from adjacent cells from interfering with one another and to speed up the conduction of neural impulses.

Neurons communicate with each other by transmission of a nerve impulse at a site called the 24._____. It includes the axon terminal of one axon, the 25._____, where the axon terminal of one neuron nearly touches a dendrite or cell body of another neuron, and the membrane of the receiving dendrite or cell body.

Certain synaptic pathways are more excitable when information is stored for the long term in a process called 26.____. On the other hand, unused connections may die; this illustrates the brain's flexibility or 27.____.

The process of neural transmission begins when a neural impulse or 28._____ travels down the transmitting axon and involves a change in electrical potential between the inside and outside of the cell causing a wave of electrical voltage. When the impulse reaches the tip of the axon terminal or 29._____ (tip of the axon terminal), 30._____ (tiny sacs in the end bulb) open and release a 31._____, a chemical substance that can alter the activity of receiving neurons. These chemical substances bind with 32._____ sites, which are special molecules in the membrane of the receiving neuron, that briefly change the membrane of the receiving cell in one of two ways. One way is a voltage shift in the positive direction, making the cell more likely to fire. This shift is described as 33.____. A voltage shift in a negative direction is 34._____, making the cell less likely to fire. Neural firing is an 35._____ event. The establishment of new synaptic connections results in new learning.

Neurotransmitters are versatile couriers of information and bind only to certain specific types of receptor sites. A well-known transmitter is 36._____, which is involved in sleep, appetite, sensory perception, temperature regulation, pain suppression, and mood. 37.____ is involved in voluntary movement, learning, memory, and emotion, and is thought to be involved in the medical disorder 38._____. This condition is characterized by tremors, muscular spasms, and muscular rigidity. Another disorder, 39._____ disease, which leads to memory loss, personality changes, and disintegration of all physical and mental abilities mainly in the elderly, is linked to the brain cells responsible for producing 40.____. More generally, this particular neurotransmitter, 41._____, is involved in muscle action, cognition, memory, and emotion. 42._____ is another neurotransmitter which is involved in cognitive and emotional functions and bodily arousal. 43._____ is the main inhibitory neurotransmitter in the brain. Finally, 44._____ is an important excitatory neurotransmitter involved in long-term potentiation of memory.

The brain also produces natural opiates or 45._____, which reduce pain and promote pleasure. They act primarily as 46._____, which increase or decrease the activity of specific neurotransmitters. They operate when the person or animal is stressed.

47._____ are chemical substances secreted by glands that affect other organs. 48._____ release hormones into the bloodstream. They are affected by nervous system impulses and can also affect the way the nervous system functions. The 49._____ system consists of the parts of the nervous and endocrine systems that interact. Hormones have many functions. For example, 50._____ hormones are involved in emotion and stress responses and enhance memory. They are produced by the 51._____ glands perched above the kidneys. The inner core of these glands produce 52._____, which causes glucose to rise in the bloodstream to enhance memory and 53._____. 54._____ regulate biological rhythms, which are regular fluctuations in various biological systems. Taking this substance has become increasingly popular as a health fad. This substance regulates 55._____ rhythms, which recur every 24 hours. In fact, various biological clocks are linked together by a "super clock" in the 56._____.

57._____ regulate the development and functioning of reproductive and sex organs and stimulate the development of sexual characteristics. There are three main types. 58._____ are feminizing hormones produced primarily in the ovaries, but also in the testes and adrenal cortex. 59._____ are also produced primarily in the ovaries, but also in the testes and adrenal cortex. Generally, 60._____ (including 61._____) are masculinizing hormones produced mainly in the testes but also in the ovaries and adrenal cortex.

Neuroscientists and medical researchers have used several methods for mapping and studying the brain including 62._____, damaging or removing sections of the brain in animals, and probing the brain with 63._____ that detect the electrical activities of neurons. Electrical activity is then translated into visual patterns called 64._____ by a device called an 65._____. A 66._____ requires injection of a glucoselike radioactive substance which accumulates in highly active brain areas. Computer-processed radioactive signals are translated into colors on a monitor. 67._____ analyzes magnetic vibrations in the nuclei of atoms which are read and analyzed using computer technology.

If one took a tour of the brain starting at the base of the skill one would find the 68._____, consisting of the 69._____, which controls functions that do not have to be consciously willed, such as heart rate and breathing, and the 70._____, which is involved in sleeping, waking, and dreaming. The 71._____ system is a dense network of neurons that extends upward from the brain stem and is involved in screening incoming information for the higher centers of the brain.

At the back of the head is the 72._____ or "lesser brain," which is involved in balance and coordination. The 73._____ is the sensory relay system at the center of the brain. It receives messages from all of the senses except for 74._____, which is processed by the 75._____ bulb. The 76._____ is involved in regulating drives such as hunger, thirst, and sex. It sends chemical messengers to the 77._____ or "master gland".

The 78._____ system is a group of structures involved in emotion and motivated behavior. It includes the 79._____, which is involved in evaluating the emotional importance of sensory information and mediates anxiety and depression. The 80._____ is involved in the storage of new information in memory and compares sensory messages with what the brain has learned to expect about the world. It is the "gateway to memory" and enables us to store 81._____ memories of facts and events.

The 82._____ is the site of higher brain functions. It is divided into two separate halves or 83._____, which are connected by a bundle of nerve fibers called the 84._____. Generally, the 85._____ hemisphere controls the left side of the body and the 86._____ hemisphere controls the right side of the body. Each hemisphere is somewhat specialized, a phenomenon known as 87._____. Right and left hemisphere functions have been discovered partly through the study of 88._____ patients, who have had their corpus callosum surgically severed. These studies have found that 89._____ is mainly processed in the left hemisphere. 90._____ area in the left 91._____ lobe is associated with speech production, while 92._____ area in the left 93._____ lobe is associated with language meaning and comprehension. Visual-spatial material is processed mainly in the 94._____ hemisphere. In real-life activities, the two hemispheres cooperate naturally as partners, rather than distinct halves.

The 95._____ is a collection of several thin layers of cells covering the cerebrum. It is divided into several areas or lobes. The 96._____ lobe in the back of the brain contains the 97._____ cortex. The 98._____ lobes at the top of the brain contain the 99._____ cortex, which receives information about body pressure, pain, and temperature. The 100._____ lobes at the sides of the head are involved in memory, perception, emotion, and language. They contain the 101._____ cortex, which processes sounds. The 102._____ lobes at the front of the brain contain the 103._____ cortex, which controls voluntary movements and are involved in planning, taking initiative, and thinking creatively. Damage to frontal lobes and the 104._____ cortex may account for personality changes and criminally violent behavior. The 105._____ cortex appears to be responsible for higher mental processes.

Neuroscientists are also interested in the biology of sleep. Sleep puts an organism at risk, yet it is necessary. A likely function of sleep is to restore the body, although one night's sleep can eliminate all fatigue. Thus, the sole purpose of sleep cannot be physiological restoration. Many researchers believe sleep is important for 106._____ function. Sleep occurs in regular cycles of 107._____ sleep during which dreaming occurs and 108._____ sleep. Each stage is characterized by certain brain wave patterns. During the relaxation stage prior to sleep, there is high 109._____ activity. In Stage 1 there are small, irregular waves of low voltage and mixed frequencies. During Stage 2 there are short bursts of rapid, high-peaking waves called 110._____. During Stage 3 there are occasional slow, high-peaked 111._____ waves during deeper sleep. During Stage 4, deep sleep, there are mostly delta waves. Following this 30-45 minute sequence, stages occur in reverse order.

There are several theories that have been advanced to explain dreaming. The 112._____ theory holds that dreams are the result of neurons firing spontaneously in the lower part of the brain and are being interpreted by the cortex. However, some theorists contend that dreaming is really a modification of what goes on while we are awake. Formerly, most theories of dreaming were psychological, emphasizing unconscious wishes or desires.

The oldest question is still yet to be answered: Where is the mind? However, many neuroscientists think that the brain is an exceedingly complex mechanism with no identifiable center for the exercise of will.

MULTIPLE CHOICE SELF-TEST

1. The nerves in your foot are part of the:

   a. primary nervous system.
   b. secondary nervous system.
   c. central nervous system.
   d. peripheral nervous system.

2. Nerves that carry messages from skin and muscle receptors to the brain are _____ nerves.

   a. reflex
   b. sensory
   d. motor
   e. central

3. Sue is capable of regulating her blood pressure on demand. When doing so, she is regulating her _____ nervous system.

   a. autonomic
   b. central
   c. somatic
   d. conscious

4. Sympathetic is to parasympathetic as:

   a. accelerator is to brake.
   b. decelerator is to restraint.
   c. quickness is to speed.
   d. instantaneous is to swift.

5. The part of the neuron that acts like an antenna, directly receiving messages from other nerve cells, is the:

   a. cell body.
   b. dendrite.
   c. axon.
   d. tract.

6. Loss of the myelin sheath is implicated in the physical symptoms of:

    a.   Huntington's chorea.
    b.   Parkinson's disease.
    c.   Alzheimer's disease.
    d.   multiple sclerosis.

7. The purpose of the myelin sheath is to ensure:

    a.   elimination of waste matter from the neuron.
    b.   nourishment of the neuron.
    c.   faster conduction of neural impulses.
    d.   whether or not the neuron should fire at all.

8. Toby recently had a stroke and finds it difficult to speak. However, his doctors expect him to be able to speak effectively within half a year. This expectation is based on the:

    a.   plasticity of the brain.
    b.   fact that language is reflexive.
    c.   lack of previous long-term potentiation in the brain.
    d.   administration of melatonin in order to regenerate brain cells.

9. Serotonin, dopamine, and acetylcholine are names for specific types of:

    a.   glial cells.
    b.   nerve cells.
    c.   receptors.
    d.   neurotransmitters.

10. Ellen is an older woman who suffers from insomnia. To alleviate this problem, her doctor should consider prescribing:

    a.   norepinephrine.
    b.   melatonin.
    c.   acetylcholine.
    d.   glutamate.

11. Kyle is a 65-year-old man suffering from Parkinson's disease. A drug that is effective in treating his symptoms is L-dopa, a precursor of:

    a.   GABA
    b.   acetylcholine.
    c.   dopamine.
    d.   norepinephrine.

12. Mariana is a marathon runner who usually feels exhilarated after completing her training sessions. Her "runner's high" is most likely due to the effect of:

    a.   levodopa.
    b.   endorphins.
    c.   melatonin.
    d.   exogenous opiates.

13. Chemical messengers that are made in one part of the body but affect another are:

    a.   neuroleptics.
    b.   endogenous opioid peptides.
    c.   hormones.
    d.   neuromodulators.

14. The hormone that is responsible for sexual arousal in men and women is:

    a.   epinephrine.
    b.   estrogen.
    c.   progesterone.
    d.   testosterone.

15. A college student wants to enhance her ability to memorize a list of words. A substance that is likely to help give her an immediate boost to her memory is:

    a.   estrogen.
    b.   melatonin.
    c.   glucose.
    d.   GABA.

16. Circadian rhythms recur in a regular time interval of every:

   a. 90 minutes.
   b. 24 hours.
   c. 36 hours.
   d. 28 days.

17. Dr. Peterson injects a person with a harmless radioactive element in order to record biochemical changes in that person's brain as they are happening. This procedure will produce a(n):

   a. PET scan.
   b. CAT scan.
   c. MRI picture.
   d. EEG record.

18. The area of the brain that primarily acts as a filter for incoming messages and arouses the higher centers of the brain when something demands its attention is the:

   a. brain stem.
   b. cerebellum.
   c. reticular activating system.
   d. limbic system.

19. Camilla has problems walking in a smooth and coordinated fashion ever since she fell and hit her head. Camilla is most likely to have sustained damage to her:

   a. thalamus.
   b. pons.
   c. medulla.
   d. cerebellum.

20. The brain structure which acts as the sensory switching station is the:

   a. medulla.
   b. pons.
   c. hypothalamus.
   d. thalamus.

21. Tashima recently hit her head against her car's steering wheel while in a car accident. Up until this time she had been able to exercise good judgement in social and intellectual situations. Now her judgmental ability has been impaired. Tashima has probably sustained damage to her _____ lobes.

    a. frontal
    b. parietal
    c. occipital
    d. temporal

22. If a person's medulla is destroyed he or she will:

    a. lose control of fine motor behavior.
    b. not be able to dream.
    c. have language problems.
    d. die.

23. Some of the highest concentrations of endorphins and endorphin receptors are located in the:

    a. cerebrum.
    b. prefrontal cortex.
    c. limbic system.
    d. parietal lobes.

24. The part of the brain that is responsible for evaluating sensory information and determining its emotional importance is the:

    a. hypothalamus.
    b. amygdala.
    c. corpus callosum.
    d. pons.

25. A man has his hippocampus removed in order to relieve severe and life-threatening seizures caused by epilepsy. The most likely effect of this surgery is to damage his ability to:

    a. form declarative memories.
    b. control the emotion of anger.
    c. engage in fine motor control and balance.
    d. hear and comprehend language.

26. A police officer is shot in the left temporal lobe in Wernicke's area. The likely result of this injury to the brain is that the officer will have difficulty in:

   a. comprehending and understanding word meanings.
   b. producing speech.
   c. learning new declarative memories.
   d. learning new procedural memories.

27. In real-life situations, severing the corpus callosum results in:

   a. severe brain damage.
   b. two separate brains each with distinct thoughts and memories.
   c. control of seizures and normal behavior except under experimental conditions.
   d. a spread of electrical activity throughout the brain.

28. Most dreaming takes place during:

   a. REM sleep.
   b. NREM sleep.
   c. stage 3 sleep.
   d. stage 4 sleep.

29. One important characteristic of REM sleep is that your:

   a. heart rate decreases.
   b. blood pressure falls.
   c. breathing becomes slow and regular.
   d. your skeletal muscles go limp.

30. The activation-synthesis theory proposes that dreams function to:

   a. make sense of the spontaneous firing of neurons.
   b. fulfill our unconscious wishes and fantasies.
   c. help us resolve deep-seated emotional conflicts.
   d. modify what goes on when we are awake.

TRUE FALSE SELF-TEST

T   F   1. The peripheral system consists of the brain and spinal cord.

T   F   2. The somatic nervous system works automatically, without a person's conscious control.

T F 3. Some people can intentionally learn to heighten or suppress autonomic responses such as heart rate or blood pressure.

T F 4. The sympathetic nervous system works to enable the body to conserve and store energy by slowing autonomic functions.

T F 5. Glial cells can carry electric or chemical signals between parts of the nervous system.

T F 6. The myelin sheath speeds the conduction of neural impulses.

T F 7. Severed axons in the spinal cords of some mammals have been regenerated by neuroscientists.

T F 8. Once a synaptic connection in the brain has been made, it is impossible to change or eliminate it.

T F 9. It is possible for a person who is incapable of recalling simple words because of a stroke to regain normal speech within several months.

T F 10. The firing of a neuron is an all-or-none event.

T F 11. Neurotransmitters exist only in the brain.

T F 12. Glutamate functions as an important inhibitory neurotransmitter in the brain.

T F 13. The degeneration of brain cells that produce serotonin appear to cause the symptoms of Parkinson's disease.

T F 14. Endorphins mimic the effects of natural opiates.

T F 15. Hormones primarily affect the part of the body they originate in.

T F 16. Men do not produce the feminizing hormone estrogen.

T F 17. Adrenal hormones are involved in memory functioning.

T F 18. A high level of arousal is best when you want to learn and remember new information.

T F 19. The sugar, glucose, can enhance memory performance.

T   F   20.   Biological clocks in our brains regulate our sleep cycle.

T   F   21.   A PET scan can record biochemical changes in the brain as they are happening.

T   F   22.   Hanging, as a method of execution, is effective because it severs nervous pathways from the cerebellum.

T   F   23.   The medulla is involved in our sense of balance.

T   F   24.   The only sense that completely bypasses the thalamus is the sense of sight.

T   F   25.   The limbic system is heavily involved in emotions, such as rage and fear, that we share with other animals.

T   F   26.   Humans will press a button thousands of times, and for many hours at a time, to receive stimulation to their limbic systems.

T   F   27.   People with damage to the amygdala often have difficulty in recognizing fear in themselves or others.

T   F   28.   The result of a split-brain operation on a human being is severe intellectual and emotional damage.

T   F   29.   The frontal lobes govern personality, self-control, and our ability to plan.

T   F   30.   A sleep-deprived person requires the same number of hours of sleep as he/she is deprived.

KEY TERMS

neuropsychology - The field of psychology concerned with the neural and biochemical bases of behavior and mental processes.

central nervous system (CNS) - The portion of the nervous system consisting of the brain and spinal cord.

peripheral nervous system (PNS) - All portions of the nervous system outside the brain and spinal cord; it includes sensory and motor nerves.

somatic nervous system - The subdivision of the peripheral nervous system that connects to sensory receptors and skeletal muscles; sometimes called the skeletal nervous system.

autonomic nervous system - The subdivision of the peripheral nervous system that regulates the internal organs and glands.

sympathetic nervous system - The subdivision of the autonomic nervous system that mobilizes bodily resources and increases the output of energy during emotion and stress.

parasympathetic nervous system - The subdivision of the autonomic nervous system that operates during relaxed states and that conserves energy.

neuron - A cell that conducts electrochemical signals; the basic unit of the nervous system. Also called a nerve cell.

glial cells - Cells that hold neurons in place, insulate neurons, and provide them with nutrients.

dendrites - Branches on a neuron that receive information from other neurons and transmit it toward the cell body.

cell body - The part of the neuron that keeps it alive and determines whether it will fire.

axon - Extending fiber of a neuron that conducts impulses away from the cell body and transmits them to other neurons.

nerve - A bundle of nerve fibers (axons and sometimes dendrites) in the peripheral nervous system.

myelin sheath - A fatty insulating sheath surrounding many axons.

synapse - The site where transmission of a nerve impulse from one nerve cell to another occurs; it includes the synaptic end bulb, synaptic cleft, and receptor sites in the membrane of the receiving cell.

long-term potentiation - A long-lasting increase in the strength of synaptic responsiveness, thought to be a biological mechanism of memory.

neurotransmitter- A chemical substance that is released by a transmitting neuron at the synapse and that alters the activity of a receiving neuron.

endorphins - Neuromodulators that are similar in structure and action to opiates. They are involved in pain reduction, pleasure, and memory, and are known technically as endogenous opioid peptides.

neuromodulators - Chemical substances in the nervous system that increase or decrease the action of specific neurotransmitters.

hormones - Chemical substances, secreted by organs called glands, that affect the functioning of other organs.

endocrine glands - Internal organs that produce hormones and release them into the bloodstream.

adrenal hormones - Hormones produced by the adrenal glands that are involved in emotion and stress; they include cortisol, epinephrine, and norepinephrine.

melatonin - A hormone secreted by the pineal gland that is involved in the regulation of daily (circadian) biological rhythms.

biological rhythm - A periodic, more or less regular fluctuation in a biological system; it may or may not have psychological implications.

circadian rhythm - A biological rhythm that recurs approximately every 24 hours.

sex hormones - Hormones that regulate the development and functioning of reproductive and sex organs and that stimulate the development of male and female sexual characteristics; they include androgens (such as testosterone), estrogens, and progesterone.

electroencephalogram (EEG) - A recording of neural activity detected by electrodes.

PET scan (positron-emission tomography) - A method for analyzing biochemical activity in the brain, using injections of a glucoselike substance containing a radioactive element.

MRI (magnetic resonance imaging) - A method for studying body and brain tissue, using magnetic fields and special radio receivers.

brain stem - The part of the brain at the top of the spinal cord; it is responsible for automatic functions such as heartbeat and respiration.

medulla - A structure in the brain stem responsible for certain automatic functions, such as breathing and heart rate.

pons - A structure in the brain stem involved in, among other things, sleeping, waking, and dreaming.

reticular activating system (RAS) - A dense network of neurons found in the core of the brain stem; it arouses the cortex and screens incoming information.

cerebellum - A brain structure that regulates movement and balance and that is involved in the learning of certain kinds of simple responses.

thalamus - The brain structure that relays sensory messages to the cerebral cortex.

hypothalamus - A brain structure involved in emotions and drives vital to survival, such as fear, hunger, thirst, and reproduction; it regulates the autonomic nervous system.

pituitary gland - A small endocrine gland at the base of the brain that releases many hormones and regulates other endocrine glands.

limbic system - A group of brain areas involved in emotional reactions and motivated behavior.

amygdala - A brain structure involved in the arousal and regulation of emotion; it may also play a role in the association of memories formed in different senses.

hippocampus - a brain structure thought to be involved in the storage of new information in memory.

cerebrum - The largest brain structure, consisting of the upper part of the forebrain; it is in charge of most sensory, motor, and cognitive processes. From the Latin for "brain."

cerebral hemispheres - The two halves of the cerebrum.

corpus callosum - The bundle of nerve fibers connecting the two cerebral hemispheres.

lateralization - Specialization of the two cerebral hemispheres for particular psychological operations.

cerebral cortex - A collection of several thin layers of cells covering the cerebrum; it is largely responsible for higher mental functions. Cortex is Latin for "bark" or "rind".

rapid eye movement (REM) sleep - Sleep periods characterized by eye movement, loss of muscle tone, and dreaming.

alpha waves - Relatively large, slow brain waves characteristic of relaxes wakefulness.

delta waves - Slow, regular brain waves characteristic of stage 3 and stage 4 sleep.

activation-synthesis theory - The theory that dreaming results from the cortical synthesis and interpretation of neural signals triggered by activity in the lower part of the brain.

Suggested Research Projects

1. Find articles in magazines, scientific journals, or on the Internet about one or more specialized topics you are interested in knowing more about.

2. Test the speed of neural impulses by having several people stand in a line and hold hands. Tell them to close their eyes and to squeeze the left hand of the person next to them when they feel their right hand being squeezed. Using a stopwatch, record the time it takes to get from one end of the line to the other. Then ask the participants to squeeze the next person's shoulder instead of his or her hand. Does the time differ? What neural explanation can you give for this difference?

Suggested Readings

Calvin, W. H., & Ojemann, G.A. (1994). Conversations with Neil's Brain. Reading, MA: Addison-Wesley. The story of a person with epilepsy who undergoes temporal lobe surgery. Describes the presurgery exploration and mapping of his brain.

Hobson, J.A. (1988). The Dreaming Brain. NY: BasicBooks. Discussion of the psychological and neurobiological aspects of sleep and dreaming.

Sacks, O. (1985). The Man Who Mistook His Wife for a Hat and Other Clinical Tales. New York: Harper & Row. A collection of case studies of people with neurological abnormalities, written in a highly engaging fashion.

Springer, S.P., & Deutsch, GJ. (1993). Left Brain, Right Brain. NY: W.H. Freeman. Exploration of what we know about the brain asymmetry.

Suggested Audio-Visuals

Annenberg/CPB. (1984). The Brain. This four volume series explores various topics relevant to the structure and function of the brain.

PBS Video, WNET, NY (1988). The Mind. This nine part series explores our sense of self, language, memory, dysfunction, and the unconscious.

CHAPTER 4

ANSWERS TO CHAPTER SUMMARY

1. neuropsychologists
2. nervous
3. central
4. brain
5. spinal cord
6. peripheral
7. sensory
8. motor
9. somatic
10. autonomic
11. biofeedback
12. sympathetic
13. parasympathetic
14. neurons
15. glial
16. dendrites
17. spines
18. cell body
19. axon
20. axon terminals
21. nerve
22. cranial
23. myelin sheath
24. synapse
25. synaptic cleft
26. long-term potentiation
27. plasticity
28. action potential
29. synaptic end bulb
30. synaptic vesicles
31. neurotransmitter
32. receptor
33. excitatory
34. inhibitory
35. all-or-none
36. serotonin
37. dopamine
38. Parkinson's disease
39. Alzheimer's

40. acetylcholine
41. acetylcholine
42. norepinephrine

43. GABA
44. glutamate
45. endorphins
46. neuromodulators
47. hormones
48. endocrine glands
49. neuroendocrine
50. adrenal
51. adrenal
52. epinephrine
53. norepinephrine
54. melatonin
55. circadian
56. hypothalamus
57. sex hormones
58. estrogens
59. progesterone
60. androgens
61. testosterone
62. lesioning
63. electrodes
64. brain waves
65. EEG (electroencephalogram)
66. PET scan (positron-emission-tomography)
67. MRI (magnetic resonance imaging)
68. brain stem
69. medulla
70. pons
71. reticular activating system (RAS)
72. cerebellum
73. thalamus
74. smell
75. olfactory
76. hypothalamus
77. pituitary gland
78. limbic
79. amygdala
80. hippocampus
81. declarative
82. cerebrum

83. cerebral hemispheres
84. corpus callosum
85. left
86. right
87. lateralization
88. split-brain
89. language
90. Broca's
91. frontal
92. Wernicke's
93. temporal
94. right
95. cerebral cortex
96. occipital
97. visual
98. parietal
99. somatosensory
100. temporal
101. auditory
102. frontal
103. motor
104. prefrontal
105. association
106. brain
107. REM (rapid eye movement)
108. NREM
109. alpha-waves
110. sleep spindles
111. delta
112. activation-synthesis

ANSWERS TO MULTIPLE-CHOICE SELF-TEST

1. D
2. B
3. A
4. A
5. B
6. D
7. C
8. A
9. D
10. B

11.	C
12.	B
13.	C
14.	D
15.	C
16.	B
17.	A
18.	C
19.	D
20.	D
21.	A
22.	D
23.	C
24.	B
25.	A
26.	B
27.	C
28.	A
29.	D
30.	A

ANSWERS TO TRUE-FALSE SELF-TEST

1.	F
2.	F
3.	T
4.	F
5.	T
6.	T
7.	T
8.	F
9.	T
10.	T
11.	F
12.	F
13.	F
14.	T
15.	F
16.	F
17.	T
18.	F
19.	T
20.	T
21.	T

22. F
23. F
24. F
25. T
26. F
27. T
28. F
29. T
30. F

CHAPTER 5

EVALUATING THE BIOLOGICAL PERSPECTIVE

CHAPTER 5 LEARNING OBJECTIVES

1. Explain several of the contributions of the biological perspective to psychological science.

2. Discuss some of the misuses and limitations of the biological perspective.

3. Discuss the controversy concerning premenstrual syndrome.

4. Compare and contrast arguments for and against sociobiology.

5. Compare and contrast the relative benefits and dangers of the use of drugs in the treatment of mental illness.

CHAPTER 5 OUTLINE

I.   In the past few decades, there has been a huge expansion of the understanding of the nervous system and brain chemistry.

II.   Contributions and Misuses of This Perspective
    A.   The biological perspective has:
        1.   rejected extreme environmentalism and improved our understanding of people as animals whose behavior is influenced by evolution, genes, and neurons.
        2.   shown that our bodies and our brains need proper care and maintenance to function well.
        3.   improved our understanding of biological contributions to mental and emotional disorders and their management.
    B.   However, <u>biological reductionism</u>, the tendency to explain complex personal and social problems solely in terms of a few physiological mechanisms, leads to three errors:
        1.   overstatement of biological findings encourages people to draw premature conclusions.
            a.   Scientists mistakenly identified a gene that was thought to cause **bipolar disorder**, a mood disorder in which depression alternates with mania.
            b.   Scientists, so far, have been unable to identify definite biological causes for **schizophrenia**, a mental disorder or group of disorders marked by symptoms such as delusions, hallucinations, inappropriate emotions, and bizarre speech.
            c.   "Hot" issues such as sex differences in the brain are especially likely to invoke premature conclusions.
        2.   there is a strong tendency to draw unwarranted conclusions about cause and effect. Biology influences behavior, but experience also alters biology.
        3.   people often exaggerate the power of genes, for example, when evaluating findings on the origins of sexual orientation.
    C.   Biological findings have great potential for being misinterpreted and misused for political reasons. Critics worry that biological findings will be used to foster racism and draw attention away from economic and environmental causes of human suffering.

III.   The appeal of the biological perspective, its pitfalls and its problems, can be seen in current debates about 3 issues: 1. the importance of hormones, 2. the validity of sociobiology, 3. the use of drugs to treat psychological disorders.

A.   Issue # 1 Hormones, Mood, and Behavior
   1.   **Premenstrual syndrome (PMS)** is described as a cluster of physiological and psychological symptoms associated with the days preceding menstruation. Research findings from double-blind studies indicate that:
      a.   physiological symptoms vary, but have a physical basis.
      b.   emotional symptoms are not reliably and universally tied to the menstrual cycle.
      c.   women and men do not differ in emotional symptoms or number of mood swings.
      d.   there is no relationship between cycle stage and performance of important real-world behaviors.
      e.   the impact of a bodily change depends on how the change is interpreted and how the person responds to it.
   2.   Men have daily testosterone fluctuations and some men have high levels of testosterone which are typically not characterized as a "syndrome".
B.   Issue # 2 Sociobiology and the Genetic Leash
   1.   In **sociobiology** the focus is on the species, and sociobiologists hold the view that individuals tend to act in ways that give one a reproductive advantage. For example, sociobiologists claim that:
      a.   men are motivated to be sexually promiscuous, dominant, and aggressive in order to propagate their genes.
      b.   women are motivated to be sexually selective because they can conceive and bear only a limited number of offspring.
   2.   Evolutionary psychologists agree with much of the sociobiology argument, except that behavioral tendencies, including mating preferences and strategies, are the end products of two evolutionary processes:
      a.   natural selection, which occurs when characteristics increase in frequency because they help individuals survive.
      b.   sexual selection, which occurs when characteristics increase in frequency because they help individuals compete for or attract sexual partners.
   3.   Not all animal behavior confirms sociobiological theory, and evolutionary theorists believe it is a mistake to argue by analogy because the origins of the behavior may not be the same in humans as compared to animals.
   4.   Sociobiological arguments have some troubling political implications.
   5.   Sociobiology's opponents dispute sociobiology's estimates of the relative power of biology versus culture. Evolutionary psychologists emphasize adaptive nature of behaviors in original environments in which they evolved, but recognize they may not be adaptive in current environments.

120

C.　Issue # 3 Medicating the Mind

1.　The biological perspective has made important contributions to the treatment of emotional disorders, including **major depression,** a serious disorder that involves chronic misery, decreased self-esteem, apathy, and a pervasive sense of hopelessness.　Drug treatments include:

　　a.　**antipsychotic drugs** (major tranquilizers) used to treat schizophrenia and other **psychoses** (extreme mental disorders that involve distorted perceptions and irrational behavior).

　　b.　**antidepressant drugs** for mood disorders and **obsessive - compulsive symptoms** including handwashing and hairpulling.　There are 3 types of antidepressants:

　　　　1.　monamine oxidase (MAO) inhibitors elevate the level of norepinephrine and serotonin in the brain.

　　　　2.　tricyclic antidepressants prevent normal reuptake of norepinephrine and serotonin.

　　　　3.　fluoxetine (Prozac) targets serotonin.

　　c.　**"minor" tranquilizers** (e.g., Valium, Xanax) for anxiety disorders or **panic attacks** (brief episodes of intense fear and feelings of impending doom or death, accompanied by intense physiological arousal).

　　d.　lithium carbonate - used to treat bipolar disorder.

2.　Despite their benefits, drugs also have several limitations:

　　a.　the placebo effect - double-blind studies comparing active placebos that mimic the physical effects of real drugs often find little difference between the real drug and the placebo.

　　b.　high relapse and high drop-out rates from taking the drug.

　　c.　dosage problems - difficult to find the "therapeutic window," an amount that is enough but not too much.

　　d.　side effects and long-term risks - include tardive (late-appearing) dyskinesia (involuntary muscle movements caused by taking antipsychotic medications) and neuroleptic malignant syndrome caused by reactions to antipsychotic drugs.

　　e.　dysthymia - a condition of chronic melancholy is one symptom helped by Prozac, but Prozac has been criticized for altering negative personality characteristics which may also be responsible for creativity and insight.

3.　Drugs are sometimes prescribed routinely, without investigation of the source of a person's problems.

4.　Biological findings are most illuminating when integrated with knowledge about personal development and cultural context.

5.　Jurassic Park Question:　Just because we *can* do something, does that mean we *should* do it?

121

EVALUATION SUMMARY

The biological perspective emphasizes the similarities between humans and other animals. However, critics of the biological perspective have spoken of the danger of biological 1._____, the tendency to explain complex issues in terms of simple physiological mechanisms. For example, scientists mistakenly identified a gene that was thought to cause 2._____, a mood disorder in which depression alternatives with mania. Scientists also have not been able to identify a definite biological cause for 3._____, a mental disorder or group of disorders marked by symptoms such as delusions, hallucinations, inappropriate emotions, and bizarre speech. People need to realize that experience and biology interact, and that there is a tendency to draw unwarranted conclusions about cause and effect from biopsychological findings. There is also a fear that research will be used to foster racism and draw attention away from the economic and environmental causes of human suffering.

The interaction of biology and environment can be illustrated by the research findings in the area of 4._____, a cluster of physiological and psychological symptoms associated with the days preceding menstruation. While physiological symptoms are well-documented, 5._____ studies have revealed that, overall, women and men do not differ in emotional symptoms or mood swings over the course of the month. The impact of any bodily change depends on the interpretation of, and response to, that change.

A small group of theorists called 6._____ have proposed that evolutionary motivations dominate human behavior, including mating patterns and differences between male and female sexual tendencies. A subfield of psychology that studies the same issues, 7._____ psychology, agrees that evolutionary motivations may influence human behavior, but argue that they may be the end result of adaptation to a particular environment and may not be as adaptive in modern society.

The biological approach has provided new insights into the biochemical and genetic bases of mental and emotional disorders, including 8._____, a serious disorder that involves chronic misery, decreased self-esteem, apathy, and a pervasive sense of hopelessness. Drug treatments include 9._____, which have transformed the treatment of schizophrenia and other psychotic disorders, and 10._____, drugs which have been helpful in the treatment of mood disorders. There are also the 11._____ for anxiety disorders or 12._____, brief episodes of intense fear and feelings of impending doom or death, accompanied by intense physiological arousal. However, these medications manage symptoms and do not provide a cure. They are also associated with serious side effects and even long-term risks. Critics of the use of medication to treat these illnesses usually cite these risks, as well as the placebo effect and high relapse and drop-out rates.

The challenge in evaluating this perspective is to learn from biology without oversimplifying by reducing all explanations to biological ones. In addition, there is the Jurassic Park question: Just because we can do something, does that mean we should do it, in applying our knowledge of the biological perspective.

CHAPTER 5 MULTIPLE CHOICE

1. Dr. Knowles is known for his argument that culture and social forces are the major determinants of behavior. This perspective is known as:

    a. biological Darwinism.
    b. social Darwinism.
    c. extreme environmentalism.
    d. eugenics.

2. People who argue that all social and psychological problems are due to physiological mechanisms are agreeing with a perspective known as:

    a. eugenics.
    b. interactionism.
    c. psychological reductionism.
    d. biological reductionism.

3. The Nazis, who exterminated 12 million people during the Holocaust, were inspired by:

    a. social Darwinism.
    b. biological reductionism.
    c. sociobiology.
    d. evolutionary psychology.

4. Research on the role of physical health in psychological functioning indicates that good nutrition and aerobic exercise:

    a. keep our bodies healthy but have little effect on mood functioning.
    b. result in lower arousal to stress and a more positive mood.
    c. do have placebo effect on mood and stress, but not a physical effect.
    d. affect the mood and stress tolerance of mainly elite athletes.

5. Even after other factors are taken into account, behavior problems and intellectual deficits among poverty-stricken children have been strongly linked to the:

    a. absence of a father.
    b. mother's IQ.
    c. mother's occupation.
    d. ingestion of lead-based paint.

6. Alzheimer's disease can most likely be attributed to:

   a. malnutrition.
   b. genetic causes.
   c. normal aging.
   d. psychological stress.

7. A current issue of the journal "Brain Science" contains a research report on a previously unstudied brain structure. The researchers found that the structure was twice as large in paranoid individuals compared to normal individuals. You should conclude that:

   a. more research needs to be done to determine the structure's relationship to paranoia.
   b. the larger brain structure causes paranoia.
   c. paranoia causes the brain structure to become enlarged.
   d. paranoia is caused by both genetic defects and the enlarged brain structure.

8. Joe is a gay man and Sally is a lesbian. Currently, the best explanation for their sexual orientation is:

   a. genetic determinism and brain structures.
   b. cultural determinism.
   c. experiential determinism and individual choice.
   d. an interaction between biology, culture, and experience.

9. Research evidence indicates that premenstrual symptoms are due to:

   a. purely biological mechanisms.
   b. purely cultural experiences.
   c. an interaction between experience and biology.
   d. an interaction between genetic abnormalities and learning.

10. The belief that psychological traits and social customs have been selected to aid individuals in propagating their genes has been advanced mainly by:

    a. sociologists.
    b. physiological psychologists.
    c. sociobiologists.
    d. medical researchers.

11. The belief that behavioral tendencies are the end products of natural selection and sexual selection and may not necessarily be adaptive in contemporary society is most likely to be held by:

a. eugenicists.
b. evolutionary psychologists.
c. sociobiologists.
d. social Darwinists.

12. Research on average sex differences in the size and shape of the splenium indicate that:

a. the female brain is definitely less lateralized than the male brain.
b. most studies find no sex differences at all.
c. this brain structure produces differences in male and female behavior with regard to the processing of auditory information.
d. the shape of the splenium is different in women as compared to men, but its size is the same.

13. Chronic misery, decreased self-esteem, apathy, and a pervasive sense of hopelessness characterize:

a. bipolar disorder.
b. schizophrenia.
c. antisocial personality disorder.
d. major depression.

14. Barney is a young college student who has been hospitalized because he lives in his own inner world, hears voices, and believes that aliens from Mars are monitoring his thoughts. He is most likely to be suffering from:

a. major depression.
b. schizophrenia.
c. an anxiety disorder.
d. obsessive-compulsive symptoms.

15. Thorazine, Haldol, and Clozaril decrease hallucinations and delusions and are used to treat:

a. neuroses.
b. phobias.
c. anxiety disorders.
d. psychoses.

16. One traditionally effective treatment for bipolar disorder is:

    a. Lithium carbonate.
    b. Haldol.
    c. Thorazine.
    d. Prozac.

17. Dr. Jenkins is conducting an experiment to determine the effect of a new antipsychotic drug. She is including a control group who will take a drug that will mimic the physical effects of the new drug. The control group will be taking a(n):

    a. active placebo.
    b. anti-depressant drug.
    c. anti-psychotic drug.
    d. inactive placebo

18. The "therapeutic window" with regard to the administration of drugs which have an impact on psychological disorders is best described as the:

    a. time period between the administration of the drug and the alleviation of symptoms.
    b. the effect of the drug above and beyond a placebo level.
    c. the dose that is most effective without causing harm.
    d. the largest possible dose that a patient may receive.

19. Joe is responding positively to his antidepressant medication. To ensure that he will not relapse, Joe's doctor should:

    a. steadily increase the dosage of the medication.
    b. withdraw the medication after a year.
    c. help Joe learn to cope with his problems and continue drug therapy.
    d. administer a second type of antidepressant medication.

20. Tardive dyskinesia and neuroleptic malignant syndrome are long-term side effects associated with:

    a. antipsychotic drugs.
    b. antidepressant drugs.
    c. stimulants.
    d. Prozac.

TRUE-FALSE

1. T   F   Most contemporary psychologists believe the environment is the sole determinant of personality.

2. T   F   Physical health plays a minimal role in psychological functioning.

3. T   F   Ordinary foods can affect mood and alertness.

4. T   F   High exposure to lead is associated with attention problems, aggression, and delinquency.

5. T   F   Alzheimer's is a normal result of the aging process.

6. T   F   Most complex personal and social problems can ultimately be explained solely in terms of a few physiological mechanisms.

7. T   F   Hormones can cause violent criminal behavior in a simple and direct manner.

8. T   F   There is one definitive biological cause of all cases of schizophrenia.

9. T   F   Research indicates that differences in the size and shape of the splenium can explain behavioral sex differences.

10. T   F   Experience can alter the biology of the brain.

11. T   F   Having a homosexual orientation is related to bad parenting practices and individual psychopathology.

12. T   F   The expression of sexual orientation is affected by cultural norms and practices.

13. T   F   Sexual orientation is too complex to be explained by a single gene.

14. T   F   There is solid evidence that millions of women suffer from mood changes during the days prior to having their menstrual period.

15. T   F   Blocking the hormonal changes that normally occur premenstrually eradicates all symptoms of PMS.

16. T   F   Women and men differ significantly in the emotional symptoms they report in the course of a month.

17. T F Menstrual cycle stage is related to work efficiency and problem solving.

18. T F Premenstrual symptoms are created by an interaction between mind and body.

19. T F Men's testosterone levels peak in the morning and fall in the evening.

20. T F Human behavior is largely motivated by instincts.

21. T F Evolutionary psychologists believe that the main motive of human beings is to perpetuate their genes. (???)

22. T F Evolutionary psychologists believe that behavioral tendencies are the end products of sexual and natural selection.

23. T F Around the world, studies have found that men are more violent than women and more socially dominant.

24. T F Because two species behave in a similar fashion, this means that the origins of the behavior must be the same in both species.

25. T F There are some female birds, fish, mammals, and primates that are sexually ardent and promiscuous.

26. T F Many sociobiologists would agree that even if there were identical education and access to all professions, men would still play a disproportionate role in political life, business, and science, compared to women.

27. T F Antipsychotic drugs cure schizophrenia.

28. T F Antipsychotic drugs rarely have negative side or long-term effects.

29. T F Prozac is an antidepressant drug.

30. T F Double-blind studies comparing the effects of active placebos to real drugs often find little difference between them.

KEY TERMS

bipolar disorder - A mood disorder in which depression alternates with mania.

schizophrenia - A mental disorder or group of disorders marked by some or all of these symptoms: delusions, hallucinations, disorganized and incoherent speech, severe emotional abnormalities, inappropriate behavior, and withdrawal into an inner world.

sociobiology - An interdisciplinary field of study that emphasizes evolutionary explanations of social behavior in animals, including human beings.

major depression - A mood disorder involving disturbances in emotion (excessive sadness); behavior (loss of interest in one's usual activities); cognition (distorted thoughts of hopelessness and low self-esteem); and body function (fatigue and loss of appetite).

antipsychotic drugs - Major tranquilizers used primarily in the treatment of schizophrenia and other psychotic disorders.

psychosis - An extreme mental disturbance involving distorted perceptions and irrational behavior; it may have psychological or physiological causes.

antidepressant drugs - A category of drugs that are used primarily in the treatment of mood disorders, especially depression and anxiety.

obsessive compulsive disorder - An anxiety disorder in which a person feels trapped in repetitive, persistent thoughts (obsessions) and repetitive, ritualized behaviors (compulsions) designed to reduce anxiety.

"minor" tranquilizers - Depressants commonly prescribed for patients who complain of unhappiness or worry; they are the least effective drugs for emotional disorders.

panic attack - a brief feeling of intense fear and impending doom or death, accompanied by intense physiological symptoms such as rapid breathing and pulse and dizziness.

Suggested Research Projects

1.   Replicate one of the experiments on premenstrual syndrome cited in your textbook under the supervision of your psychology experiment. You will have to read the original research article to study how the experiment was done. Ask your professor for guidance regarding how you might replicate the experiment as an independent study project. You may even find that you have an original idea for a research study on this topic. Make sure you complete any human subjects ethics form required by your college and university. In addition, obtain the approval of your college or university's ethics committee before you start your research project. Did you obtain the same results as the original researchers? What may account for any differences between your results and the original research?

Suggested Readings

Campbell, A. (1993). <u>Men, Women and Aggression</u>. NY: HarperCollins. Discussion of the roots of aggression with emphasis on gender differences in aggression and ways of viewing aggression.

Kluger, J. (1996). <u>Demonic Males</u>. Examines the behavior of Bonobo primate society and examines the implications of their social and sexual behavior for human society. In particular, examines the peacekeeping role of female Bonobos.

Kramer, P.D. (1993). <u>Listening to Prozac</u>. NY: Penguin Books. This psychiatrist examines the personality altering nature of the drug Prozac.

Ornstein, R. (1991). <u>The Evolution of Consciousness: The Origins of the Way We Think</u>. NY: Simon & Schuster. Reviews the evolution of the mind.

ANSWERS TO CHAPTER 5 SUMMARY

1. reductionism
2. bipolar disorder
3. schizophrenia
4. premenstrual syndrome (PMS)
5. double-blind
6. sociobiologists
7. evolutionary
8. major depression
9. antipsychotic drugs
10. antidepressant drugs
11. minor tranquilizers
12. panic attacks

ANSWERS TO MULTIPLE CHOICE SELF-TEST

1. C
2. D
3. A
4. B
5. D
6. B
7. A
8. D
9. C
10. C

11.	B
12.	B
13.	D
14.	B
15.	D
16.	A
17.	A
18.	C
19.	C
20.	A

ANSWERS TO TRUE-FALSE SELF-TEST

1.	F
2.	F
3.	T
4.	T
5.	F
6.	F
7.	F
8.	F
9.	F
10.	T
11.	F
12.	T
13.	T
14.	F
15.	F
16.	F
17.	F
18.	T
19.	T
20.	F
21.	F
22.	T
23.	T
24.	F
25.	T
26.	T
27.	F
28.	F
29.	T
30.	T

CHAPTER 6

BEHAVIORAL LEARNING

LEARNING OBJECTIVES

After reading and studying this chapter, you should be able to:

1.   Explain the basic theoretical stance of behaviorism.

2.   Explain the terminology and procedures involved in classical conditioning.

3.   Apply classical conditioning principles to real-life learning situations in humans and animals.

4.   Explain and understand the terminology, components, and procedures of operant conditioning.

5.   Apply operant conditioning principles to real-life learning situations in humans and animals.

6.   Compare and contrast classical and operant conditioning.

7.   Identify the major scientific contributions of B.F. Skinner to psychology.

8.   Discuss the problems with implementing punishment and reward in real-life learning situations.

9.   Explain behaviorist views of superstition, insight, and separation anxiety.

CHAPTER 6 OUTLINE

I. Introduction

    A.   **Learning** is any relatively permanent change in behavior that occurs because of experience (excluding changes due to maturation, fatigue, injury, or disease).

    B.   The **behaviorist** view is that learning, especially conditioning, is the most important influence on behavior.

    C.   Basic learning called **conditioning** involves associations between environmental stimuli and responses.

II. Classical Conditioning

    A.   **Classical Conditioning** is the process by which a previously neutral stimulus acquires the capacity to elicit a response through association with a stimulus that already elicits a similar response. It is also called **Pavlovian** or **respondent conditioning**.

    B.   Russian physiologist Ivan Pavlov's original experiments on salivation in dogs demonstrate how classical conditioning works:

        1.   food is an **unconditioned stimulus (US)** because animals react naturally to food by salivating before any learning has taken place; a US is anything that elicits a response automatically or reflexively.

        2.   the original salivary reflex is the **unconditioned response (UR)**; a UR is automatically produced.

        3.   learning occurs when a neutral stimulus becomes a **conditioned stimulus (CS)** after it is regularly paired with the unconditioned stimulus.

        4.   when the original stimulus is removed, the dog will salivate in response to the conditioned stimulus presented alone--a **conditioned response (CR)** similar to the original unlearned response.

    C.   Other classical conditioning principles include the following:

        1.   the optimal interval between the presentation of the CS, <u>before</u> the presentation of the US depends on the type of response being conditioned; generally in the laboratory the interval is less than 1 second.

        2.   nearly any involuntary response can become a CR (e.g. heartbeat, blinking, etc.)

        3.   mere pairing is *not* enough to produce learning; the stimulus (CR) must reliably <u>signal</u> or <u>predict</u> the US. The CR enables the organism to prepare for an event that is about to happen and provides information.

        4.   **extinction** occurs when the CS is repeatedly presented without the US; the CR weakens and eventually disappears.

        5.   after a time period following extinction, the response may reappear in a phenomenon called **spontaneous recovery**.

6.   when a neutral stimulus is paired with an already established CS, it can become a conditioned stimulus itself, through the process of **higher-order conditioning.**

7.   in **stimulus generalization,** stimuli similar to the original CS produce the same reaction.

8.   in **stimulus discrimination,** if a stimulus is different enough from the original CS, different responses will occur.

III.   Classical Conditioning in Real Life

A.   Emotional reactions to words may be learned through higher-order conditioning.

B.   Taste aversions can be learned when various foods or odors are paired with nausea-inducing stimuli.

C.   Some allergic reactions can be learned by classical conditioning.

D.   Sexual masochism may result when a particular object or a painful stimulus is repeatedly paired with an unconditioned stimulus for sexual arousal.

E.   The pairing of products with music, attractive people, etc. in marketing is a common application of classical conditioning.

F.   A phobia is an acquired, irrational fear of a specific object or situation.

1.   The classical conditioning of a phobia was first demonstrated by John Watson and Rosalie Raynor in the "Little Albert" study.

2.   **Counterconditioning,** a treatment for phobias, involves pairing a CS with a stimulus that elicits a response that is incompatible with an unwanted CR. Systematic desensitization is a therapy variant of counterconditioning used to treat phobias in adults.

IV.   Operant Conditioning

A.   **Operant conditioning** (also called instrumental conditioning) is the process by which a response becomes more or less likely to occur, depending on its consequences.

B.   Comparison and contrast of operant conditioning versus classical conditioning:

1.   in classical conditioning, responses are elicited, automatic and reflexive; the animal or person's behavior does not have an environmental consequence.

2.   in operant conditioning, the organism <u>operates on</u> the environment to produce effects, and those effects influence whether or not the response will occur again; responses are complex and not reflexive and involve the entire organism; consequences control behavior.

C.   Thorndike's study of cat learning behavior in "puzzle boxes" enabled him to discover the law of effect which states that:

1.   behaviors followed by satisfying effects tend to be "stamped in."

2.   behaviors followed by unsatisfying or annoying effects tend to be "stamped out."

D. B.F. Skinner, one of America's most famous psychologists and a radical behaviorist, elaborated and extended Thorndike's general principle, but eliminated terms such as "satisfying" and "annoying".
1. Skinner believed focusing on mind or internal states was unproductive in understanding human behavior; however, he considered private events as early stages of behavior, before any action by the organism on the environment; these are less accessible and harder to describe.
2. A misconception is that Skinner denied the influence of genes and biology.
3. Skinner argued that free will is an illusion and thus argued in favor of determinism.
E. Reinforcement and Punishment
1. **Reinforcement** - increases the probability or strength of the response that it follows.
2. **Punishment** - decreases the probability or strength of the response that follows.
3. **Positive reinforcement** - involves presenting something pleasant following a desired response.
4. **Negative reinforcement** - involves removing something unpleasant following a desired response.
5. **Positive punishment** - involves presenting or applying something unpleasant following an undesired response.
6. **Negative punishment** - involves removing something pleasant following an undesired response.
7. **Primary reinforcers** - typically satisfy a biological need (like food) and are inherently reinforcing.
8. **Primary punishers** - include extreme hot or cold stimuli and are inherently punishing.
9. **Secondary reinforcers** and **secondary punishers** acquire their ability to influence behavior through repeated pairings with primary reinforcers and punishers.
10. Negative reinforcement may explain some behaviors that are self-defeating or injurious.
11. In operant conditioning, "positive" and "negative" characterize procedures rather than "good" or "bad".
12. Secondary reinforcers can be as potent as primary ones but will eventually lose their ability to affect behavior if they are not occasionally paired with the original stimulus.

F. Principles of Operant Conditioning
    1. Scientists often use a **Skinner box** to study operant conditioning. It is a device consisting of a cage equipped with a mechanism to deliver reinforcement whenever an animal makes a desired response. Attached to the Skinner box is a **cumulative recorder** which automatically records each response and produces a graph showing the cumulative number of responses across time.
    2. **Extinction** takes place when the reinforcer that has maintained the response is removed. At first, there is a spurt of responding, followed by a decrease in responding. After a period of time, the response may reappear, a phenomenon known as **spontaneous recovery**.
    3. In general, the sooner a reinforcer or punisher follows a response, the greater its effect.
    4. In **stimulus generalization**, responses generalize to stimuli that were not present during the original learning situation, but that resemble the original stimuli.
    5. If a stimulus differs significantly from the original stimulus, there may be no response, a situation known as **stimulus discrimination**.
    6. A **discriminative stimulus** signals when a particular type of response is likely to be followed by a certain consequence. The discriminative stimulus exerts **stimulus control** over the response, but is not compelled as in classical conditioning; the response becomes more probable.
    7. Reinforcers can be delivered according to different schedules.
        a. In **continuous reinforcement**, every response is reinforced.
        b. **Partial** or **intermittent schedules of reinforcement** involve reinforcing only some responses. These schedules produce responses that are more resistant to extinction.
    8. **Ratio schedules** deliver a reinforcement after a certain number of responses have occurred.
        a. On a **fixed-ratio (FR)** schedule, reinforcement occurs after a fixed number of responses, producing a high rate of responding with a performance drop-off just after reinforcement.
        b. On a **variable-ratio (VR)** schedule, reinforcement occurs after some average number of responses, but the number varies from time to time, producing high, steady rates of responding that are highly resistant to extinction.
    9. **Interval schedules** deliver a reinforcement if a response is made after the passage of a certain amount of time since the last reinforcement.
        a. On a **fixed-interval (FI)** schedule, the time period is the same from reinforcement to reinforcement, producing high rates of response around the end of an interval, with decreased responses following reinforcement.

b. On a **variable-interval (VI)** schedule, the time periods vary, producing low but steady response rates.

10. Learning curves describe the characteristic pattern of response produced by different schedules of reinforcement and can be plotted with a cumulative recorder.

11. **Shaping** is the rewarding of **successive approximations**, behaviors that are ordered in terms of increasing similarity or closeness to a desired response. Shaping can be used to establish a complex behavior.

V. Operant Conditioning in Real Life

A. **Behavior modification** is the use of conditioning techniques to teach new responses and/or reduce or eliminate maladaptive or problematic behavior in real-world settings.

1. A **token economy** involves the use of secondary reinforcers (tokens) to reinforce desired behaviors. Tokens can be exchanged for primary or other secondary reinforcers.

B. The Problem with Punishment

1. It is often administered inappropriately.

2. Negative emotional side effects often accompany punishment. They may even produce an increase in the undesired behavior.

3. The effects of punishment are sometimes temporary, depending on the presence of the punisher or the circumstances.

4. Much misbehavior is hard to punish immediately.

5. Punishment conveys little information about appropriate behavior.

6. The attention that accompanies punishment may be reinforcing.

7. Punishment can be effective if it:

a. does not involve physical abuse.

b. is accompanied by information about appropriate behavior.

c. is administered following the undesired behavior very closely in time.

d. is followed by reinforcement of desired or alternative behaviors.

e. involves mild punishment which may be as effective as strong punishment.

f. is based on knowing the reasons for misbehavior.

C. The Problem with Reward

1. **Extrinsic reinforcers** come from an outside source and are unrelated to the activity being reinforced.

2. **Intrinsic reinforcers**, such as enjoyment of a task, are inherent <u>only</u> in the activity being reinforced.

3. Extrinsic reinforcement can sometimes undermine intrinsic reinforcement. There are three reasons for this:

a. we interpret enjoyable activities as work.

137

　　　　b.　　extrinsic rewards are perceived as controlling and undermine autonomy.

　　　　c.　　it may raise the rate of responding above an optimal, enjoyable level.

　　4.　　The short-term effectiveness of extrinsic reinforcers should be balanced with the long-term effectiveness of intrinsic reinforcers.

VI.　　The World as the Behaviorist Views It
　　A.　　Superstitions
　　　　1.　　Superstitions may arise if a response is rewarded coincidentally.
　　　　2.　　The response may be intermittently reinforced, making it resistant to extinction.
　　　　3.　　Superstitions may persist because attention is paid only to confirming evidence, and because they are reinforced by the agreement of others.
　　B.　　Insight
　　　　1.　　**Insight** involves the apparently sudden understanding of how to solve a problem.
　　　　2.　　The behaviorist views insight as the combination of previously learned responses, and does not invoke mentalistic notions to explain it.
　　C.　　Separation Anxiety
　　　　1.　　Between 7 and 9 months of age, many children develop a fear of unfamiliar people, called **stranger anxiety**, as well as a fear of being left by their primary caregiver, called **separation anxiety**.
　　　　2.　　The behavioral view is that when the caregiver returns to a protesting child, the protesting is reinforced. Ainsworth's study in Chapter 3 can be reinterpreted such that separation anxiety is not necessarily the natural result of attachment, but is learned through operant conditioning.
　　　　3.　　When the caregiver responds only to behavior other than crying and protesting, signs of separation anxiety stop.

CHAPTER SUMMARY

1._____ is any relatively permanent change in behavior that occurs because of experience. Russian physiologist Pavlov discovered a kind of learning called 2._____ conditioning. In his original experiments, Pavlov paired a neutral stimulus with food, which is called the 3._____ stimulus because it elicits a response (salivation) without any learning. The response to food is called the 4._____ response. After repeated pairings with food, the neutral stimulus becomes a 5._____ stimulus. Even when the food was no longer present, the dog still salivated – a 6._____ response. In order for classical conditioning to be effective, the conditioned stimulus must 7._____ the unconditioned stimulus.

After conditioning takes place, the conditioned response will disappear if the conditioned stimulus is presented by itself repeatedly. This procedure is called 8. _____ . Curiously, the response may reappear the next day, a phenomenon known as 9. _____ .

If the CS-US connection is already learned, one can add another layer to learning by pairing a new neutral stimulus with an established CS, a procedure known as 10. _____ conditioning. Also, animals and humans may make a CR to stimuli that are similar to an established CS. This is known as stimulus 11. _____ , which contrasts with stimulus 12. _____ , in which neutral stimuli are different enough from the CS to elicit responses different from the CR.

The classical conditioning model can be used to account for a variety of phenomena, including taste aversion, sexual fetishism, and phobias. It also explains why advertisers associate attractive people or pleasant music with their products in marketing efforts.

The famous case of "Little Albert" is an illustration of how classical conditioning procedures can be used to produce a phobia. In this (unethical) experiment, John Watson used a 13. _____ as an unconditioned stimulus and a 14. _____ as a conditioned stimulus. The reversal of a phobia was accomplished some years later with another subject, using the technique of 15. _____ . This procedure involves pairing the conditioned stimulus with another stimulus that elicits a response that is incompatible with the fear response.

While classical conditioning always involves reflexive responses, 16. _____ conditioning involves responses that produce effects on the environment. In this type of learning, the 17. _____ of certain responses affect the likelihood of the recurrence of those responses.

There are two kinds of consequences, pleasant and unpleasant. A pleasant stimulus presented following a desired response is called 18. _____ , and the likelihood of repeating the response 19. _____ . When an unpleasant stimulus follows an undesired response, 20. _____ has taken place, and the frequency of the response 21. _____ . Both of these procedures are termed 22. _____ because a stimulus is presented after the response. However, we can also affect behavior by removing an unpleasant stimulus in order to increase a desired response, or by removing a pleasant stimulus in order to decrease an undesired response. These operations are called 23. _____ and 24. _____ respectively. These terms are confusing, but they can be clearer if one remembers that the words "positive" and "negative" refer to whether the frequency of the response 25. _____ or 26. _____ .

Some reinforcers, such as food, satisfy biological needs and are called 27. _____ reinforcers. 28. _____ reinforcers, such as money, gain reinforcement value from being repeatedly paired with primary reinforcers. Punishers can also be categorized in this way. In general, reinforcers and punishers will be most effective when they are applied immediately following the target behavior.

When a response has been learned, but stops occurring because reinforcement has been removed, 29._____ has taken place. When reinforcement is first withdrawn, there is usually a spurt of responding, followed by a gradual decline in the rate of response.

As in classical conditioning, an animal or human may respond to stimuli that were not present during the original learning, but which resemble the original stimuli. As in classical conditioning, this phenomenon is known as stimulus 30._____. If new stimuli are different enough from the original stimuli, then stimulus 31._____ will occur. In the learning environment, a stimulus that signals the availability of a consequence is called a 32._____ stimulus. This stimulus is said to exert 33._____ over the response.

The procedure in which every target response is reinforced is called 34._____ reinforcement. However, one does not have to reinforce every response in order to build or maintain a response. In fact, partial reinforcement makes a response more resistant to 35._____. Therefore, it is important to resist reinforcing a response intermittently if you want to get rid of it.

Reinforcement can be applied according to four basic 36._____, each of which produces a characteristic pattern of responding. 37._____ schedules deliver a reinforcer after a certain number of responses have occurred. 38._____ schedules deliver a reinforcer after the passage of some amount of time since the last reinforcer. The number of responses or the interval between responses can be either 39._____ or 40._____.

41._____ schedules deliver reinforcement after an invariant number of responses. For instance, a schedule in which an animal receives a food pellet after every 50 responses is called an 42._____ schedule. This schedule produces very high rates of responding. We can also deliver reinforcement on the average of once for every 50 responses, but vary that number from reinforcement to reinforcement. This particular 43._____ schedule is abbreviated 44._____. This kind of schedule produces a high, steady response rate that is more resistant to extinction than a fixed schedule.

When an interval schedule is used with an invariant interval of 60 seconds, the schedule is abbreviated 45._____ (seconds). Animals on this kind of schedule show high rates of responding toward the end of each interval, with a sharp drop in response rate immediately following reinforcement. When the interval is varied, which in this case would be a 46._____ schedule, the response rate is low but steady.

Because complex behaviors are not usually produced spontaneously, they must often be built using a procedure called 47._____. In this procedure, the person or animal is first rewarded for making 48._____ to the target behavior. For example, if you want to get a rat to press a bar for food, you might first reinforce it for coming closer to the bar, then for touching the bar, etc.

The use of conditioning techniques to affect behavior in real-world settings is known as 49._____. A common technique is the 50._____ in which target behaviors are rewarded by markers that can later be used to buy things like money or privileges.

Although punishment can be a powerful technique for controlling behavior, it is not without its problems. First, punishment, especially physical punishment, can be inappropriately applied, resulting more from the rage of the punisher than from a real effort to teach a new behavior. Second, the person being punished may have negative 51._____ reactions, such ad negative emotions which can create more problems. Third, the effects of punishment depend heavily on the presence of the punishing person. If misbehavior is not punished immediately, the punishment might have only a temporary effect. Conversely, 52._____ given by this person can also be inadvertently reinforcing. Finally, punishment conveys little or no information about appropriate alternative behaviors. Therefore, if punishment is to be used, it should be accompanied by the opportunity for, and reinforcement of, appropriate alternative responses.

Rewarding appropriate behaviors seems like a better option than punishment. However, it is not without its own problems. Often a person will work for 53._____ rewards, like money or praise. At other times, the person works for 54._____ reinforcers, which are inherent in the activity itself. Research has demonstrated that intrinsic motivation may decrease when extrinsic rewards are applied. Therefore, there is a trade-off between the short-term effectiveness of 55._____ rewards and the long-term effectiveness of 56._____ rewards.

The behaviorist view of superstitious behavior is that coincidental 57._____ has followed the behavior at some time. Recall that a behavior does not have to be rewarded every time; superstitious behaviors are not. They may persist because they are rewarded 58._____, which makes them highly resistant to extinction.

Behaviorists are also interested in 59._____, which appears to involve a sudden realization about how to solve a problem. While this phenomenon appears to be antithetical to the behaviorist view of learning as a trial-and-error process, behaviorists argue that insight really reflects the use of previously learned responses to solve problems. It merely requires combining these responses in new ways.

One can also apply the behavioral model to explain 60._____, which is evidenced by a child's protests and cries when his or her caregiver leaves the room. Behaviorists have suggested that these behaviors are actually reinforced by the caregiver, who picks up and soothes the crying baby. Researchers have demonstrated not only that crying can be extinguished by not rewarding it, but that rewarding the child for alternative behaviors is also a useful strategy.

MULTIPLE CHOICE SELF-TEST

1. In Ivan Pavlov's original classical conditioning experiment, dogs learned to salivate to the presence of a food dish and to the person who delivered their food. In this experiment the US is the:

    a. salivation.
    b. food dish.
    c. food.
    d. experimenter.

2. A behavior that is most likely to become a conditioned response is:

    a. studying.
    b. reading.
    c. swimming.
    d. blinking.

3. The type of conditioning that depends on the consequences of behavior is _____ conditioning:

    a. classical
    b. instinctive
    c. higher-order
    d. operant

4. Derek loves his cat "Jezebel" who is soft and affectionate. Derek's similar, positive reaction to a guinea pig is probably a result of:

    a. higher-order conditioning.
    b. extinction.
    c. spontaneous recovery.
    d. stimulus generalization.

5. A cat associates food with the sound of an electric can opener and salivates when he hears the noise. What type of learning is this?

    a. classical conditioning.
    b. operant conditioning.
    c. social learning.
    d. instrumental learning.

6. On a trip to the dentist, Jason notices that he cringes when he hears the sound of the dentist's drill in the waiting room. In classical conditioning terms, the sound of the drill is a(n):

   a. unconditioned stimulus
   b. unconditioned response.
   c. conditioned stimulus.
   d. conditioned response.

7. In classical conditioning terms, cringing at the sound of a dentist's drill is a(n):

   a. unconditioned stimulus.
   b. unconditioned response.
   c. conditioned stimulus.
   d. conditioned response.

8. Dr. Jones eats goat cheese in a fancy restaurant and gets sick later on that night from the flu. The next time he is served goat cheese he is most likely to:

   a. refuse to eat it because he has developed a taste aversion.
   b. eat the cheese because it had no connection to his illness.
   c. refuse to eat goat cheese when he has the flu, but eat it on other occasions.
   d. eat the goat cheese only if it is served in a situation other than a restaurant.

9. In her animal learning laboratory, Dr. Michaels has trained a rabbit to blink at the sound of a buzzer by repeatedly pairing the buzzer with a puff of air to the rabbit's eye. If she wants to achieve higher-order conditioning she will:

   a. repeatedly present the buzzer alone.
   b. intermittently present the buzzer alone.
   c. pair another neutral stimulus with the buzzer.
   d. present the buzzer alone several times, wait a day, and present the buzzer alone again.

10. Jim has developed a phobia of snakes. According to the principle of counterconditioning the best way of eliminating Jim's phobia is to:

   a. put him in a room with a lot of snakes so that he can see that they will not harm him.
   b. gradually expose him to snakes in the presence of a pleasant stimulus.
   c. teach him to avoid snakes until he feels ready to face them.
   d. put him in a room with a lot of snakes and then remove them in his presence.

11. Kelly's dog, "Chopper" has learned to cower and defecate in fear everytime he sees a newspaper. It is most likely that this behavior developed due to:

   a. classical conditioning.
   b. operant conditioning.
   c. higher-order learning.
   d. shaping.

12. The best way of eliminating Chopper's fear of newspapers would be to use the technique of:

   a. systematic desensitization.
   b. counterconditioning.
   c. operant conditioning.
   d. higher-order conditioning.

13. In order for optimal conditioning to occur, the conditioned stimulus should:

   a. follow the unconditioned stimulus.
   b. occur simultaneously with the unconditioned stimulus.
   c. precede the unconditioned stimulus.
   d. occur with a voluntary response.

14. Erica's fear of flying was successfully "cured" in therapy last year. Yet today, in a new airplane, this fear returned. This reappearance of an extinguished classically conditioned response is called:

   a. spontaneous recovery.
   b. stimulus generalization.
   c. higher-order conditioning.
   d. reinforcement.

15. A device that Thorndike used to establish the "law of effect" was the:

   a. Skinner box.
   b. cumulative recorder.
   c. reinforcement machine.
   d. puzzle box.

16. A squirrel learns to climb into your bird feeder and obtain food. This behavior was probably learned by:

    a. classical conditioning.
    b. operant conditioning.
    c. reflexive learning.
    d. higher-order learning.

17. B.F. Skinner, a radical behaviorist, would have been most likely to make which one of the following statements?

    a. "Our behavior is a product of our free will and we can consciously control our behavior."
    b. "Biology and genetics have no place in scientific psychology."
    c. "We should focus psychology mainly on observable behavior rather than mental states."
    d. "We must determine if consequences of behavior are satisfying or annoying to an organism."

18. Coach Cooper makes his football team members do laps when they are late to practice. This is an example of:

    a. positive reinforcement.
    b. negative reinforcement.
    c. positive punishment.
    d. negative punishment.

19. A dog has learned to go to a corner in the kitchen when he has done something bad. He sits there impatiently until his owner lets him leave. This "time out" is an example of:

    a. negative reinforcement.
    b. positive reinforcement.
    c. positive punishment.
    d. negative punishment.

20. Jennifer praises her dog "Spike" whenever he fetches her slippers. Praise is an example of a(n):

    a. primary reinforcer.
    b. secondary reinforcer.
    c. conditioned stimulus.
    d. unconditioned stimulus.

21. You are angry at your cat for jumping on the kitchen counters where food is stored in canisters. The most effective action to specifically curb only this behavior would be to:

    a. yell every time you see your cat present in the kitchen.
    b. immediately spray water from a squirt gun at him when he's on the counter top.
    c. hit him severely when you catch him on the counter top.
    d. ignore the behavior entirely.

22. If you are teaching your daughter to ice skate using the method of shaping, you might begin by:

    a. explaining to her why she will be able to skate.
    b. letting her see other children who are skating.
    c. praising her for standing upright with the skates on.
    d. taking her to an ice rink and tell her to start skating.

23. A manager wants her sales people to sell more cars. She tells one group of employees they will be rewarded with a commission for each car they sell. The other group of employees will be paid a salary. Your boss is comparing the productivity of which two schedules of reinforcement?

    a. fixed-ratio and variable-ratio.
    b. variable-ratio and variable-interval.
    c. fixed-interval and fixed-ratio.
    d. variable-interval and fixed-ratio.

24. A token economy is based on giving what kind of reinforcers to shape desired behavior?

    a. primary
    b. secondary
    c. negative
    d. intrinsic

25. A young child loves to play the piano. Her parents begin rewarding her for every hour she spends practicing the piano. A potential effect of this reward is to make practicing a:

   a.   more intrinsically reinforcing activity.
   b.   less intrinsically reinforcing activity.
   c.   less extrinsically reinforcing activity.
   d.   primary reinforcing activity.

26. A pigeon on a variable-ratio schedule learns to peck at a circle. Under this type of schedule, the responding of the pigeon is best described as:

   a.   extremely high and steep.
   b.   random.
   c.   slow and steady.
   d.   a scalloped pattern.

27. Employees in a shirt factory all work at a low but steady rate. Which of the following statements is most likely to be true?

   a.   Employees receive payment for every 30 shirts made.
   b.   The boss comes out of his office exactly every 15 minutes to check on the worker's productivity.
   c.   The boss comes out of his office approximately every 15 minutes or so to check on the workers, but each time interval varies.
   d.   The workers get paid on a regular fixed schedule.

28. Tina wants to eliminate her daughter's use of sexual slang words. To most effectively accomplish this goal, Tina should:

   a.   use physical punishment every time her daughter uses "dirty" words.
   b.   use guilt and shame as punishment.
   c.   put her daughter on a token economy.
   d.   teach her daughter the correct words and reward their use.

29. Alonzo can never predict when his mail will arrive. Sometimes the mail truck comes to his home early in the morning, while on other days the mail does not arrive until late in the evening. Therefore, Alonzo checks his mailbox periodically throughout the day and evening. Alonzo is being reinforced on a:

   a. VI schedule.
   b. VR schedule.
   c. FR schedule.
   d. FI schedule.

30. Geraldo is trying to toilet train his two-year-old son. He begins by praising the boy for sitting on the toilet at Geraldo's direction without fussing. Then, he stops praising the boy for this behavior, instead praising him only for sitting on the toilet without being told to do so. Finally, he withdraws this praise for merely sitting on the toilet, instead praising the boy only for using the toilet properly. What process is taking place?

   a. reinforcement of successive approximations.
   b. stimulus discrimination.
   c. intermittent reinforcement.
   d. a variable-ratio schedule of reinforcement.

TRUE FALSE SELF-TEST

T F 1. Learning is a change in behavior caused by maturation.

T F 2. In classical conditioning, conditioned responses are usually different than the original, unlearned response.

T F 3. Classical conditioning is also called respondent conditioning.

T F 4. Nearly any involuntary response can become a conditioned response.

T F 5. Eliminating a conditioned response usually requires only one extinction session.

T F 6. Emotional responses and phobias are usually acquired through operant conditioning.

T F 7. Some allergic reactions may be classically conditioned.

T F 8. A stimulus that is similar to a conditioned stimulus can elicit a similar response.

T F 9. Counterconditioning is similar to punishment.

T F 10. In operant conditioning responses are reflexive.

T F 11. B.F. Skinner regarded human free will as an illusion.

T F 12. Negative reinforcement lessens the probability of a response.

T F 13. Negative punishment involves applying a negative stimulus in order to decrease the probability of a behavior.

T F 14. Praise and money are examples of primary reinforcers.

T F 15. In general, the later a reinforcer or punisher follows a response, the greater its effect.

T F 16. Stimulus discrimination inhibits adaptive learning.

T F 17. Shaping involves both differential reinforcement and successive approximation.

T F 18. Responses learned on continuous schedules of reinforcement are more resistant to extinction than responses learned on intermittent schedules.

T F 19. Ratio schedules of reinforcement are more resistant to extinction than interval schedules.

T F 20. A person who receives a paycheck every month is being reinforced on an FI schedule.

T F 21. Interval schedules produce extremely high and steady rates of responding.

T F 22. A factory worker who works on a "piecework" system is working under a fixed-interval schedule.

T F 23. The use of operant techniques in applied settings is called behavior modification.

T   F   24.   In school systems, punishment is more likely to be used against middle-class white girls, than boys, poor children, or minorities.

T   F   25.   Mild punishers are just as effective and may be even more effective than strong punishers.

T   F   26.   Research studies have demonstrated that arrests of abusers are effective at deterring domestic violence in the long run.

T   F   27.   Physical punishment of children tends to be a highly effective method of instilling positive social behaviors.

T   F   28.   An action intended to punish may instead be reinforcing because it brings attention.

T   F   29.   Extrinsic rewards, such as grades, are particularly effective in instilling long-term motivation to learn.

T   F   30.   The behaviorist views insight as the result, rather than the cause, of learning.

KEY TERMS

behaviorism - An approach to psychology that emphasizes the study of observable behavior and the role of the environment as a determinant of behavior.

conditioning - A basic kind of learning that involves associations between environmental stimuli and the organism's responses.

unconditioned stimulus (US) - The classical-conditioning term for a stimulus that elicits a reflexive response in the absence of learning.

unconditioned response (UR) - The classical-conditioning term for a reflexive response elicited by a stimulus in the absence of learning.

conditioned stimulus (CS) - The classical-conditioning term for an initially neutral stimulus that comes to elicit a conditioned response after being associated with an unconditioned stimulus.

conditioned response (CR) - The classical-conditioning term for a response that is elicited by a conditioned stimulus; occurs after the conditioned stimulus is associated with an unconditioned stimulus.

classical conditioning - The process by which a previously neutral stimulus acquires the capacity to elicit a response through association with a stimulus that already elicits a similar or related response; also called Pavlovian and respondent conditioning.

extinction - The weakening and eventual disappearance of a learned response; in classical conditioning, it occurs when the conditioned stimulus is no longer paired with the unconditioned stimulus.

spontaneous recovery - The reappearance of a learned response after its apparent extinction.

higher-order conditioning - In classical conditioning, a procedure in which a neutral stimulus becomes a conditioned stimulus through association with an already established conditioned stimulus.

stimulus generalization - After conditioning, the tendency to respond to a stimulus that resembles one involved in the original conditioning; in classical conditioning, it occurs when a stimulus that resembles the conditioned stimulus elicits the conditioned response.

stimulus discrimination - The tendency to respond differently to two or more similar stimuli; in classical conditioning, it occurs when a stimulus similar to the CS fails to evoke the CR.

counterconditioning - In classical conditioning, the process of pairing a conditioned stimulus with a stimulus that elicits a response that is incompatible with an unwanted conditioned response.

operant conditioning - The process by which a response becomes more or less likely to occur, depending on its consequences.

reinforcement - The process by which a stimulus or event strengthens or increases the probability of the response that it follows.

punishment - The process by which a stimulus or event weakens or reduces the probability of the response that it follows.

positive reinforcement - A reinforcement procedure in which a response is followed by the presentation of, or increase in intensity of, a reinforcing stimulus; as a result, the response becomes stronger or more likely to occur.

negative reinforcement - a reinforcement procedure in which a response is followed by the removal, delay, or decrease in intensity of an unpleasant stimulus; as a result, the response becomes stronger or more likely to occur.

primary reinforcer - A stimulus that is inherently reinforcing, typically satisfying a physiological need; an example is food.

primary punisher - A stimulus that is inherently punishing; an example is electric shock.

secondary reinforcer - A stimulus that has acquired reinforcing properties through association with other reinforcers.

secondary punisher - A stimulus that has acquired punishing properties through association with other punishers.

extinction - The weakening and eventual disappearance of a learned response; in operant conditioning, it occurs when a response is no longer followed by a reinforcer.

stimulus generalization - In operant conditioning, the tendency for a response that has been reinforced (or punished) in the presence of one stimulus to occur (or be suppressed) in the presence of other, similar stimuli.

stimulus discrimination - In operant conditioning, the tendency of a response to occur in the presence of one stimulus but not in the presence of other, similar stimuli that differ from it on some dimension.

discriminative stimulus - A stimulus that signals when a particular response is likely to be followed by a certain type of consequence.

stimulus control - Control over the occurrence of a response by a discriminative stimulus.

continuous reinforcement - A reinforcement schedule in which a particular response is always reinforced.

intermittent (partial) schedule of reinforcement - A reinforcement schedule in which a particular response is sometimes but not always reinforced.

shaping - An operant conditioning procedure in which successive approximations of a desired response are reinforced; it is used when the desired response has a low probability of occurring spontaneously.

successive approximations - In the operant-conditioning procedure of shaping, behaviors that are ordered in terms of increasing similarity or closeness to the desired response.

behavior modification - The application of conditioning techniques to teach new responses or reduce or eliminate maladaptive or problematic behavior.

token economy - A behavior-modification technique in which secondary reinforcers, called tokens, can be collected and exchanged for primary or other secondary reinforcers to shape behavior.

extrinsic reinforcers - Reinforcers that are not inherently related to the activity being reinforced, such as money, prizes, and praise.

intrinsic reinforcers - Reinforcers that are inherently related to the activity being reinforced, such as enjoyment of the task and the satisfaction of accomplishment.

insight - A form of learning that occurs in problem solving and appears to involve the (often sudden) understanding of how elements of a situation are related or can be reorganized to achieve a solution.

Suggested Research Projects

1. Select a social problem (e.g., teenage pregnancy, increased violent crime) that you have read about in the newspaper or have viewed on television. Describe the problem in operant terms (i.e., what are the reinforcers, punishers, discriminative stimuli, etc.) Using operant principles, devise a plan to remedy the problem. What practical and ethical problems or considerations might affect your plan?

2. Think of a habit that you would like to get rid of. Describe the habit in operant terms. Chart the occurrence of the undesired response over some time period. For example, if you want to quit smoking, keep a log of how many cigarettes you smoke, as well as the circumstances, such as eating or getting out of class, that accompany the response (these are discriminative stimuli). Then, using operant principles (such as punishing the behavior or rewarding incompatible behaviors), devise a behavioral plan to change your habit.

Suggested Readings

Skinner, B.F. (1948). *Walden Two*. New York: Macmillan. A novel about the application of behavioral technology in an utopian community.

Skinner, B.F. (1974). *About Behaviorism*. New York: Knopf. A description of behaviorist research and theory.

Nye, R.D. (1992). The Legacy of B.F. Skinner: Concepts and Perspectives, Controversies and Misunderstandings. Pacific Grove, CA: Brooks/Cole. Reviews Skinner's life, the basic concepts of his theory, and its relevance for today's society.

Watson, D.L., & Tharp, R.G. (1985). *Self-Directed Behavior: Self-Modification for Personal Adjustment* (4th ed.). Monterey, CA: Brooks/Cole. Suggestions for changing one's own behavior through the application of learning principles.

Suggested Audio-Visuals

B.F. Skinner. (1966). From Insight Media. In this two part video series, B.F. Skinner discusses his views on a variety of behaviorist topics and their implications for societal change.

CHAPTER 6

ANSWERS TO CHAPTER SUMMARY

1.   learning
2.   classical (respondent)
3.   unconditioned
4.   unconditioned
5.   conditioned
6.   conditioned
7.   precede
8.   extinction
9.   spontaneous recovery
10. higher-order
11. generalization
12. discrimination
13. loud noise
14. white rat
15. counterconditioning
16. operant
17. consequences
18. reinforcement
19. increases
20. punishment
21. decreases
22. positive
23. negative reinforcement
24. negative punishment
25. increases
26. decreases
27. primary
28. secondary
29. extinction
30. generalization
31. discrimination
32. discriminative
33. control
34. continuous
35. extinction
36. schedules
37. ratio
38. interval
39. fixed (variable)
40. variable (fixed)

41. FR
42. FR-50
43. variable-ratio
44. VR-50
45. FI-60
46. VI-60
47. shaping
48. successive approximations
49. behavior modification
50. token economy
51. emotional
52. attention
53. extrinsic
54. intrinsic
55. extrinsic
56. intrinsic
57. reinforcement
58. intermittently
59. insight
60. separation anxiety

ANSWERS TO MULTIPLE CHOICE SELF-TEST

1. C
2. D
3. D
4. D
5. A
6. C
7. D
8. A
9. C
10. B
11. A
12. B
13. C
14. A
15. D
16. B
17. C
18. C
19. D
20. B
21. B

22.	C
23.	C
24.	B
25.	B
26.	A
27.	C
28.	D
29.	A
30.	A

ANSWERS TO TRUE FALSE SELF-TEST

1.	F
2.	F
3.	T
4.	T
5.	F
6.	F
7.	T
8.	T
9.	F
10.	F
11.	T
12.	F
13.	F
14.	F
15.	F
16.	F
17.	T
18.	F
19.	T
20.	T
21.	F
22.	F
23.	T
24.	F
25.	T
26.	F
27.	F
28.	T
29.	F
30.	T

CHAPTER 7

SOCIAL AND COGNITIVE LEARNING

LEARNING OBJECTIVES

After reading and studying this chapter, you should be able to:

1. Compare and contrast social learning theory with behaviorism.

2. Explain the concept of reciprocal determinism.

3. Describe the process of observational learning.

4. Describe the sources of self-efficacy.

5. Describe the various factors involved in gender development.

6. Describe the various factors involved in moral development.

CHAPTER 7 OUTLINE

I. Introduction
    A. **Social learning theories** emphasize learning that is acquired by observing other people in a social context. Major proponents include: Albert Bandura, and Walter Mischel.
        1. Researchers differ in the emphasis they place on cognitive processes.
        2. Researchers differ in how much they distance themselves from behaviorism.
    B. Social learning theorists agree with behaviorists about the effects of consequences on behavior, but add an emphasis on:
        1. learning acquired in the absence of consequences.
        2. the influence of the psychological meaning of situations and the choices people make about what situations to get into.
        3. the influence of attitudes, beliefs, and expectations on behavior.
    C. Social learning theorists emphasize **reciprocal determinism** , the interactions between individuals and their environments.
        1. Environmental factors affect motivating beliefs and behaviors.
        2. Motivating beliefs affect environmental factors and behaviors.
        3. Behaviors affect environmental factors and motivating beliefs.

II. Beyond Behaviorism
    A. **Observational learning** is the process of learning new responses by observing the behavior of a **model**. (Behaviorists call this vicarious conditioning).
        1. Behaviorists explain observational learning in stimulus-response terms. But social learning theorists also try to take into account the thought processes of the learner.
        2. The learned response may be displayed immediately or remain unexpressed until circumstances are favorable for its expression.
    B. Cognitive processes occur between stimulus and response.
        1. **Latent learning** is a form of learning that is not immediately expressed in an overt response; it occurs without obvious reinforcement, and implies that what is learned is knowledge about responses and their consequences.
        2. In some situations, this knowledge takes the form of a **cognitive map** which is a mental representation of the spatial layout of the environment.
        3. An individual's behavior is affected by perceptions, which are influenced by:
            a. knowledge.
            b. assumptions.
            c. attention.

C. **Motivating beliefs** are cognitions that cause an organism to move toward a goal.

1. **Motivation** is an inferred process within an animal or person that causes that individual to move toward a goal.

2. Motivating beliefs may be formed by reward and punishment.

3. In the social learning view, motivating beliefs come to exert their own effects on behavior.

4. An example of an important type of motivating belief is **locus of control,** a general expectation about whether one can control one's own rewards and punishments (i.e., consequences of one's actions).

   a. These expectations can create a **self-fulfilling prophecy** in which a person behaves in a way that confirms his or her expectations.

   b. People with an external locus of control tend to believe that they are victims of luck, fate, or situational influences. People with an internal locus of control tend to believe that they are responsible for what happens to them.

   c. To measure people's attitudes and beliefs about locus of control, Julian Rotter developed the Internal/External (I/E) scale.

   c. Having an internal locus of control has important advantages, psychological and physical. An internal locus of control is strongly related to adjustment to surgery and illness, recovery from diseases, and achievement, especially academic achievement, but it is not necessarily beneficial in all situations.

   d. A person's locus of control is affected by one's culture, and one's position and experiences in society. Having an external locus of control may help to preserve self-esteem and cope with objective difficulties.

5. A second important motivating belief is **explanatory style** - a characteristic way of explaining one's successes and failures.

   a. People with pessimistic styles, which are associated with depression, attribute failures to internal, stable, and global factors.

   b. People with optimistic styles, which are associated with achievement, attribute failures to external and unstable factors that are limited in impact.

   c. Optimism is a predictor of achievement and resilience.

6. A third important motivating belief is **self-efficacy,** the fundamental belief that one can successfully accomplish what one has set out to do. Self-efficacy affects task performance, commitment to goals, persistence, career choice, problem-solving ability, health, and ability to handle stress.

   a. Self-efficacy is acquired from four sources:

160

1. experiences in mastering new skills and overcoming obstacles by learning from occasional failures.
2. vicarious experiences provided by competent people similar to one's self.
3. encouragement and persuasion from others.
4. judgements of one's own physiological state.

    b. People with high self-efficacy interpret failure as a learning opportunity.

    c. People with high self-efficacy emphasize learning goals more than performance goals. People who are motivated by **performance goals** are concerned with doing well, being judged highly, and avoiding criticism. In contrast, people who are motivated by **learning (mastery) goals** are concerned with increasing their competence and skills.

7. Locus of control, explanatory style, and self-efficacy are closely interrelated.

III. Learning the Rules of Gender
    A. **Sex** refers to the anatomical and physiological attributes of the sexes.
    B. **Gender** refers to human attributes that are culturally and psychologically defined as more appropriate for one sex than the other.
    C. Social learning theories attempt to explain **gender identity**, the sense of one's own maleness or femaleness, and **gender socialization** (sometimes called <u>sex typing</u>), the process by which people come to learn about "masculine" and "feminine" qualities in their culture.
    D. <u>Transsexuals</u> are people whose gender identity is out of sync with their biological sex.
    E. Behavioral learning
        1. Behavioral learning theories emphasize reinforcement and punishment of "sex-appropriate" and "sex-inappropriate" behavior and imitation.
            a. Meta-analytic studies demonstrate that parents do not treat sons and daughters differently.
            b. Children are selective of whom they imitate.
            c. Children often do not imitate a same-sex parent's nontraditional behavior.
        2. Parents respond to their children's interests and behavior as well as shape them.
        3. Parents and teachers may reinforce behavior subtly.
        4. Parents' expectations influence children in their gender development.
    F. Gender Schemas
        1. Children acquire information about sex-appropriate behavior and internalize it in the form of **gender schemas**, networks of beliefs and expectations which:

a. are learned early in life. Their development is especially evident from ages 2 to 4.

b. regulate behavior.

c. are used partly as the basis for self-evaluations by age 4 or 5.

d. can change throughout life to accommodate new experiences.

2. Studies show that children voluntarily sex-type themselves.

G. The Specific Situation

1. Some situations evoke sex-typed behavior, while others do not.

a. Children adjust their behavior to the gender of the child they are playing with.

b. Acquisition of sex-typed behavior may be affected by factors other than the maintenance of the behavior, because people continue to have varied experiences throughout life.

c. Knowing details about situations allows for better prediction of behavior than knowing the sexes of participants.

d. People are more likely to attribute behavior to a person's sex when the person is not the only female or male in a group.

e. When women are not tokens, or a small percentage of a group, they are perceived as being diverse.

IV. Learning to be Moral

A. Morality involves kindness, fairness, responsibility, empathy, consideration, conscience, and good intentions.

B. Behavioral and cognitive theories

1. Behaviorism overlooks the importance of developing cognitive categories of right and wrong that can be applied to new situations.

2. Kohlberg's cognitive stage theory of moral development proposed three levels of moral reasoning:

a. preconventional - based on punishment, direction of authority, and desire to obey or disobey.

b. conventional - based on trust, caring, and loyalty.

c. postconventional - based on principles of justice.

3. Gilligan's criticism was that women tend to base moral decisions on the basis of compassion and caring, whereas men base moral decisions on abstract principles of law and justice. However, research indicates that people of both sexes use both approaches.

4. Other critics argue that Kohlberg's hierarchy reflects verbal sophistication, not moral judgement; it assumes too much consistency across situations and cultures, and does not explain or predict moral behavior.

C. Social Learning Theories
  1. Social learning theories hold that:
     a. moral behavior is learned.
     b. children internalize parents' moral standards through the attachment process.
     c. the basic capacity for moral feelings is inborn, but is encouraged or inhibited by a child's experiences.
     d. empathy is essential for internalizing morality.
        1. Early empathy is global - general distress at another person's misery.
        2. Egocentric empathy is understanding that another person is in distress but assuming that the other person must feel as you do.
        3. Empathy for another's feelings, when these feelings are different from one's own, can develop in 2- to 3-year-olds.
        4. Empathy for another's life condition can develop by late childhood.
  2. The moral emotions of shame, a wound to the self-concept, and guilt, remorse for wrongdoing, are also essential to moral development.
  3. Children internalize moral standards as much from how parents act as from what they teach.
     a. Many parents use **power assertion** to correct a child's behavior, a method which consists of punitive measures such as threats, physical punishment, depriving the child of privileges, and taking advantage of being bigger and stronger. Power assertion is associated with a lack of moral behavior and feeling.
     b. In using **Induction,** a method of correcting a child's misbehavior the parent appeals to the child's sense of responsibility and feelings for others; this method tends to produce moral children.
     c. Prohibitions of bad behavior are most effective when accompanied by explanations, moralizing, consistent discipline, affection, and high parental expectations.
     d. Culture has an impact on moral development. The most altruistic children come from societies in which children are assigned many tasks, they know their work makes a contribution to the welfare of their family, parents depend on children's contributions, mothers work inside and outside the home, and children respect parental authority.

CHAPTER 7 SUMMARY

Social learning theory holds that most learning is acquired through the 1._____ of other people in social context. Its proponents agree with 2._____ that people are subject to the laws of classical and operant conditioning, but add that attitudes, beliefs, and expectations also affect learning. We know that situations affect behavior. However, as intelligent beings, people choose situations and assess the psychological 3._____ of situations. Social learning theory emphasizes the 4._____ between individuals and their environments. Beliefs, environmental factors, and behavior all affect one another. Albert Bandura termed these mutual effects 5._____.

6._____ learning involves watching others as the basis for the acquisition of behavior. The person one learns from is called a 7._____. If that person is reinforced or punished for some response, an observer may be 8._____ conditioned, although he or she may not exhibit the response for some time. Even very young children seem to have a propensity for observing and imitating others.

Social learning theorists also believe that observational learning cannot be fully understood without taking into account the 9._____ processes of the learner. For instance, Tolman demonstrated that an organism can learn in the absence of reinforcement and without an overt response, a phenomenon he called 10._____ learning. His classic research involved rats learning mazes without being reinforced. Tolman argued that these rats acquired cognitive 11._____, knowledge about the spatial layout of the maze. It is important to remember that two people may observe the same situation and have different interpretations of it. This explains why observational learning does not produce the same results in everybody.

Beliefs are learned through experience, and, in turn, they also exert their own influences on interpretations and behavior, sometimes overcoming the effects of rewards and punishers. 12._____, an inferred process within a person (or animal) that causes movement toward a goal, is powerfully affected by beliefs.

Researchers have described several types of beliefs that have pervasive influences on behavior. Rotter concluded that people develop generalized 13._____ about which situations and acts will be rewarded. A person with an internal 14._____ expects rewards and punishments to depend on his or her behavior, while a person with an 15._____ feels like he or she is at the mercy of fate, luck, chance, or other forces outside of the self. These expectations can create a 16._____, in which a person acts in such a way as to confirm his or her expectations. An internal locus of control is strongly related to achievement, but critics have argued that an internal sense of control reflects the experience of middle-class people, who have often been rewarded for hard work, in sharp contrast to poor and minority peoples.

17. _____ people tend to believe that positive events are the result of good luck, but that negative events are their own fault. Seligman suggested that this pathological belief system is a product of learned 18. _____, which has resulted from experiences of not being able to escape from pain and unhappiness. However, people differ not only in the actual experiences, but also in their interpretations of those experiences. 19. _____ style is the typical way in which a person accounts for negative events. Depressed people tend to have a 20. _____ style in which they explain these events as 21. _____ (being one's own fault), 22. _____ (lasting forever), and 23. _____ (affecting everything). In contrast, people with an 24. _____ explanatory style see negative events as more temporary, external, and limited in impact.

25. _____ is the fundamental belief that one is competent and able to achieve desired goals through personal effort. It affects a wide variety of behaviors, including persistence, health habits, and career choice. According to Bandura, it is acquired from four sources: experiences in mastering new skills, encouragement from others, positive judgements of one's 26. _____ state, and 27. _____ experiences provided by successful models who are similar to the self. Occasional failure is important to the development of this sense, as long as it is interpreted positively. People who set 28. _____ goals want to increase their competence and skills. Therefore, they are not as bothered by failures (if they have learned something) as are people who set 29. _____ goals and who tend to take failure more personally.

While sex is a biological distinction, 30. _____, the cultural attributes assigned to males and females, is a 31. _____ distinction. Social leaning theorists are interested in several associated issues, including the development of 32. _____ (the fundamental sense of oneself as male and female) and 33. _____ (the process of learning what it means to be "masculine" or "feminine").

While behavioral and early social learning theories depicted children as passive participants in the gendering process, we now know that children selectively imitate adults of the same sex, and that they respond differentially to reinforcers from the same-sex and other-sex. Although parents may be egalitarian in their views, they may subtly reinforce gender-stereotyped behaviors. Early in their lives, children acquire networks of beliefs about which behaviors are gender appropriate and which are not. These beliefs, called gender 34. _____, regulate behavior. For instance, five-year-old children tend to be strongly self-critical if they behave in a cross-gendered fashion.

Sex-typed behavior is more salient in some situations than in others. Maccoby discovered that behaviors such as those associated with passivity or independence may be more influenced by the sex of the playmate than by internalized gender standards. Social learning theorists make an important distinction between acquisition of gendered behavior and its 35._____ in adulthood. Some researchers have noted that situational variables usually allow better prediction of behaviors than knowing the sex of the actors. People tend to attribute behavior to a person's sex when there are very few or only one person of that sex in a group.

Social learning theorists are also interested in the study of 36._____, which is described as kindness, fairness, responsibility, and good intention. Behavioral theories overlook the importance of developing cognitive categories of right and wrong that can be applied to new situations. Kohlberg outlined a stage theory of moral development based on a cognitive model. In the first level, called 37._____ morality, a person behaves in a certain way in order to avoid being punished or because of his or her own desires. 38._____ morality is based on trust, caring and loyalty, and 39._____ morality is based on higher principles, such as justice and universal human rights. Gilligan criticized this model as biased towards masculine definitions of morality. She theorized that women tend to base moral decisions on compassion and care, and that these could be as moral as decisions based on abstract principles as justice. A good deal of research, however, has revealed that most people take both compassion and justice into account.

These cognitive theories have been criticized by social learning theorists. For instance, it has bee argued that Kohlberg's stages reflect 40._____ sophistication rather than moral development, and that cognitive approaches overestimate consistency across situations. More important, these theories were developed from interviews rather than from the observation of actual behavior. Social learning theories have shown that the development of morality depends on empathy, shame, guilt, attachment to the caregiver, parental child-rearing styles, and the behavior required of children in everyday situations.

The capacity for morality seems to be inborn, as evidenced by emphatic behaviors exhibited by even very young children. Empathy seems to develop in predictable ways. Very young children exhibit 41._____ empathy, a general distress at another person's misery. Later, they develop 42._____, which is characterized by attempts to make the other person feel better. Next comes the development of empathy for another's feelings. By late childhood, children are capable of having empathy for another's 43._____, and for entire groups of people who are less fortunate.

According to social learning theorists, children internalize moral standards as much from their parent's behaviors as from the lessons their parents teach. 44. _____ assertion by parents, which controls the behavior of children through punishment, is associated with a lack of moral feeling. On the other hand, 45. _____, in which a parent appeals to the child's resources, affection for others, and responsibility, tends to have a positive impact on the development of moral feelings. Punishments are only effective when they are accompanied by 46. _____. Morality also appears to be positively influenced by consistent discipline, parental affection, high parental standards, and requiring children to behave in helpful ways.

MULTIPLE CHOICE SELF-TEST

1. The belief that psychological meaning cannot be separated from behavior is an important tenet of:

    a.   operant conditioning theory.
    b.   social-learning theory.
    c.   behaviorism.
    d.   classical conditioning theory.

2. Social-learning theorists believe that an individual's behavior depends on the interaction of the person and the environment. This is called:

    a.   radical behaviorism.
    b.   stimulus-response conditioning.
    c.   environmental determinism.
    d.   reciprocal determinism.

3. Dr. LaShawn believes that human responses are strictly dependent on a person's reinforcement history. Dr. LaShawn would best be categorized as a(n):

    a.   social learning theorist.
    b.   modified social-learning theorist.
    c.   interactionist.
    d.   radical behaviorist.

4. Monique, an 8-year-old girl, is an avid fan of professional wrestling, which she, watches on television. After watching several matches, she then "body slams" her little brother on the living room carpet. Monique has learned this behavior through:

    a.   vicarious observation.
    b.   classical conditioning.
    c.   operant conditioning
    d.   reciprocal conditioning.

5. The "Rocky and Johnny show" experiment demonstrated that children who watched violent models:

    a.   imitated behavior only if provided with direct reward.
    b.   became more aggressive in their play compared to a control group.
    c.   who are less than five years old, do not imitate very successfully.
    d.   were not able to transfer learning to new situations.

6. The saying that children do as their parents do and not as they say reflects the principle of learning by:

   a. observation.
   b. reinforcement of stimulus-response chains.
   c. classical conditioning.
   d. induction.

7. Learning that is not immediately expressed but is instead expressed at a later time under more appropriate circumstances is known as:

   a. programmed instruction.
   b. instinctive drift.
   c. expert learning.
   d. latent learning.

8. Edward Tolman's (1938) classic study demonstrated a problem with behaviorist theory because it found:

   a. intermittent reward was less effective than consistent reward.
   b. operant conditioning was less important for animal learning than was previously believed.
   c. subjects demonstrated latent learning even when they had not been conditioned.
   d. animal models of behavior do not apply to humans.

9. With regard to the debate about media violence, a social learning theorist would agree with the statement that:

   a. the relationship between media violence and real violence is very strong.
   b. images of violence in the media have the same effect on everyone.
   c. it is important to consider the psychological meaning of the violent images to the individual.
   d. media models are more influential than parents, peers, and teachers.

10. Your friend does not expect to do well in a job interview that is to take place that day. Later that evening you discover that the interview was a disaster. This is an example of:

    a. counterconditioning.
    b. a demotivating complex.
    c. vicarious learning.
    d. self-fulfilling prophecy.

11. Ian doesn't believe in wearing seat belts in the car because he thinks that accidents are pretty much a result of being in the wrong place at the wrong time. This illustrates a(an):

    a. internal locus of control.
    b. external locus of control.
    c. optimistic outlook.
    d. high sense of self-efficacy.

12. Suppose you recently had a heart attack. You would expect to have a speedy recovery and you would follow carefully the instructions of the doctor about your condition if you had a(n):

    a. internal locus of control.
    b. external locus of control.
    c. pessimistic outlook.
    d. low sense of self-efficacy.

13. Depressed people are likely to explain what happens to them by saying that:

    a. good things that happen to them are accidents and that bad things are their own fault.
    b. good things are a result of their own efforts and that bad things are accidents.
    c. both good things and bad things are accidental happenings.
    d. both good things and bad things are a result of their own efforts or mistakes.

14. According to Seligman, people who are pessimistic when faced with bad events make attributions that are:

    a. external, unstable, and limited.
    b. internal, stable, and global.
    c. external, unstable, and global.
    d. internal, unstable, and limited.

15. Based on her past successes with similar work projects, Shirdena believes that she can successfully accomplish a new work project. According to Bandura, she is exhibiting:

    a. delusional thinking.
    b. a high level of self-efficacy.
    c. egotistic thinking.
    d. extreme overconfidence.

16. In all respects, both Bill and Sam have equal ability. However, Bill overcomes failures by persistence and masters a task while Sam stops trying and gives up. The most likely explanation for this occurrence is that Bill sets:

   a. mastery goals and Sam sets performance goals.
   b. performance goals and Sam sets mastery goals.
   c. easy performance goals and Sam sets difficult performance goals.
   d. easy mastery goals and Sam sets difficult mastery goals.

17. An important component in the development of self-efficacy is:

   a. the experience of easy successes.
   b. observing similar models fail.
   c. occasional failure.
   d. overcoming persistent failures.

18. An athlete performs poorly in a skating competition. According to Julian Rotter, an athlete with an external locus of control would believe her poor performance was due to:

   a. the judges' dislike of her music.
   b. her lack of practice.
   c. her lack of motivation.
   d. her poor technique.

19. Gilbert is a 30-year-old transsexual. He was once a man, but has now had surgery to become a woman. He now functions successfully in the role of a woman. Jack most likely had a problem with his gender:

   a. schema.
   b. identity.
   c. locus.
   d. role.

20. An individual's sense of maleness or femaleness is his or her:

   a. gender schema.
   b. gender identity.
   c. sex role.
   d. gender type.

21. Jenny is in the most important period for developing strong and elaborate gender schemas. She is probably in the age range of:

    a. 9 months to 1 year.
    b. 1 to 2
    c. 2 to 4.
    d. 4 to 6.

22. Boys and girls have a tendency to act in stereotypical ways, even though parents or teachers insist they treat both the sexes the same. Social learning theorists believe this result is often due to:

    a.   subtle reinforcement of appropriate gender behavior.
    b.   natural biological sex differences.
    c.   strong punishments for opposite-sex behavior.
    d.   lack of non-traditional role models.

23. Nadia is discussing medical career options with her mother. If Nadia has developed strong gender schemas about male and female behavior, she is most likely to believe that:

    a.   girls can be both nurses and doctors, but boys cannot be nurses.
    b.   girls and boys can choose any career they want.
    c.   only girls can be nurses and only boys can be doctors.
    d.   boys can be both nurses and doctors, but only girls can be nurses.

24. The best predictor of how a person will behave is knowledge of the:

    a.   person's gender identity.
    b.   person's sex.
    c.   situation.
    d.   person's gender schema.

25. During World War II, Oskar Schindler helped save Jews from being deported to concentration camps and murdered. According to Kohlberg's theory of moral development, Oskar Schindler's actions exhibit a _____ level of morality.

    a.   subconventional.
    b.   preconventional.
    c.   conventional.
    d.   postconventional.

26. A person is presented with a moral dilemma: A man's wife is dying and he wants to steal an expensive drug to save her life because he can't afford to buy it. When asked if the man should steal the drug, a person at the <u>conventional</u> level of morality would respond:

    a.   "Stealing is against the law and therefore he shouldn't do it no matter what!"
    b.   "He should steal the drug because his wife's life is more important than any law."
    c.   "He can't help the fact that he is poor and the druggist is immoral for not giving it to him for free!"
    d.   "Life-saving drugs should be available to all people for low cost as a matter of principle."

27. According to social learning theorists, parents can best teach morality to children by:

    a.   teaching them to obey without question and instilling fear of punishment.
    b.   discouraging the emotions of guilt and shame.
    c.   using corporal punishment and threats.
    d.   using induction and instilling a sense of empathy for others.

28. Research indicates that when men and women make decisions about ethical dilemmas:

    a.   men base moral choices on principles of justice, while women tend to reason based on care and compassion.
    b.   men base moral choices on care and compassion, while women tend to base moral choices on principles of justice.
    c.   both men and women base moral choices on principles of justice and on principles of care and compassion.
    d.   both men and women base moral choices only on principles of justice.

29. A two-year-old child believes her cat "Fluffy" needs a cold water bath because it's hot outside and the cat is uncomfortable. The child is exhibiting:

    a.   global empathy.
    b.   conventional empathy.
    c.   empathy for the cat's discomfort.
    d.   egocentric empathy.

30. Children who are the most moral come from families where parents use:

   a.   power assertion.
   b.   a permissive style.
   c.   induction.
   d.   few explanations.

TRUE FALSE SELF-TEST

T   F   1.   Social-learning theorists differ from radical behaviorists by arguing that people often choose the situations they are in.

T   F   2.   In social-learning approaches, the psychological meaning of a behavior is emphasized.

T   F   3.   Reciprocal determinism means that behavior follows directly from environmental consequences.

T   F   4.   Observational learning can begin even when children are too young to speak.

T   F   5.   Research shows that even though very young children may see a model play with a toy only once, they can correctly imitate the model's behavior.

T   F   6.   In most studies, the relationship between media violence and real violence is very strong.

T   F   7.   Social-learning theorists believe that learned habits and beliefs may supersede the power of external rewards and punishers.

T   F   8.   Learning can remain latent for long periods of time.

T   F   9.   According to social learning theory, people influence environments.

T   F   10.   Persons with an internal locus of control believe that they are the victims of luck or fate.

T   F   11.   An internal locus of control can help reduce chronic pain and help people recover from diseases.

T   F   12.   An external locus of control is related to high achievement.

T   F   13.   People who are pessimistic tend to explain events as being due to external factors which are limited in impact.

T   F   14.   Optimism is a good predictor of goal achievement.

T   F   15.   Occasional failures undermine a person's sense of self-efficacy.

T   F   16.   People best develop self-efficacy from models who are similar to them.

T   F   17.   People who are motivated by learning goals are concerned with doing well, being judged highly, and avoiding criticism.

T   F   18.   The term gender refers to anatomical and physiological attributes of the sexes.

T   F   19.   Gender identity is strongly developed by age one.

T   F   20.   Transsexuals are people whose gender identity is discrepant from their biological sex.

T   F   21.   Adults start sex-typing as soon as a baby is born.

T   F   22.   Meta-analytic research shows that parents treat sons and daughters quite differently.

T   F   23.   Children are generally passive imitators of same-sex models.

T   F   24.   Even young boys and girls whose behavior is the same are treated differently by adults.

T   F   25.   Rudimentary gender schemas can develop as early as age nine months.

T   F   26.   There is evidence that children voluntarily sex-type themselves.

T   F   27.   If you want to know how a person will behave in a particular situation, you would do better to know that person's sex rather than the details of the situation.

T   F   28.   Gender rules acquired in childhood are "stamped-in" and are very difficult to modify.

T   F   29.   A boy with a secure gender identity will necessarily behave in sex-appropriate ways.

T   F   30.   Parental induction is associated with negative psychological outcomes in children.

KEY TERMS

social-learning theories - Theories of learning that typically emphasize a person's reciprocal interaction with the environment and that focus on observational learning, cognitive processes, and motivational beliefs.

observational learning - A learning process in which an individual learns new responses by observing the behavior of another (a model) rather than through direct experience; in behaviorism, it is called <u>vicarious conditioning</u>.

latent learning - A form of learning that is not immediately expressed in an overt response; it occurs without obvious reinforcement.

cognitive map - A mental representation of the environment.

motivation - An inferred process within a person or animal that causes that individual to move toward a goal.

self-fulfilling prophecy - An expectation that comes true because of the tendency of the person holding it to act in ways that confirm it.

locus of control - A general expectation about whether the results of one's actions are under one's own control (<u>internal</u> locus) or beyond one's control (<u>external</u> locus).

self-efficacy - The belief that one is capable of producing, through one's own efforts, desired results, such as mastering new skills and reaching goals.

performance goals - Motivational goals that emphasize external rewards, such as doing well, being judged highly, and avoiding criticism.

learning (mastery) goals - Motivational goals that emphasize the intrinsic satisfaction of increasing one's competence and skills.

gender identity - The fundamental sense of being male and female, regardless of whether or not one conforms to the rules of sex typing.

gender socialization (sex typing) - The process by which children learn the behaviors, attitudes, and expectations associated in their culture with being masculine or feminine.

gender schema - A cognitive schema (mental network) of knowledge, beliefs, metaphors, and expectations about what it means to be male or female.

power assertion - A method of correcting a child's behavior in which the parent uses punishment and authority.

induction - A method of correcting a child's behavior in which the parent appeals to the child's own abilities, sense of responsibility, and feelings for others.

Suggested Research Projects

1. A frequent topic of conversation is "the difference between men and women." Assemble one group of all males, one group of all females, and one group of both males and females of different ages, and hold general discussions on this topic. What gender schemas do you discover? Are there differences in gender schemas among groups or across generations? What do you attribute these differences to?

2. Take a negative life event (such as a car accident, an unwanted pregnancy, relationship break-up, the attainment of a low grade point average, etc.) and make a list of possible interpretations for the event. Identify each interpretation using Seligman's three dimensions: stable-unstable, internal-external, global-specific.

Suggested Readings

Gilligan, C. (1982). *In a Different Voice: Psychological Theory and Women's Development.* Cambridge, MA: Harvard University Press. A feminist approach to understanding moral development.

Shulman, M., & Mekler, E. (1994). *Bringing up a Caring Child.* NY: Doubleday. An excellent critique of exclusively behavioral approaches to moral development and a social-learning analysis of how children learn to be kind, fair, and responsible.

Pryor, K. (1985). Don't Shoot the Dog: The New Art of Teaching and Training. New York: Bamtam. This book explains in an entertaining way how to train anyone: human and animal.

Suggested Audio-Visuals

Albert Bandura (1988). This two part series examines Bandura's social learning theory and his classic Bobo doll experiment, morality, and the effects of violence in the media. From Insight Media.

CHAPTER 7

ANSWERS TO CHAPTER SUMMARY

1. observation
2. behaviorists
3. meaning
4. interaction
5. reciprocal determinism
6. observational
7. model
8. vicariously
9. thought (cognitive)
10. latent
11. maps
12. motivation
13. expectations
14. locus of control
15. external locus of control
16. self-fulfilling prophecy
17. depressed
18. helplessness
19. explanatory
20. pessimistic
21. internal
22. stable
23. global
24. optimistic
25. self-efficacy
26. physiological
27. vicarious
28. learning
29. performance
30. gender
31. psychological
32. gender identity
33. gender socialization
34. schemas
35. maintenance (expression)
36. morality
37. preconventional
38. conventional
39. postconventional

40. verbal
41. global
42. egocentric
43. life condition
44. power
45. induction
46. explanations

ANSWERS TO MULTIPLE CHOICE SELF-TEST

1. B
2. D
3. D
4. A
5. B
6. A
7. D
8. C
9. C
10. D
11. B
12. A
13. A
14. B
15. B
16. A
17. C
18. A
19. B
20. B
21. C
22. A
23. C
24. C
25. D
26. A
27. D
28. C
29. D
30. C

ANSWERS TO TRUE FALSE SELF-TEST

1. T
2. T
3. F
4. T
5. T
6. F
7. T
8. T
9. T
10. F
11. T
12. F
13. F
14. T
15. F
16. T
17. F
18. F
19. F
20. T
21. T
22. F
23. F
24. T
25. T
26. T
27. F
28. F
29. F
30. F

CHAPTER 8

EVALUATING THE LEARNING PERSPECTIVE

LEARNING OBJECTIVES

After reading and studying this chapter, you should be able to:

1. Discuss the contributions and criticisms of the learning perspective.

2. Examine the implications of the learning perspective in the areas of psychotherapy, education, and child rearing.

CHAPTER 8 OUTLINE

I.   Contributions and Misuses of the Learning Perspective.
    A.   Contributions of the learning perspective
        1.   A major contribution is that behavioral studies are among psychology's most reliable and useful.
        2.   Behaviorists recognize that we all influence others and in turn are influenced by others.
        3.   The learning perspective teaches that merely naming a behavior does not explain it.
        4.   Social learning research findings are applicable to solving a variety of personal and social problem
            a.   Self-efficacy can be acquired and improved through programs that teach skills, provide models, and supply appropriate rewards.
            b.   Setting goals that are demanding, but realistic and focused, improves performance.
            c.   Health habits can be improved by raising self-efficacy and internal locus of control, and by providing positive role models.
    B.   Limitations of the learning perspective
        1.   Critics regard deliberate efforts at manipulation as cold and mechanistic, but behaviorists argue that influencing others is unavoidable, and so should be done systematically and intelligently to improve our lives.
        2.   Critics accuse behaviorists of regarding people as passive pawns of the environment.
        3.   Environmental reductionism, the tendency to attribute all behavior to situational factors, ignores biological attributes that are known to affect behavior, such as physical characteristics of the body, biological preparedness to learn a particular task, and **instinctive drift** (the reversion to instinctive behavior).
        4.   Learning theorists are attractive to advocates of egalitarianism, but as in the biological perspective, political motivations can lead to an incomplete view of reality (e.g., of gender development). There is the error of assuming that if something is learned it can be easily changed.
        5.   Behavioral researchers tend to study one influence on behavior at a time, but in real life, hundreds of influences interact in complex ways.
        6.   There is often a tendency to apply learning principles in oversimplified ways. Some applications have focused on extrinsic rather than intrinsic motivators of behavior.

II.   Issue #1: Psychotherapy
    A.   The learning perspective has contributed many useful techniques to psychotherapy.
        1.   Psychologists practice <u>behavior therapy</u> to change behaviors and attitudes using a variety of methods derived from behavioral principles.
        2.   Behavioral records and contracts identify rewards that maintain unwanted habits and establish behavioral goals with new reinforcers.
        3.   <u>Systematic desensitization</u> combines relaxation training with systematic exposure to feared stimuli, in order to extinguish fear. Based on the principles of counterconditioning (See Chapter 6).
        4.   <u>Aversive conditioning</u> substitutes punishment for the positive reinforcement that perpetuates a bad habit.
        5.   <u>Flooding</u> exposes a person to a feared situation so that the person can experience a lack of negative consequences. Behavioral techniques are used to treat <u>agoraphobia,</u> the fear of leaving a safe place and being in an unfamiliar, unprotected situation.
        6.   Skills training provides practice in specific behaviors.
    B.   Research demonstrates the efficacy of behavior therapies. Behavior therapy has been especially successful in the treatment of fears, management of chronic pain, teaching of self-control strategies, and treatment of child and adolescent behavioral problems.
    C.   Therapies based on learning principles have not been very successful in treating trauma, severe depression, sex offenders, unmotivated people, or **antisocial personality disorder,** a condition that is characterized by antisocial behavior (such as lying, stealing, and sometimes violence), lack of social emotions (empathy, shame, and guilt), and impulsivity, and that may involve biological abnormalities.
    D.   Antisocial personalities are slow to develop classically conditioned responses of fear or anxiety and may exhibit a lack of <u>behavioral inhibition,</u> the ability to control responses to frustration or to inhibit a pleasurable action that may have unpleasant consequences.

III.   Issue #2: Education
    A.   Learning principles can be applied to classrooms.
        1.   Programmed instruction and other programs have used operant approaches to teach new skills.
        2.   However, because of practical problems and misunderstandings of concepts, behavioral approaches have not been used to their full effect in schools.
            a.   Using frequent reinforcement requires a great deal of extra planning and work, and teachers are often not rewarded for implementing operant approaches.

        b.   School systems overemphasize extrinsic rewards and performance (grades) rather than learning goals, which promote a lifelong interest in learning.

        c.   Efforts to boost self-esteem use indiscriminate rewards which are ineffective and do not increase self-efficacy.

IV.   Issue #3: Child Rearing

    A.   The learning perspective has identified three basic styles of parenting:

        1.   <u>authoritarian</u> parents exercise too much power and give too little nurturance. This style tends to produce children with poor social skills, low self-esteem, poor academic achievement, and either timidity or aggressiveness.

        2.   <u>permissive</u> parents are nurturant but exercise too little control and make too few demands. This style tends to produce children who are impulsive, immature, and irresponsible. There are two varieties of permissiveness: indulgent (responsive to children while making few demands), and neglecting (making few demands and being unresponsive; this style is associated with more severe problems).

        3.   <u>authoritative</u> parents exercise appropriate control, nurture, have high but reasonable expectations for their children, and encourage two-way communication. This style tends to produce children who show good self- control,high self-esteem, high self-efficacy, cooperation, independence, social maturity, academic achievement, cheerfulness, and thoughtfulness.

    B.   Ethnicity and life circumstances may affect the consequences of a particular parenting style.

    C.   The contextual model of parenting style suggests that a parent's style affects the child by making the parent's actions more or less effective, and by making the child more or less open to those practices.

    D.   The learning perspective shows that good parenting includes the following:

        1.   consistency in enforcing rules and demands.

        2.   modeling of desired behaviors.

        3.   high expectations.

        4.   respect for the child.

        5.   explanations of rules.

        6.   approval and reinforcement of desired behaviors.

        7.   use of <u>induction</u>, rather than power assertion, to call attention to the effect of hurtful actions on others and teach the child to take another person's point of view.

CHAPTER 8 SUMMARY

The learning perspective has been useful in many circumstances. Critics argue that its approach is cold and manipulative, but learning theorists counter that people will inevitably be influenced by their environments, and so we would do well to design those environments so that this influence is positive.

The benefits of learning research have included the development of programs for raising self-efficacy, helping people set goals that are demanding but realistic, and improving health habits. Like other perspectives, however, the learning perspective has its dangers, including environmental 1._____, the tendency to explain every behavior by situational influences. It has been well demonstrated that all organisms are biologically prepared to learn some responses more easily than others. In mammals the tendency to gravitate toward these types of behaviors, regardless of reinforcers, is known as 2._____.

People who advocate egalitarianism and social change are drawn to the learning perspective because of its assumption that human behavior is malleable. This gives them hope that inequalities can be rectified by changes in environments. Some biological psychologists disagree, especially with regard to gender differences. However, even if there are biologically based 3._____ differences between the sexes, they should never be used to restrict the opportunities of any individual.

Learning researchers tend to study one influence at a time, but in actual environments there are almost always a complex variety of influences on any given behavior. Also, people who try to apply learning theories sometimes do so in oversimplified ways. Despite these problems, learning theorists are probably correct in their belief that society does not take as much advantage as it could of what we have learned in this area.

Psychotherapy has been a major beneficiary of behavioral findings. Behavior therapists use a variety of methods. For example, a therapist who is treating someone with a self-control problem might direct the person to keep records about the behavior. Techniques include 4._____, a treatment for phobia that combines relaxation training with systematic presentation of the feared stimuli. This is similar to the classical conditioning technique of 5._____. Another technique is 6._____, where punishment is substituted for the reinforcement that perpetuates the bad habit. 7._____, also known as exposure treatment, is the technique of putting the clients into actual feared situations so that they can learn that the situation need not be fearsome. For example, a person suffering from 8._____, a fear of leaving a safe place and being in an unfamiliar unprotected situation, would be taken right into a large shopping mall or other new situation. Some people need practice in learning specific kinds of behavior, and behavioral skills training can provide it.

Behavior therapies have been especially successful in helping people eliminate fears and unwanted habits, as well as the management of chronic pain. They have not been very successful in the treatment of post-traumatic reactions or severe depression, nor have they been effective in changing the behavior of sex offenders, people who do not want to change, and people with 9._____ disorder, which is characterized by behavior such as lying, stealing, manipulating others, a lack of social emotions, and sometimes violence. Some researchers believe that there is a common, inherited condition among antisocial, hyperactive, or overly extroverted people who have a problem with 10._____, the ability to control responses to frustration or to inhibit a pleasurable action that may have unpleasant consequences.

In education, one very promising behavioral approach is to break down skills into small units and reinforce the learner for acquiring each unit. This technique, called 11._____, makes use of the behavioral principle of frequent reinforcement. Unfortunately, classroom teachers do not usually use this technique enough, often because it makes too much work for them to handle. Another problem in the American educational system is the overreliance on grades, an 12._____ reward that may dissuade students from developing learning goals. Some theorists believe that schools put too much emphasis on self-esteem and not enough emphasis on self-efficacy.

Behavioral science has also made significant contributions to the study of child rearing. Baumrind had described three basic styles of child rearing and their effects. The 13._____ parent exercises a good deal of power, but gives little nurturance. Children of these parents often suffer from low self-esteem and do poorly in school. 14._____ parents nurture but exercise too little control. Their children are more likely to be impulsive and immature. One type of permissive parent is 15._____, who makes few demands but does reinforce desirable behavior. Another parenting type is 16._____, who neither makes demands nor gives appropriate reinforcement. 17._____ parents strike a balance between nurturance and discipline. They also encourage two-way communication with their children, who often grow up with many characteristics of psychological health: self-control, self-efficacy, social maturity, and thoughtfulness.

These styles may have different effects in different ethnic groups because of social contexts, but some general parenting guidelines seem to be universal. Children respond most positively when parents provide consistent discipline, modeling of desirable behavior, high expectations, respect, explanations for rules, appropriate positive reinforcement, and the use of 18._____ rather than power assertion.

MULTIPLE CHOICE SELF-TEST

1.   The purpose of the "Air-crib" invented by B.F. Skinner was to provide his daughter Deborah with:

     a.   her own Skinner box to be used to operantly condition her.
     b.   a "time-out" area when she was misbehaving.
     c.   a place that she could move around in and be comfortable.
     d.   her own programmed instruction device.

2.   A good explanation for a child's refusal to keep his room clean according to a behaviorist would be that fact that he:

     a.   is just lazy.
     b.   has an unconscious desire to get back at his parents.
     c.   has psychological problems.
     d.   is being reinforced to do something that's more fun.

3.   In order to help you with a problem a behavior therapist is most likely to:

     a.   tell you what you can do to change.
     b.   help you analyze your motives.
     c.   figure out your unconscious desires.
     d.   give you a chance to talk about your problem.

4.   A college student wants to improve her grade in her beginning psychology class. From a behavioral perspective, a good goal for her to set would be to:

     a.   study more.
     b.   read two hours every evening instead of one.
     c.   procrastinate less.
     d.   read the entire book the first day of class.

5.   Mr. Kaminsky has high blood pressure, is 40 pounds overweight, and has high cholesterol, making him a prime candidate for a heart attack. From a behavioral perspective, the best approach to help him would be to:

     a.   discuss with him the dangers of poor health habits and scare him into thinking he might die if he doesn't take care of himself.
     b.   provide him with several pamphlets explaining the dangers of a high-fat diet.
     c.   help him to gradually increase his daily exercise and modify his diet.
     d.   tell his wife to monitor everything he eats.

6. An animal trainer is trying to teach a raccoon to pick up an apple and deposit it in a bin. However, the raccoon insists on "washing" the apple with its paws rather than picking it up and taking it to the bin. The raccoon's behavior is best explained by:

   a. instinctive drift.
   b. a failure of operant conditioning.
   c. distractions from the environment.
   d. counterconditioning.

7. A college professor decides to award only one "A" grade in order to motivate students to perform better. This reward scheme illustrates:

   a. environmental reductionism.
   b. oversimplification in applying learning techniques.
   c. the assumption that if something is learned, it can easily be changed.
   d. a focus on learning rather than performance.

8. As part of a program to stop smoking, a woman charts the number of times she lights up a cigarette over the course of a day. This is an example of the technique of:

   a. behavioral recording.
   b. exposure.
   c. systematic desensitization.
   d. skills training.

9. Gretchen is terrified of cats. In order to help her overcome her fear, her therapist takes her to a room in a local animal shelter where there are at least a hundred cats. The therapist is using the technique of:

   a. skills training.
   b. systematic desensitization.
   c. aversive conditioning.
   d. flooding.

10. Carmine is afraid of heights. If his therapist is using systematic desensitization to help him, he would first ask Carmine to:

   a. go up to the top of the Empire State Building.
   b. relax and then look at pictures of tall buildings.
   c. snap a rubberband around his wrist whenever he feels fear.
   d. keep a record of his feelings about his fear of heights.

11. A prison psychologist is trying to change the behavior of a pedophile by showing him pictures of children and then administering a brief electric shock to him. The prison psychologist is using the behavioral technique of:

   a.   skills training.
   b.   systematic desensitization.
   c.   aversive conditioning.
   d.   flooding.

12. Milton is a man who has several wives in different states, all of whom he has swindled out of large sums of money. He feels no remorse about his behavior. Milton is likely to have:

   a.   antisocial personality disorder.
   b.   bipolar disorder.
   c.   schizophrenia
   d.   major depression.

13. Mr. Sims is trying to teach basic math to his classroom of first-graders using programmed instruction. He would structure the learning situation by:

   a.   making sure that all the children learn at the same rate.
   b.   breaking down the lessons into small chunks.
   c.   using constant verbal praise for all behaviors.
   d.   giving high grades in order to boost self-esteem.

14. A good way to enhance self-efficacy in the classroom is by:

   a.   providing extrinsic reinforcers.
   b.   using effusive praise.
   c.   punishing failures.
   d.   setting challenging goals.

15. Timmy's parents believe that children should be "seen and not heard". They also believe that Timmy should obey them without question. Because of this parenting style, Timmy is more likely to:

   a.   have high-self esteem.
   b.   be less socially skilled.
   c.   be a high achiever.
   d.   have high self-control.

16. Betty is an adolescent girl who cares little for school, is immature, very impulsive, and frequently gets into trouble with the law. It is most likely her parents are:

  a. authoritative.
  b. authoritarian.
  c. indulgent.
  d. neglecting.

TRUE FALSE SELF-TEST

T   F   1. B.F. Skinner reared his daughter in a Skinner box.

T   F   2. According to a behaviorist, a good explanation for why someone cannot control his drinking is that he is an alcoholic.

T   F   3. Learning theorists regard people as passive pawns of the environment.

T   F   4. Behavior modification techniques have been applied successfully in many settings.

T   F   5. People who see managerial ability as a learned skill tend to have a high sense of self-efficacy and better performance as a manager.

T   F   6. Setting realistic but demanding goals can improve performance on a task.

T   F   7. A focus on performance rather than learning is more likely to result in persistence in the face of failure.

T   F   8. A criticism of the behavioral approach is that researchers tend to focus on one influence on behavior at a time.

T   F   9. All behavior can be ultimately reduced to environmental influences.

T   F   10. An animal learning a "trick" through operant conditioning may revert to its natural instinctive behavior, rather than performing the trick in the manner desired by the trainer.

T   F   11. Human beings are biologically prepared to learn taste aversions rather than aversions to light or sound.

T   F   12.   Girls exposed to prenatal androgens are more likely to prefer to play with masculine toys.

T   F   13.   Average gender differences in certain skills typically indicate an individual man or woman's strengths and weaknesses.

T   F   14.   Extrinsic reinforcers are best used for developing long-term motivation.

T   F   15.   In using systematic desensitization to treat agoraphobia, the person is presented with the feared stimulus all at once.

T   F   16.   Systematic desensitization is based on counterconditioning principles.

T   F   17.   Aversive conditioning substitutes punishment for positive reinforcement in order to eliminate a bad habit.

T   F   18.   Agoraphobia is a fear of heights.

T   F   19.   Meta-analytic studies show the exposure techniques are more effective in reducing fears than any other treatment.

T   F   20.   Behavior therapies are useful for recovering from trauma or from severe depression.

T   F   21.   Sex offenders are effectively treated by behavior therapy alone.

T   F   22.   Antisocial personality disorder appears to be entirely learned.

T   F   23.   A person who commits antisocial behaviors always can be classified as having antisocial personality disorder.

T   F   24.   A heavy emphasis on grades tends to promote a life-long interest in learning.

T   F   25.   Self-esteem appears to be the main ingredient of success and achievement.

T   F   26.   Teachers with a greater sense of self-efficacy tend to maintain a more positive climate in the classroom.

T   F   27.   Authoritative parents exercise too much power and give too little nurturance.

T	F	28.	Permissive parents tend to be nurturant but exercise too little control.

T	F	29.	Explaining the reasons for rules helps children internalize them.

T	F	30.	Using power assertion is a good way to teach empathy and consideration for others.

KEY TERMS

instinctive drift - The tendency of an organism to revert to an instinctive behavior over time; it can interfere with learning.

agoraphobia - A set of phobias (irrational fears) involving the basic fear of being away from a safe place or person.

antisocial personality disorder - A disorder characterized by antisocial behavior such as lying, stealing, manipulating others, and sometimes violence; a lack of social emotions (guilt, shame, and empathy); and impulsivity. (Sometimes called psychopathy or sociopathy).

Suggested Research Projects

1. Interview students who are education majors or professors at your college. Alternatively interview teachers in elementary and secondary education. Ask them their opinions on the relative emphasis on intrinsic rather than extrinsic reinforcers in American schools.

2. Design a program to teach parenting skills in the high school curriculum. What would be the contributions and limitations of a learning perspective in designing such a program?

Suggested Readings

Brazelton, T.B. (1984). To Listen to a Child: Understanding the Normal Problems of Growing Up. Reading, MA: Addison-Wesley. A self-help book on parenting that reviews methods for dealing with common problems and issues during the childhood years.

Turecki, S. (1995). Normal Children Have Problems, Too: How Parents Can Understand and Help. New York: Bantam. This self-help book discusses a variety of childhood problems and offers insights for effective intervention.

CHAPTER 8

ANSWERS TO CHAPTER SUMMARY

1. reductionism
2. instinctive drift
3. gender
4. systematic desensitization
5. counterconditioning
6. aversive conditioning
7. flooding
8. agoraphobia
9. antisocial personality
10. behavioral inhibition
11. programmed instruction
12. extrinsic
13. authoritarian
14. permissive
15. indulgent
16. neglecting
17. authoritative
18. induction

ANSWERS TO MULTIPLE CHOICE SELF-TEST

1. C
2. D
3. A
4. B
5. C
6. A
7. B
8. A
9. D
10. B
11. C
12. A
13. B
14. D
15. B
16. D

ANSWERS TO TRUE FALSE SELF-TEST

1.   F
2.   F
3.   F
4.   T
5.   T
6.   T
7.   F
8.   T
9.   F
10.   T
11.   T
12.   T
13.   F
14.   F
15.   F
16.   T
17.   T
18.   F
19.   T
20.   F
21.   F
22.   F
23.   F
24.   F
25.   F
26.   T
27.   F
28.   T
29.   T
30.   F

CHAPTER 9

THINKING AND REASONING

LEARNING OBJECTIVES

After reading and studying this chapter, you should be able to:

1. Define how information is represented internally in the form of concepts, propositions, and cognitive schemas.

2. Distinguish conscious, subconscious, and nonconscious thought.

3. Distinguish inductive, deductive, and dialectical reasoning.

4. Distinguish divergent thinking from convergent thinking.

5. Discuss the importance of creativity for psychological functioning.

6. Describe Piaget's stage theory of cognitive development.

7. Discuss research calling into question some specific aspects of Piaget's theory.

8. Describe stages in the development of reflective thinking in adults.

9. Identify common cognitive biases that hinder reasoning and creative thought; for example, the confirmation bias, the hindsight bias, cognitive dissonance reduction, and the fundamental attribution error.

10. Describe some recent research findings on animal cognition and discuss the controversy about how to interpret these findings.

CHAPTER 9 OUTLINE

I.   Introduction
      A.   Information-processing theories of cognition recognize the fact that the brain does not passively record information but actively alters and organizes it.
      B.   Functions of thinking:
            1.   allows the person to go beyond the present.
            2.   allows for the manipulation of mental representations of objects, situations, and activities.
            3.   aids problem-solving by simplifying and summarizing information from the environment.
      C.   How information is represented mentally
            1.   **Concepts** are mental categories that simplify the world by grouping objects, relations, activities, abstractions, or qualities that have common properties. We form concepts by:
                  a.   direct contact with objects and situations.
                  b.   contact with symbols (things that represent or stand for objects, operations, and qualities).
            2.   **Propositions** are units of meaning that are made up of concepts and express a unitary idea.
            3.   **Cognitive schemas** are complex networks of propositions that serve as mental models of various aspects of the world.

II.   How Conscious is Thought?
      A.   **Subconscious processes** lie outside of awareness but can be brought into consciousness when necessary.
      B.   **Nonconscious processes** remain out of awareness but affect behavior, and seem to be involved in the experience of intuition.
      C.   **Conscious processes** are needed for deliberate choices, unexpected events, or when events cannot be handled automatically.
      D.   Much of our thinking is conscious, but still may be mindless; in other words, we may act out of habit without analyzing our behavior. <u>Mindlessness</u> is a type of lapse in conscious thought which keeps people from recognizing when a change in context requires a change in behavior.

III. Reasoning and Creativity
      A.   Reasoning is purposeful mental activity that involves operating on information in order to reach conclusions. Two types of reasoning involve drawing conclusions from a series of observations or propositions (<u>premises</u>).
            1. In **deductive reasoning**, the conclusion must be true if certain premises are true. Deductive reasoning takes the form of a <u>syllogism</u>, a simple argument consisting of two premises and a conclusion.

2. In **inductive reasoning**, premises provide support for a conclusion, but the conclusion could still be false; science depends heavily on inductive reasoning.

B. Even when they are logical, people may reach different conclusions if their premises differ or information is incomplete. Logic does not tell us which premise is, in fact, true.

C. **Dialectical reasoning** is the ability to evaluate opposing ideas or points of view and is necessary when dealing with informal reasoning problems.

D. A **mental set** is a tendency to try to solve new problems by using the same procedures that worked before. They may be efficient but are not generally useful for new problems.

E. Creativity involves going beyond present knowledge and habit to produce new solutions.

1. Creative thinkers use **divergent thinking**, the generation of new hypotheses, interpretations and connections among pieces of information.

2. Less creative people rely solely on **convergent thinking**, following prescribed steps in an attempt to find a single correct solution to a problem

E. Tests have been devised to measure creativity. These include:

1. the Alternate Uses test, which asks you to think of as many uses as possible for common items.

2. the Remote Associates Test, which presents sets of 3 words and asks you to find an associated word for each set.

3. the Lifetime Creativity Scales, in which a skilled interviewer examines a person's accomplishments based on his or her actual history of creativity in work and leisure activities. The scale measures:

a. peak creativity - major enterprises or activities.

b. extent of involvement - pervasiveness of creativity.

F. Creativity flourishes when people:

1. have control over how to perform a task or solve a problem.

2. are evaluated unobtrusively.

3. work independently.

G. Various personality traits are related to creativity:

1. nonconformity.

2. independence.

3. confidence.

4. curiosity.

5. persistence.

IV. The Development of Thought and Reasoning
  A. Piaget's Stages: How Children Think
    1. Piaget proposed that thought involves:
      a. <u>organization</u> of observation and experience into a coherent set of meanings.
      b. <u>adaptation</u> to new observations and experiences, which takes place in two ways:
        1. **assimilation** - fitting new information into existing mental schemas.
        2. **accommodation** - modifying existing schemas to incorporate new information.
    2. Piaget's four stages of cognitive development.
      a. The <u>sensory motor stage</u> (birth - 2 years) involves:
        1. learning through concrete actions.
        2. coordinating sensory information with bodily movements.
        3. attaining **object permanence**, the understanding that objects continue to exist even when they cannot be seen or touched. This is the major accomplishment of this stage, as it is the beginning of <u>representational thought</u>, the capacity for using mental imagery and other symbolic systems.
      b. In the <u>preoperational stage</u> (ages 2 - 7):
        1. children show accelerated use of symbols and language.
        2. children show evidence of **conservation**, the understanding that physical properties of objects do not necessarily change when their form or appearance changes.
        3. Piaget believed that preoperational children cannot reason or perform **operations** (reversible actions performed in the mind), and that their thinking is **egocentric**, so they cannot take another's perspective.
      c. In the <u>concrete operations stage</u> (ages 6 or 7-11), children gain the ability to:
        1. understand conservation, reversibility, cause and effect, identity, and serial ordering.
        2. perform some mental operations, such as mathematical ones.
        3. understand some abstract principles, although their thinking is still grounded in concrete experience.

d. The <u>formal operations stage</u> (age 12 - adulthood) is characterized by :
   1. abstract reasoning.
   2. systematic problem solving.
   3. the comparison and classification of ideas.
3. Research has called into question some aspects of Piaget's theory.
   a. Stage changes are not as sweeping or clear-cut as Piaget thought.
   b. Some reasoning is influenced by its content.
   c. Many children demonstrate more cognitive skills than Piaget gave them credit for, including earlier object permanence, use of symbols, and perspective taking.
   d. By age 4 or 5, children develop a <u>theory of mind</u>, a theory about how one's own and other people's minds work and how people are affected by their beliefs and feelings.
   e. Not all adolescents or adults develop the ability for formal operational thought.
B. Beyond Piaget: How Adults Think
   1. <u>Reflective judgment</u> involves:
      a. critical thinking.
      b. evaluating and integrating evidence.
      c. relating evidence to theory.
      d. reaching reasonable and plausible conclusions that can be defended.
      e. questioning assumptions.
      f. considering alternative explanations.
      g. reassessing conclusions when new evidence becomes available.
   2. Research indicates that many adults, even when they are capable of formal operations, do not think reflectively.
   3. King & Kitchner have identified stages in the development of reflective thinking.
      a. In the <u>prereflective stage</u>, the person assumes that a single correct answer exists and can be known through the senses, and makes no distinction between knowledge and belief.
      b. In the <u>quasi-reflective stage</u>, the person recognizes that some things cannot be known with certainty, but is unsure of how to deal with this.
         1. The person realizes that judgments should be supported with reasons, but attention is paid only to evidence that supports a current belief.
         2. Because knowledge is uncertain, the person wrongly assumes that all opinions are equally valid.

        c.   A person capable of reflective judgment:
- 1. understands that some judgments are better supported and more valid than others.
- 2. is able to defend conclusions based on currently available evidence.

4. Reflective judgment is not usually exhibited until the middle or late twenties, if at all. Support for reflective thinking (such as education) can help build this skill.

V. Barriers to Logical and Creative Thought
    A. Cognitive Biases
        1. **Algorithms** are methods that are guaranteed to produce a solution. For many problems, algorithms do not exist or are unwieldy.
        2. To solve most problems, you need **heuristics**, which are rules of thumb that suggest, but do not guarantee, a solution. They are usually helpful, but they are also subject to cognitive biases.
            a. The **availability heuristic** is the tendency to judge the probability of a type of event by ease in thinking of examples.
            b. **Loss aversion** is overattention to the avoidance or minimization of losses.
            c. People reject risky but more rewarding solutions in favor of a sure gain. However, people will seek risk if they see it as a way to avoid loss.
            d. The **confirmation bias** is the tendency to attend only to evidence that confirms existing expectations.
            e. Biases due to expectations affect how we take in information (perceptual set - the tendency to perceive what one expects) and what we do with information once it has been perceived.
            f. The **hindsight bias** is the tendency to overestimate one's ability to have predicted an event, once the outcome is known.
            g. **Cognitive dissonance reduction** is the tendency to reject or alter beliefs or change behavior in order to reduce cognitive dissonance, the state of tension that occurs when a person holds two inconsistent beliefs or holds a belief that is incongruent with the person's behavior. People are motivated to reduce this tension:
                1. when they feel that they have made a choice freely.
                2. when they believe that the decision is important and irrevocable.
                3. when they feel responsible for the negative consequences of their choices.

4.   when they have expended a lot of effort in making a decision, only to find the results disappointing; people often engage in <u>justification of effort</u>, which involves a mental reevaluation of a belief or experience; it is one of the most popular methods for reducing dissonance.

5.   when what people do threatens their self-concept.

3.   **<u>Attribution theory</u>** states that we are constantly searching for causes to which we might attribute our own behavior or the behavior of others.

     a.   Biases in **attributions** can result in errors when judging the cause of behavior. Attributions fall into two categories:

         1.   <u>situational attributions</u>, which are made when we regard an action as caused by something in the environment.

         2.   <u>dispositional attributions</u>, which are made when we regard an action as caused by a trait or motive within the person.

     b.   Attributional biases include:

         1.   the **fundamental attribution error**, which is the overestimation of dispositional factors and the underestimation of situational factors in explaining another's behavior.

         2.   the **self-serving bias**, which occurs when we make dispositional attributions (take credit) for our good actions and situational attributions for our mistakes or bad actions.

4.   Research on human reasoning has shown that :

     a.   people often reach the right conclusion even if they are not aware of the process.

     b.   people are not irrational in all situations,

     c.   understanding biases can help us reduce or eliminate them.

VI.   Animal Minds

     A.   **Cognitive ethology** is the study of cognitive processes in nonhuman animals.

         1.   Some animals may be capable of remembering the past and anticipating future events, making plans and choices, and coordinating efforts with others of their species, although scientists disagree about the extent of the cognition involved in apparently intelligent behavior.

         2.   Many animals are capable of using objects in the natural environment as rudimentary tools.

         3.   In the laboratory, nonhuman primates have shown surprising abilities, including summing abilities.

4.   Nonhuman primates, and even some nonprimates, have shown an ability to acquire some aspects of language, including simple grammatical ordering rules.

B.   In evaluating findings on animal cognition, it is important to avoid both <u>anthropomorphism</u>, the tendency to falsely attribute human qualities to nonhuman beings, and anthropocentrism, the tendency to attribute animal qualities to human beings.

C.   We are the only species that tries to understand its own misunderstandings.

CHAPTER 9 SUMMARY

Thinking frees us from the confines of the present by allowing us to mentally manipulate internal representations of objects, events, and situations. These representations simplify and summarize information from the environment.

1._____ are the building blocks of thought. They are mental categories that are formed through direct contact with the environment, and also through contact with symbols, which are representations that stand for the objects, operations, relationships, or qualities. We can represent the relationship of concepts to one another by combining them in 2._____, units of meaning that express a unitary idea. These may be linked together in complicated cognitive networks called 3._____.

We can handle a good deal of information and perform many complex tasks because a portion of mental processing takes place outside of our awareness. 4._____ processes can be brought into consciousness when necessary, whereas 5._____ processes remain outside of awareness but nevertheless affect behavior, as during the experience of "intuition." Fully 6. _____ processing is only needed when automatic processing is inadequate, as when a person must make a deliberate choice or handle an unexpected situation. Much of our thinking is conscious, but may still involve 7._____, a type of lapse in conscious thought which keeps people from recognizing when a change in context requires a change in behavior.

Reasoning is a purposeful mental activity that involves operating on information in order to reach conclusions. In 8._____ reasoning, conclusions must be true if certain premises are true. This type of reasoning takes the form of a 9._____, a simple argument consisting of two premises and a conclusion. In 10._____ reasoning, premises support, but do not guarantee, the conclusion. Science depends heavily on this latter type of reasoning. A person's logic may be impeccable, but the person's conclusions may still be wrong if his or her 11._____ are not true. 12._____ reasoning is the ability to weigh and evaluate opposing points of view. Reasoning can sometimes be inhibited by a 13._____, a tendency to try to solve new problems by using the same procedures that worked before. They may be efficient but are not useful for new problems.

14. _____ involves going beyond present knowledge and habit in order to produce novel solutions. This involves 15. _____ thinking, the ability to generate new hypotheses and interpretations and to make connections that are not immediately obvious. Less creative people rely on 16. _____ thinking, which involves following orderly steps in hopes of reaching a single correct answer.

Jean Piaget was a pioneer in the study of cognitive development. He proposed that mental functioning depends on two processes, 17. _____, the arranging of experiences into a set of meanings, and 18. _____ to new observations and experiences. This latter process takes two forms, 19. _____, the fitting of new information into existing schemas, and 20. _____, the modification of schemas to deal with new information.

Piaget proposed four stages of cognitive development. During the 21. _____ stage, the infant learns only through concrete actions. The major development in this stage is 22. _____, which is the understanding that objects continue to exist even though they cannot be seen or felt. This is the beginning of 23. _____ thought, the capacity for using mental imagery and other symbolic systems.

Most children aged 2 to 7 are in the 24. _____ stage, in which the use of language and most symbols accelerates. Piaget mistakenly believed that children at this stage could not reason, and that they are 25. _____, or incapable of taking another person's perspective.

During the 26. _____ stage (ages 6 - 7 to 11), children come to acquire the concept of 27. _____, the notion that physical properties do not necessarily change when their form or appearance changes. They learn mental operations and can understand cause and effect. They are capable of a few abstract concepts, but their thought is still grounded in observable events.

Around age 12, children enter the 28. _____ stage, in which they become capable of abstract reasoning. They can now compare and classify ideas and imagine multiple possibilities. They also become capable of searching systematically for solutions to problems.

Piaget's critics have argued that changes from one stage to the next are not as clear-cut or sweeping as he proposed, and that children's reasoning depends to some extent on what they are reasoning about. Research findings have demonstrated that object permanence, perspective taking, and the use of symbols develop earlier in life than Piaget suggested.

29. _____ involves the ability to evaluate and integrate evidence, relate evidence to theory, and reach conclusions that can be defended as reasonable and plausible. King and Kitchner have demonstrated that people can reach the stage of formal operations without having acquired these skills. They described stages of development of these skills. In the earliest, 30. _____ stages, individuals believe that a single correct answer always exists and can be known, and they cannot distinguish between belief and evidence. In the 31. _____ stages, people recognize that some things cannot be known with certainty, and that judgments should be supported, but they pay attention only to evidence that supports their beliefs and assume that all beliefs are purely subject and therefore equal.

When a person becomes capable of reflective judgment, he or she is willing to consider evidence from different sources, see inquiry as an ongoing process, and make coherent and defensible judgments. Most people do not show evidence of reflective judgment until their middle or late twenties. However, the skills involved in reflective judgment can be improved when students have opportunities to practice them and are encouraged to do so.

Finding solutions to some problems requires only that the person apply an 32. _____, which is a method guaranteed to produce a solution. For most problems, however, a person must use a rule of thumb, or 33. _____, that suggests, but does not guarantee, a solution.

Usually these strategies are helpful, but occasionally they are influenced by cognitive biases that hinder problem solving. For example, people sometimes exaggerate the probability of rare events because of the 34. _____ heuristic, which is the tendency to judge the probability of events on the basis of how easy it is to think of examples. People are also biased toward making decisions that minimize or avoid 35. _____, which makes them less likely to take risks in order to gain something.

Another cognitive bias, called the 36. _____ bias, is the tendency to selectively attend to evidence that confirms one's belief, while ignoring evidence to the contrary. People can also make errors of judgment by having a certain readiness, or 37. _____, to perceive a situation in a particular way. There is also a tendency to use one's knowledge of past events as evidence that one could have predicted those events in advance. This kind of distortion is known as the 38. _____ bias.

People become uncomfortable when their behavior does not conform to their beliefs or when they hold two incompatible beliefs. This cognitive 39. _____ motivates a person to reduce discomfort by rejecting or changing beliefs, altering behavior, or making excuses. People tend to be especially motivated to reduce this tension when they think that their decisions are freely chosen, important, and irrevocable, when they feel they are responsible for negative consequences, and when they have put a lot of effort into something that has had a disappointing outcome. A person who has worked hard to achieve a goal may mentally reevalaute and overvalue that goal in order to reduce dissonance, a phenomenon called the 40. _____.

41. _____ theory is the study of the way people assign causes for events. There are two basic types of attributions, 42. _____, where the cause is judged to be within the person, and 43. _____, where the cause is judged to be in the environment. People from Western cultures tend to overestimate 44. _____ when judging the causes of another person's behavior. A related tendency is the 45. _____ bias, the inclination to take credit for positive outcomes of one's own behavior and make 46. _____ attributions for negative ones.

Although these biases distort a good deal of thinking, there is evidence that people often reach correct conclusions, even if they do not understand the process by which they do so. People are not equally irrational in all situations, and understanding a bias can help a person reduce or eliminate it.

The field of 47. _____ is the study of cognitive processes in nonhuman animals. Although it was once assumed that cognitive processes do not exist in animals, recent research has suggested that some animals can use symbols and tools, construct novel language utterances, make plans and choices, anticipate the future, and understand basic summation. However, in evaluating findings on animal cognition, it is important to avoid both 48. _____, the tendency to falsely attribute human qualities to nonhuman beings, and anthropocentrism. Humans are the only animals that seek to understand their own misunderstandings.

MULTIPLE CHOICE SELF-TEST

1.   All football fans are mortal. I am a football fan. Therefore, I am mortal. This is an example of a(n) _____ argument.

    a.   dialectical.
    b.   deductive.
    c.   symbolic.
    d.   inductive.

2.   Mitzi's car has a full tank of gas and still will not start. It is likely that her battery is dead. This is an example of a(n) _____ argument.

    a.   dialectical.
    b.   deductive.
    c.   symbolic.
    d.   inductive.

3.   The statements "All cows eat grass" and "Holsteins are types of cows" are:

    a.   concepts.
    b.   symbols.
    c.   schemas.
    d.   propositions.

4.   The word "flower" is an example of a(n):

    a.   proposition.
    b.   symbol.
    d.   concept.
    e.   schema.

5.   The complex network of knowledge and beliefs we have about gender are:

    a.   schemas.
    b.   symbols.
    c.   propositions.
    d.   concepts.

6. Practiced basketball players can make shots without thinking about them. However, if you asked them to tell you about their shooting techniques, they could readily describe them because their shooting is a(n) _____ process.

      a. conscious
      b. subconscious
      c. nonconscious
      d. deductive

7. Gary is driving in his car on the expressway. All of a sudden he realizes he has driven past his exit. This would be an example of:

      a. assimilation.
      b. divergent thinking.
      c. mindlessness.
      d. dialectical reasoning.

8. Melinda is taking a multiple choice test in which there are four possible choices. Completing the test requires _____ thinking:

      a. divergent
      b. creative
      c. convergent
      d. dialectical

9. Newton is pondering the many arguments for and against abortion in order to formulate a conclusion. He is engaging in _____ reasoning.

      a. dialectical
      b. convergent
      c. pre-reflective
      d. assimilative

10. Research on creativity finds that people who are creative are most likely to:

      a. tend to prefer working alone.
      b. have one very narrow interest in life.
      c. value success highly.
      d. care about the opinion of others.

11.   Dr. Wang, a research psychologist, is studying creativity. She administers a test which examines a person's history of creativity in their work and leisure activities: She is giving the:

        a.   Remote Associates Test.
        b.   Alternate Uses Test.
        c.   Lifetime Creativity Scales.
        d.   Creative Personality Inventory.

12.   Lisa, a young girl, just learned the word "doggie". Now Lisa refers to every animal she sees as a "doggie". This is an example of:

        a.   assimilation.
        b.   conservation.
        c.   egocentrism.
        d.   accommodation.

13.   You show a baby her favorite toy, allow her to look at the toy, and then hide it under a blanket. The baby does NOT look for the toy. This shows that she has NOT achieved:

        a.   conservation.
        b.   object permanence.
        c.   assimilation.
        d.   egocentrism.

14.   According to Piaget, the ability to understand abstract proverbs such as "a stitch in time save nine" and "the early bird gets the worm" depends on one being at least in the _____ stage.

        a.   sensory-motor
        b.   preoperational
        c.   concrete operations
        d.   formal operations

15.   Karen watches as her mother rolls a lump of clay into a long, skinny tube. According to Piaget, if Karen knows there is no more clay than there was before, she is <u>at least</u> in the _____ stage.

        a.   sensory-motor
        b.   preoperational
        c.   assimilation
        d.   concrete operations

16. Research by King and Kitchener on critical thinking in adults found that:

    a. after reaching age 18 the majority of people are capable of reflective judgement.

    b. good thinkers pay attention to evidence that fits their preexisting ideas.

    c. people who are advanced thinkers realize there is always one final correct answer.

    d. advanced higher education moves people closer to reflective judgement.

17. A college student states, "I just <u>know</u> homosexuality is wrong. My parents said so." This is an example of _____ thinking:

    a. reflective
    b. pre-reflective
    c. quasi-reflective
    d. formal operational

18. When people overestimate the number of deaths from earthquakes and underestimate deaths due to asthma, this is an example of the _____ heuristic.

    a. representativeness.
    b. availability.
    c. algorithm.
    d. confirmation.

19. People will be more likely to reduce cognitive dissonance when:

    a. they believe they have been forced into making a decision.
    b. when the decision is trivial.
    c. when they believe they are not responsible for consequences.
    d. when they have to justify effort expended to reach a goal.

20. When people who are told the actual outcome of an event tend to be overly certain that they "knew it all along" they are exhibiting _____ bias.

    a. divergent
    b. availability
    c. hindsight
    d. confirmation

21. Research on decision making shows we may change from risk-seeking to risk-aversive depending on:

    a.   logic and reason.
    b.   the context or framing of the loss.
    c.   the warning of a potential loss.
    d.   the expectations of others.

22. Reggie goes through an elaborate and boring hazing ritual in order to join a fraternity. If asked about his attitude toward the fraternity, cognitive dissonance theory would predict that Reggie would say:

    a.   "I want to drop out because their initiation is stupid."
    b.   "I really like the fraternity even more than I did before."
    c.   "I don't really have an attitude one way or the other."
    d.   "Maybe I'll join next year instead."

23. Politician Jones is against welfare because he believes that women have more children to purposely gain more benefits. He reads a professional study that states that only a very small percentage of women on welfare have more than one or two children. He dismisses the study as "liberal nonsense". In making his judgement he is relying on:

    a.   the confirmation bias.
    b.   dialectical reasoning.
    c.   the availability heuristic.
    d.   cognitive dissonance.

24. Russell's classmate Michelle failed her Psychology test. Due to the fundamental attribution error, Russell is most likely to think that his classmate failed the test because:

    a.   she was ill and couldn't study.
    b.   the class is very difficult.
    c.   she isn't very smart.
    d.   the grading was unfair.

25. Russell fails a Psychology test. Russell is most likely to think that he failed because:

    a.   he didn't take the time to study enough.
    b.   he isn't very smart.
    c.   the professor's grading is unfair.
    d.   he is very lazy.

26. Eric crashes his car into a tree. If he holds the self-serving bias, he will say that he had the accident because he:

    a. is a lousy driver.
    b. was not paying attention.
    c. was driving too recklessly and too fast.
    d. believes the road is poorly designed.

27. An attribution identifying the cause of an action as something in a person is termed:

    a. dispositional.
    b. situational.
    c. self-serving.
    d. confirmatory.

28. The field that studies thinking processes in nonhuman animals is:

    a. sociobiology.
    b. cognitive ethology.
    c. eugenics.
    d. behavioral genetics.

29. A weakness of animal communication research has been a lack of:

    a. objectivity.
    b. public acceptance of findings.
    c. motivation in animal subjects.
    d. suitable technology.

30. Chimpanzee language research teaches animals to communicate by:

    a. imitation of human speech.
    b. a written alphabet and words.
    c. American Sign Language.
    d. informal body language.

TRUE FALSE SELF-TEST

T   F   1.   Subconscious processes allow us to handle more information than if we depended entirely on conscious thought.

T   F   2.   A concept is a mental category that groups objects, qualities, and activities.

T   F   3.   We form concepts only through direct contact with objects and situations.

T   F   4.   Users of American Sign Language are more skilled at generating complex visual images than non-signers.

T   F   5.   The experience of intuition is a disorderly and entirely nonsystematic process.

T   F   6.   Mindless processing of information does have some benefits.

T   F   7.   Inductive conclusions are probabilistic.

T   F   8.   In deductive reasoning, if the premises are true then the conclusion is definitely true.

T   F   9.   Inductive reasoning involves only the drawing of general conclusions from specific observations.

T   F   10.   Science depends heavily on inductive reasoning.

T   F   11.   Logic will tell us whether or not premises are, if fact, true.

T   F   12.   Dialectical reasoning involves applying a formula to find the one correct solution.

T   F   13.   Mental sets are helpful for problems which require fresh insights and methods.

T   F   14.   Divergent thinking involves following a particular set of steps that lead to one definite solution.

T   F   15.   The Remote Associates Tests ask a person to think of as many uses as possible for common items.

T   F   16.   Creativity involves conformity to prevailing viewpoints.

T   F   17.   Accommodation involves fitting new information into existing mental schemas.

T   F   18.   The sensory-motor stage takes place during ages 2 to 7.

T   F   19.   Object permanence develops during the sensory-motor stage.

T   F   20.   Representational thought develops at age 5 or later.

T   F   21.   The concrete operations stage marks the beginning of abstract reasoning.

T   F   22.   Some people never develop reflective thinking capabilities.

T   F   23.   Reflective thinking is well-established at age 12 for most people.

T   F   24.   A person in a prereflective stage is typically good at distinguishing between knowledge and belief.

T   F   25.   Higher education promotes reflective judgement.

T   F   26.   Deaths from tornadoes are much more likely than are deaths from asthma.

T   F   27.   People tend to take risks to avoid losses.

T   F   28.   College students are more likely to criticize studies that confirm their beliefs and opinions.

T   F   29.   People who make a public commitment to a failed prediction are more likely to abandon their beliefs.

T   F   30.   You are more likely to experience cognitive dissonance for a poor decision made about something important.

KEY TERMS

concept - A mental category that groups objects, relations, activities, abstractions, or qualities having common properties.

proposition - A unit of meaning that is made up of concepts and expresses a unitary idea.

cognitive schema - An integrated network of knowledge, beliefs, and expectations concerning a particular topic or aspect of the world.

subconscious processes - Mental processes occurring outside of conscious awareness but accessible to consciousness when necessary.

nonconscious processes - Mental processes occurring outside of and not available to conscious awareness.

deductive reasoning - A form of reasoning in which a conclusion follows necessarily from certain premises; if the premises are true, the conclusion must be true.

inductive reasoning - A form of reasoning in which the premises provide support for a certain conclusion, but it is still possible for the conclusion to be false.

dialectical reasoning - A process in which opposing facts or ideas are weighed and compared, with a view to determining the best solution or to resolving differences.

mental set - A tendency to solve problems using procedures that worked before on similar problems.

divergent thinking - Mental exploration of unconventional alternatives on similar problems.
convergent thinking - Thinking aimed at finding a single correct answer to a problem.

assimilation - In Piaget's theory, the process of absorbing new information into existing cognitive structures, modifying them if necessary to fit.

accommodation - In Piaget's theory, the process of modifying existing cognitive structures in response to experience and new information.

object permanence - The understanding, which develops in the first year of life, that an object continues to exist even when you can't see it or touch it.

operations - In Piaget's theory, mental actions that are cognitively reversible.

egocentric thinking - Seeing the world from only one's own point of view; the inability to take another person's perspective.

conservation - The understanding that the physical properties of objects - such as the number of items in a cluster or the amount of liquid in a glass - can remain the same even when their form or appearance changes.

theory of mind - A theory about how one's own mind and other people's minds work and how people are affected by their beliefs and feelings.

algorithm - A problem-solving strategy guaranteed to produce a solution, even if the user does not know how it works.

heuristic - A rule of thumb that suggests a course of action or guides problem-solving but does not guarantee an optimal solution.

availability heuristic - The tendency to judge the probability of a type of event by how easy it is to think of examples or instances.

confirmation bias - The tendency to look for or pay attention to only information that confirms one's beliefs.

hindsight bias - The tendency to overestimate one's ability to have predicted an event, once the outcome is known; the"I knew it along" phenomenon.

cognitive dissonance - A state of tension that occurs when a person simultaneously holds two cognitions that are psychologically inconsistent, or when a person's belief is incongruent with his or her behavior.

attribution theory - The theory that people are motivated to explain their own and other people's behaviors by attributing causes of those behaviors to a situation or a disposition.

fundamental attribution error - The tendency, in explaining other people's behavior, to overestimate personality factors and underestimate the influence of the situation.

self-serving bias - The tendency, in explaining one's own behavior, to take credit for one's good actions and rationalize one's mistakes.

cognitive ethology - The study of cognitive processes in nonhuman animals.

Suggested Research Projects

1.   If you know of a relative or friend who has a child that is less than 6 months old, test the child for object permanence. Show an interesting toy to the child and then hide it. See whether or not the child looks for it. Try the same task with a child of 8 or 9 months. Is there any difference in response between the younger and the older child?

2.   Under the supervision of your professor, ask people of different age ranges and educational levels to respond to some of the questions Kitchner and King asked in their original research. Analyze the responses of the subjects in terms of Kitchner and King's research on reflective judgment.

Suggested Readings

Adams, J.L. (1991). Conceptual Blockbusting: A Guide to Better Ideas. Reading, MA: Addison-Wesley. A guide to creative thinking with exercises and problems to practice. This book examines blocks to problem-solving and creativity.

Freeman, A., & DeWolf, R. (1992). The Ten Dumbest Mistakes Smart People Make and How to Avoid Them. NY: HarperCollins. A cognitive approach for aboiding self-defeating and irrational thoughts in everyday life.

Gardner, H. (1995). The Mind's New Science: A History of the Cognitive Revolution. NY: BasicBooks. The originator of the theory of multiple intelligences, traces the history of the cognitive revolution of psychology.

Gardner, H. (1995). Creating Minds. NY: BasicBooks. Applies the theory of multiple intelligences to understanding creativity in famous people including Freud, Einstein, Picasso, and Ghandi.

Suggested Audio-Visuals

Insight Media (1992). Piaget's Developmental Theory: An Overview. This 30 minute video reviews Piaget's developmental theory and features psychologist David Elkind.

CHAPTER 9

ANSWERS TO CHAPTER SUMMARY

1. concepts
2. symbols
3. propositions
4. cognitive schemas
5. subconscious
6. conscious
7. mindlessness
8. deductive
9. syllogism
10. inductive
11. premises
12. dialectical
13. mental set
14. creativity
15. divergent
16. convergent
17. organization
18. adaptation
19. assimilation
20. accommodation
21. sensory-motor
22. object permanence
23. representational
24. preoperational
25. egocentric
26. concrete operations
27. conservation
28. formal operations
29. reflective judgement
30. prereflective
31. quasi-reflective
32. algorithm
33. heuristic
34. availability
35. loss
36. confirmation
37. perceptual (mental) set
38. hindsight
39. dissonance
40. justification of effort

41. attribution
42. dispositional
43. situational
44. dispositions
45. self-serving
46. situational
47. cognitive ethology
48. anthropomorphism

ANSWERS TO MULTIPLE CHOICE SELF-TEST

1. B
2. D
3. D
4. D
5. A
6. B
7. C
8. C
9. A
10. A
11. C
12. A
13. B
14. D
15. D
16. D
17. B
18. B
19. D
20. C
21. B
22. B
23. A
24. C
25. C
26. D
27. A
28. B
29. A
30. C

ANSWERS TO TRUE FALSE SELF-TEST

1.   T
2.   T
3.   F
4.   T
5.   F
6.   T
7.   T
8.   T
9.   F
10.   T
11.   F
12.   F
13.   F
14.   F
15.   F
16.   F
17.   F
18.   F
19.   T
20.   F
21.   F
22.   T
23.   F
24.   F
25.   T
26.   F
27.   T
28.   F
29.   F
30.   T

CHAPTER 10

MEMORY

LEARNING OBJECTIVES

After reading and studying this chapter, you should be able to:

1. Explain the concept of memory as a reconstructive process.

2. Discuss the relationship between reconstructed memories and hypnosis, flashbulb memories, and eyewitness testimony.

3. Describe the difference between explicit and implicit memories and the various ways in which psychologists measure them.

4. Compare and contrast the various models of memory.

5. Define the three types of memory in the "three-box" model.

6. Explain the organization of long-term memory and the kinds of information stored there.

7. Explain the serial position effect.

8. Describe some methods of improving memory.

9. Compare and contrast four theories of forgetting.

10. Discuss the hypotheses about childhood amnesia.

11. Discuss the relationship between memory and narrative.

CHAPTER 10 OUTLINE

I.   Reconstructing the Past
        A.   The Manufacture of Memory
                1.   Memory is a <u>reconstructive</u> process; information is added, deleted, and changed in order to make sense of material, based on previous knowledge and beliefs (sometimes called <u>confabulation</u>).
                        a.   **Anterograde amnesia** is the inability to form lasting memories for new events and facts. To cope with this devastating condition, patients will try to reconstruct events.
                        b.   People may not be able to separate what they originally experienced from what they have added after the fact, called <u>source amnesia</u>.
                        c.   Certain conditions are associated with confusions between imagined events and actual ones. An imagined event or experience is most likely to be misremembered when:
                                1.   the person has thought about the imagined event many times.
                                2.   the image of the event contains a lot of details.
                                3.   it is easy to imagine the event.
                                4.   the person focuses on his or her emotional reactions to the event rather than on what actually happened.
                        d.   Studies of hypnosis do not support the idea that memories are stored permanently and accurately; many hypnotically induced memories are reconstructed and false.
                        e.   Contrary to widespread belief, studies of electrical brain stimulation also do not support the permanent storage of memories.
                        f.   Even "flashbulb" memories are not always complete or accurate, and involve reconstruction.
        B.   When Seeing Isn't Believing
                1.   Because of the reconstructive nature of memory, eyewitness testimony isn't always accurate.
                2.   Reconstructions of events are highly influenced by the way questions about those events are put to us.

II.   Measuring Memory
        A.   **Explicit memory** is the conscious recollection of information. It is measured by tests of:
                1.   recall - retrieval of information.
                2.   recognition - identification of information.
        B.   **Implicit memory** is the material that is recognized unconsciously but nonetheless affects thoughts and actions. It is measured by:

1. **priming** - exposing a person to information and testing to see if the information is activated on a later task.
2. the **relearning method** (<u>savings method</u>) - comparison of the amount of time it takes to learn something originally and the amount of time it takes to relearn the same material after it is no longer recalled or recognized.

III. Models of Memory
   A. The <u>information processing</u> model of memory likens the mind to a highly complex computer.
      1. **Encoding** is the conversion of information into a form that can be stored and retrieved by the brain. The forms in which information can be retained in the long run include:
         a. units of meaning such as propositions.
         b. auditory or visual images.
         c. kinesthetic instructions.
      2. Some encoding takes place automatically, but <u>effortful</u> encoding is required for other types of information, such as learning material from a difficult textbook.
      3. <u>Storage</u> is the maintenance of material in memory.
      4. <u>Retrieval</u> is the recovery of stored material.
   B. The **parallel distributed processing model** (PDP, or the connectionist model) holds that knowledge is represented by connections among interacting neural units, all operating in parallel.
      1. This model reverses the notion that the human brain is like a computer. PDP theorists say that a truly intelligent computer will have to be modeled after the brain.
      2. This model is playing an important role in the field of <u>artificial intelligence</u>.
   C. The three-box model, in contrast, points to three separate memory systems.

IV. The Three-Box Model
   A. **Sensory memory** briefly and accurately retains incoming sensory information.
      1. Visual images (icons) remain for up to half a second in the visual register.
      2. Auditory images (echos) remain for up to two seconds in the auditory register.
      3. <u>Pattern recognition</u>, the preliminary identification of a stimulus on the basis of information already contained in long-term memory, occurs during the transfer of information from sensory memory to short-term memory.
   B. **Short-term memory** (STM) holds information for up to 30 seconds, according to most estimates.

1. Information not transferred from STM to long-term memory is lost.
2. Because it holds information retrieved from long-term memory for use, STM is also known as <u>working memory</u>.
3. Estimates of the capacity of STM range from 2 to 20 items, with most at the lower end.
4. Grouping units into larger units called **chunks** increases the capacity of STM.

C. **Long-term memory** (LTM) lasts from a few minutes to an indefinite period of time.
1. There appears to be no practical limit to the capacity of LTM.
2. Many models of LTM assume that semantic or conceptual information is organized into complex networks based on meaning, but other types of organization, for example, based on sound or appearance of words, also takes place. For instance, <u>tip-of-the-tongue states</u> involve such groupings.
3. Most theories of LTM distinguish between "knowing how" (skills and habits) and "knowing that" (abstract representational knowledge).
   a. **Procedural memories** are memories for the performance of actions and skills.
   b. **Declarative memories** are memories of facts, rules, concepts, and events; they include **semantic memories** (general knowledge) and **episodic memories** (personally experienced events).

D. The three-box model has been invoked to account for the **serial position effect** - the tendency to recall items at the beginning (<u>primacy effect</u>) or at the end (<u>recency effect</u>) of a list better than the items in the middle of a list.
1. Primacy may be due to the "emptiness" of STM, which makes transfer to LTM easier for early items.
2. Recency may be due to items remaining in STM at recall.
3. However, the recency effect is often still seen when testing occurs later.

V. How to Remember
A. <u>Rehearsal</u> is the review or practice of material.
1. **Maintenance rehearsal** is rote repetition. It usually only maintains information in STM.
2. **Elaborative rehearsal** associates new information with already present LTM information, and is better for long-term retention.

B. **Deep processing** is going beyond the processing of the physical or sensory qualities of stimuli to process the meaning of the stimuli.

C. **Mnemonics** are formal strategies for encoding, storing, and retaining information; they encourage active, thorough processing of information.

1.   Mnemonics include easily memorized rhymes, formulas, visual images, word associations, chunking strategies, or stories that help to make the material more meaningful.
2.   Complicated mnemonics used by stage performers are not usually helpful in everyday life.

D.   **Metamemory** is the ability to monitor and be aware of one's retention.

E.   Overlearning is continuing to study material after it has been learned.

VI.   Why We Forget

    A.   Theories of Forgetting

        1.   The **decay theory** holds that memory traces fade with time if they are not used. This theory does not, by itself, account for lapses in LTM.

        2.   New information can completely wipe out old information.

        3.   Interference theory holds that similar items of information interfere with one another in storage and retrieval.

            a.   **Retroactive interference** occurs when new information decreases the ability to recall old information.

            b.   **Proactive interference** occurs when old information decreases the ability to recall new information.

        4.   **Motivated forgetting** theory holds that forgetting is an unconscious self-protective device.

            a.   Some cases of **retrograde amnesia** may be due to the motivated forgetting of painful incidents.

            b.   The concept of motivated forgetting is based mostly on clinical reports of people in psychotherapy.

        5.   **Cue-dependent forgetting** is the inability to recall information because of insufficient cues.

            a.   **State-dependent memory** is the tendency to recall material when one is in the same mood or physical state in which the original learning took place; the state acts as a retrieval cue.

            b.   Contextual cues are especially helpful in recall, but they may also account for <u>deja vu</u>, a false sense of having been in the same situation before.

VII.   Childhood Amnesia

    A.   **Childhood amnesia** (<u>infantile amnesia</u>) is the inability to recall events from the first two or three years of one's life. Several theories have been advanced to explain it:

        1.   brain areas involved in the storage of events, especially the hippocampus, may not be well developed enough to store long-term episodic memories.

        2.   cognitive self-recognition may be necessary for the establishment of autobiographical memory.

        3.   later schemas may not be useful for reconstruction of early events.

4.   children may not focus on the distinctive aspects of an event that would make it memorable in the long run.

VIII.   Memory and Narrative: The Stories of Our Lives
   A.   Narratives (stories) provide unifying themes to organize and give meaning to life events.
   B.   Many of our memories are actually based on our present traits and beliefs and also on our implicit theories about how much certain traits or beliefs can change; theories are "implicit" because we may never have expressed them to anyone, including ourselves.
   C.   Narratives rely on memory, but also on interpretation and imagination.

CHAPTER 10 SUMMARY

While it is common to think of memory as functioning like a tape recorder, research has demonstrated that memory is a 1._____ process. People alter incoming information in order to make sense of it, and often they cannot separate the original experience from the added information. People who have lost their ability to retain new information (a condition called 2._____ amnesia) exhibit behavior that dramatically illustrates the reconstruction of events.

Most people report that they have very vivid memories of some events, but even these so-called 3._____ memories are subject to distortion. Not only do we alter memories in the process of recalling them, but we also do so in the process of storing them. What we notice and integrate into our memories depends in strong measure on our existing knowledge, which is organized in the form of cognitive 4._____. Our reconstructions of past events are even influenced by the manner in which we are questioned about them.

Psychologists measure memory in a variety of ways. If they want to test for conscious memory of an event or item of information, which is called 5.____ memory, they can either ask the person to recall the information, or have the person identify the information in a 6.____ task. Recall is usually more difficult.

Some material is stored without a person's conscious awareness, as an 7._____ memory. Assessing this kind of memory sometimes involves how fast the person learns the material a second or third time, after apparently having forgotten it. This technique is known as the 8._____ or savings method. Researchers can also measure this same type of memory by using a technique called 9.____, in which a person has an opportunity to make responses in the form of implicitly remembered material.

Some cognitive psychologists liken the memory system to the functioning of a computer. These 10._____ models depict memory in terms of inputs and outputs, and organizing of information. In these models, the first process of memory is 11._____, in which incoming information is converted into a form the brain can store and retrieve, such as visual icons, auditory echos, and kinesthetic instructions. Some kinds of information are encoded automatically, but other kinds require more effortful processing. Next comes the process of 12._____, which allows the material to be maintained over time. Finally, memories are recovered through the process of 13.____.

When information is first encountered, it is stored for a few seconds in 14.____ memory. Then, some material may go on to 15.____ memory where it is retained for up to about 30 seconds by most estimates. This type of memory is also called 16.____ memory, because it holds information that has already been stored and is being retrieved for temporary use. Information that makes its way into 17.____ memory may be maintained indefinitely, and there appears to be no practical limit to the amount of material that can be stored there.

The computer model of memory is useful, but its critics have noted that the brain has pattern recognition and other functions that are far more sophisticated than those of any computer. Some cognitive scientists use a 18._____ processing, or connectionist, model, which depicts the memory system as a vast neural network of interconnected processing units. This model comes closer to the brain's actual makeup and is applicable to several functions besides memory, but it is not currently as useful as information-processing models in explaining a single memory of a single event.

According to the information-processing, or "three-box" model, information from sensory memory is first transferred to short-term memory (STM). This material can be maintained through rehearsal, and either transfers to long-term memory (LTM) or decays and is lost. The capacity of STM has usually been reported as 7 items plus or minus 2. However, estimates range from 2 to 20 items. The capacity of STM can be enlarged by grouping items into bigger units called 19.____.

Items in STM that are meaningful in some way usually enter LTM relatively easily. LTM is organized and indexed. Most theorists describe several different kinds of information in LTM. 20.____ memories are memories for the performance of actions or skills. Knowledge about specific pieces of information, such as facts and events, is stored in 21.____ memory, which can be further subdivided into 22.____ memory (general knowledge), and 23.____ memory (internal representations of personally experienced events).

When given a list of things to remember, people tend to remember best the items that are presented at the beginning and the end of the list, a phenomenon called the 24.____ effect. Theoretically, the 25.____ effect (the tendency to recall early items) is due to the emptiness of STM at the beginning of the tasks. The 26.____ effect (the tendency to recall later items) may be due to the presence of these items in STM at the time of recall. However, this effect persists even if the recall task is not undertaken immediately.

Long-term retention of material usually requires 27._____, the review and practice of information. There are two strategies used in this process. 28._____ involves rote repetition of the material. 29._____, a more effective strategy, involves relating the new material to information that is already stored in LTM. 30._____ is a related technique in which one processes the meaning of the material rather than just its form.

31._____ are formal devices for encoding, storing, and retaining information. They often include chunking or strategies that make the material more meaningful. It is also helpful, when trying to improve memory, to have good awareness of one's own retention and to be able to monitor one's memory, a capacity called 32._____. Sometimes it is helpful to make use of 33._____, that is, to continue studying the material that has already been learned.

There are several different theories of forgetting. The 34._____ theory is that material that is not used simply fades away. This theory alone does not account for information and skills that seem to persist for decades even if they are not used. 35._____ theory holds that some items impede the retention of others. When new information gets in the way of one's ability to recall old information, the interference is called 36._____. 37._____ interference occurs when old information inhibits the ability to remember new material. At other times, our forgetting may be motivated by an unconscious desire to avoid painful memories. This motivated forgetting may be taking place in some instances of 38._____ amnesia. The most common type of forgetting may be 39._____ forgetting, in which contextual cues from the original learning situation are no longer present to aid us in retrieving the specific information we are looking for. When such a contextual cue is one's mood or physical state, the memory is said to be 40._____.

Theories of memory and forgetting have been applied to 41._____, the inability to recall information from the first two or three years of life. Some researchers believe that this phenomenon is due to undeveloped synaptic connections in the brain. Some cognitive scientists, however, tend to emphasize the necessity of cognitive sense of self for the formation of autobiographical types of memory. Others believe that information strategies in early childhood are so markedly different from later ones that few recall cues exist for later retrieval.

MULTIPLE CHOICE SELF-TEST

1. A review of Wilder Penfield's electrical brain stimulation studies by Elizabeth Loftus found that:

    a. brain stimulation successfully results in exact, sharp memories from the past.
    b. a few patients recreated elaborate "memories."
    c. children can remember exact situations but adults cannot.
    d. most patients remembered clearly only emotional or shocking events.

2. Eyewitness testimony is often <u>NOT</u> accurate because:

    a. people frequently lie.
    b. long-term memory involves reconstruction.
    c. of failure in short-term storage.
    d. of an inability to form visual images.

3. Juanita thinks she can remember exactly the day when Martin Luther King was shot. She remembers where she was standing and who she was talking to. This is an example of what type of memory?

    a. state-dependent.
    b. procedural.
    c. flashbulb.
    d. semantic.

4. H.M., the man who was unable to form long-term memories for new events and facts suffered from:

    a. retrograde amnesia.
    b. anterograde amnesia.
    c. complex amnesia.
    d. source amnesia.

5. People are more likely to confuse imagined events and real ones when:

    a. the person has often thought about the imagined event.
    b. the image of the event contains few details.
    c. it is difficult to imagine the event.
    d. people ignore emotional reactions to the event.

6.   Suppose you experience a fight in a bar and then later in the evening you see a television news account of the fight. When asked about your memory of the fight you are unable to separate what you personally experienced from the information in the news account. Psychologists call this phenomenon:

    a.   flashbulb memory.
    b.   episodic memory amnesia.
    c.   source amnesia.
    d.   induction.

7.   Studies of hypnotic regression indicate that people who have regressed to childhood:

    a.   have brain-wave patterns that are childlike.
    b.   reason exactly like children do.
    c.   are willing to play a role.
    d.   are actually reliving their childhood.

8.   Explicit memory can be measured using both:

    a.   recall and recognition.
    b.   recall and free association.
    c.   recognition and hypnosis.
    d.   hypnosis and the polygraph.

9.   A researcher plays a taped list of word pairs to a group of subjects. Most of these words concern the topic of sports. The subjects do NOT have time to rehearse the words. The subjects are then given the task of completing a series of word stems and the researchers find that more of the words are sports-related than would be expected by chance. This illustrates the _____ effect.

    a.   priming
    b.   encoding
    c.   explicit recall
    d.   confabulation

10.   The game of Trivial Pursuit requires what type of memory ability?

    a.   recall
    b.   recognition
    c.   reconstruction
    d.   relearning

11. Michael is answering an essay examination which asks him to list the three major components of memory. The essay examination is a _____ task.

      a.   recognition
      b.   recall
      c.   reconstruction
      d.   serial position

12. Belinda looks at a list of suspects and is asked to pick out the one that stole her purse. This is a(n) _____ task.

      a.   recognition.
      b.   recall.
      c.   serial position.
      d.   implicit memory.

13. Asking you to pick out the names of the Seven Dwarfs who befriended Snow White from a list given to you would involve _____ memory.

      a.   implicit
      b.   eidetic
      c.   recognition
      d.   recall

14. Belinda listens to a song over and over again on the radio, but she does NOT consciously try to remember the words. However, when given a memory test, she finds she can remember most of the words to the song. This is an example of _____ memory.

      a.   implicit
      b.   explicit
      c.   reconstructive
      d.   episodic

15. That aspect of memory that accounts for relatively permanent storage is _____ memory.

      a.   sensory
      b.   short-term
      c.   long-term
      d.   converted

16. The maximum amount of time information can be retained in sensory memory appears to be:

    a.   two seconds.
    b.   twenty seconds.
    c.   thirty seconds.
    d.   1 minute.

17. The conversion of information into a form the brain can process and store is called:

    a.   encoding.
    b.   cueing.
    c.   priming.
    d.   confabulation.

18. According to the three box model of memory, information passes in order from:

    a.   short-term memory, to sensory memory, to long-term memory.
    b.   sensory memory, to episodic memory, to long-term memory.
    c.   iconic memory, to episodic memory, to long-term memory.
    d.   sensory memory, to short-term memory, to long-term memory.

19. Knowing that "Rudy" is a furry dog and that a dog is a mammal is an example of what type of memory?

    a.   episodic
    b.   procedural
    c.   semantic
    d.   declarative

20. Knowing how to use a fork, write with a pencil, or cut with a pair of scissors is referred to as _____ memory.

    a.   declarative
    b.   procedural
    c.   semantic
    d.   episodic

21. Alfred read his psychology textbook only once before the test. He did poorly on the test. To study adequately requires:

    a. automatic encoding.
    b. effortful encoding.
    c. sensory storage.
    d. effortless retrieval.

22. Childhood amnesia involves losses in _____ memory.

    a. iconic
    b. semantic
    c. procedural
    d. episodic

23. For easy memorization, how would you best group the following letters: V,M,F,T,B,I?

    a. I B T F V M
    b. V M F T B I
    c. VTF MBI
    d. MTV FBI

24. A student must memorize the Gettysburg Address. He finds that he can remember the opening phrases and the closing phrases. This phenomenon is called the _____ effect.

    a. elaboration
    b. serial position
    c. encoding
    d. chunking

25. Karen has just learned some basic Japanese phrases for her trip to Tokyo. However, her knowledge of French interferes with her ability to learn Japanese. This is an example of what type of interference?

    a. retroactive
    b. proactive
    c. cue-dependent
    d. reminiscence

26. Professor Grimble has successfully learned the names of the students in his 9 o'clock class. Unfortunately, now he can't remember the names of the students he learned earlier in his 8 o'clock class. This is an example of what type of interference?

    a. motivated
    b. proactive
    c. cue-dependent
    d. retroactive

27. Anita always drinks three cups of coffee before her 8:00 a.m. class. On the day of the test, she oversleeps a little, has no time for coffee, and barely makes it to class. She does poorly on the test, but curiously remembers a good deal of the information when she is having coffee after the test is over. Anita's performance can be explained by:

    a. retroactive interference.
    b. proactive interference.
    c. motivated forgetting.
    d. state-dependent memory.

28. If you were to take an introductory psychology class again, you would find that you would remember the information much better the second time around because of the phenomena of:

    a. memory networking.
    b. chunking.
    c. explicit memory.
    d. relearning.

29. Melvin "forgets" an embarrassing incident at a fraternity party in which he danced around in only his underwear. This type of memory loss would most likely be caused by what type of process?

    a. interference.
    b. decay.
    c. motivated forgetting.
    d. cue-dependent forgetting.

30. Ollie knows when he has studied enough for a test because he has developed good:

    a. rehearsal strategies.
    b. mnemonic devices.
    c. overlearning techniques.
    d. metamemory capabilities.

TRUE FALSE SELF-TEST

T   F   1.   Memories are permanently stored in the brain with perfect accuracy.

T   F   2.   Anterograde amnesia is the inability to form lasting memories for new events and facts.

T   F   3.   An imagined event is more likely to be misremembered when the person has thought about the event infrequently.

T   F   4.   If forming an image of an event takes a lot of effort, then we tend to think the event was real.

T   F   5.   Emotional reactions to an imagined event can resemble those that would have occurred to a real event.

T   F   6.   When people are hypnotically regressed to an earlier age, their mental and moral performance becomes childlike in nature.

T   F   7.   Hypnosis reliably improves memories for specific early experiences.

T   F   8.   The majority of patients whose brains were electrically stimulated by neurosurgeon Wilder Penfield recalled clear, vivid memories of actual events.

T   F   9.   Flashbulb memories are always complete and accurate records of the past.

T   F   10.   Giving a polygraph test to an eyewitness to a crime who is mentally reconstructing the event from memory is a good way of ensuring the accuracy of recall.

T   F   11.   Reconstructive memories of past events can be heavily influenced by the way questions about those events are asked.

T   F   12.   Conscious recollection of an event is called implicit memory.

T   F   13.   Recall involves the ability to identify information you have previously observed, read, or heard about.

T   F   14.   Recognition involves the ability to retrieve and reproduce information encountered earlier.

T   F   15.   Information that is retained and affects our thoughts and actions even when there is no conscious or intentional remembering is called implicit memory.

T   F   16.   Priming is a method used to investigate implicit memory.

T   F   17.   Information you previously studied typically takes the same amount of time to relearn as it did originally.

T   F   18.   Learning new and difficult information requires effortful encoding.

T   F   19.   Sensory memory retains information up to thirty seconds or more.

T   F   20.   Auditory images are retained for a slightly longer time than are visual images in sensory memory.

T   F   21.   Short-term memory can hold information that has been retrieved from long-term memory for temporary use.

T   F   22.   Short-term memory is also called working memory.

T   F   23.   Chunking increases the capacity of short-term memory.

T   F   24.   Declarative memories are memories of "knowing how" rather than "knowing that".

T   F   25.   Semantic memories are internal representations of personally experienced events.

T   F   26.   Items in the middle of a list are better remembered than items at the beginning or end.

T   F   27.   Elaborative rehearsal involves the rote repetition of material.

T   F   28.   Retroactive interference occurs when old information interferes with the ability to remember new information.

T   F   29.   Motivated forgetting can explain some cases of retrograde amnesia.

T   F   30.   Most people can easily remember events from infancy.

KEY TERMS

anterograde amnesia - The inability to form lasting memories for new events and facts.

flashbulb memory - A vivid, detailed recollection of a significant or startling event, or the circumstances in which a person learned of such an event.

explicit memory - Conscious, intentional recollection of an event or of an item of information.

recall - The ability to retrieve and reproduce from memory previously encountered material.

recognition - The ability to identify previously encountered material.

implicit memory - Unconscious retention in memory, as evidenced by the effect of a previous experience or previously encountered information on current thoughts or actions.

priming - A method for measuring implicit memory in which a person reads or listens to information and is later tested to see whether the information is "activated" on another type of task.

relearning method - A method for measuring retention that compares the time required to relearn material with the time used in the initial learning of the material.

encoding - The conversion of information into a form that can be stored in and retrieved from memory.

cognitive schema - An integrated network of knowledge, beliefs, and expectations about a particular topic or aspect of the world.

parallel distributed processing (PDP) - An alternative to the information processing model of memory, in which knowledge is represented not as propositions or images but as connections among thousands of interacting units, distributed in a vast network all operating in parallel.

sensory memory - A memory system that momentarily preserves extremely accurate images of sensory information.

short-term memory (STM) - In the three box model of memory, a limited capacity memory system involved in the retention of information for brief periods of time; it is also used to hold information retrieved from long-term memory for temporary use.

chunk - A meaningful unit of information; it may be composed of smaller units.

long-term memory (LTM) - In the three box model of memory, the memory system involved in the long-term storage of information.

procedural memories - Memories for the performance of actions or skills ("knowing how").

declarative memories - Memories for facts, rules, concepts, and events ("knowing that"); they include semantic and episodic memories.

semantic memories - Memories of general knowledge, including facts, rules, concepts, and propositions.

episodic memories - Memories for personally experienced events and the contexts in which they occurred.

serial position effect - The tendency for recall of the first and the last items on a list to surpass recall of items in the middle of the list.

maintenance rehearsal - Rote repetition of material in order to maintain its availability in memory.

elaborative rehearsal - Association of new information with already stored knowledge and analysis of the new information to make it memorable.

deep processing - In the encoding of information, the processing of meaning rather than simply the physical or sensory features of a stimulus.

mnemonics - Strategies and tricks for improving memory, such as the use of verse or a formula.

metamemory - The ability to monitor and be aware of one's own retention of information.

decay theory - The theory that information in memory eventually disappears if it is not accessed; it applies more to short-term than to long-term memory.

retroactive interference - Forgetting that occurs when recently learned material interferes with the ability to remember similar material stored previously in memory.

proactive interference - Forgetting that occurs when previously stored material interferes with the ability to remember similar, more recently learned material.

motivated forgetting - Forgetting that occurs because of a desire to eliminate awareness of painful, embarrassing, or otherwise unpleasant experiences.

retrograde amnesia - Loss of the ability to remember events or experiences that occurred before some particular point in time.

cue dependent forgetting - The inability to retrieve information stored in memory because of insufficient cues for recall.

state-dependent memory - The tendency to remember something when one is in the same physical or mental state as during the original learning experience.

childhood (infantile) amnesia - The inability to remember events and experiences that occurred during the first two or three years of life.

Suggested Research Projects

1.   Ask some family members or friends to write detailed accounts of some event that was mutually experienced without first discussing the event with each other. Afterwards, look for discrepancies in the accounts.

2.   Keep a "forgetting and remembering" journal for several weeks. Write down instances in which you have forgotten something and try to discover any memory principles that might be involved, such as the serial position effect or retroactive interference. You should also write down unusual instances of remembering, such as suddenly remembering a school classmate whom you had long forgotten. Try to explain the sudden remembering with memory principles, such as contextual cueing.

(Source: Terry, W.S. (1984). A "forgetting journal" for memory courses. Teaching of Psychology, 11, 111-112.)

Suggested Readings

Ceci, S.J., & Bruck, M. (1995). Jeopardy in the Courtroom: A Scientific Analysis of Children's Testimony. American Psychological Association. Reviews the issue of children's testimony from a scientific perspective.

Loftus, E.F. (1980). Memory: Surprising New Insights Into How We Remember and Why We Forget. Reading, MA: Addison-Wesley. A classic overview of human memory.

Loftus, E.F., & Ketcham, K. (1994). Witness for the Defense: The Accused, the Eyewitness, and the Expert Who Puts Memory on Trial. NY: St. Martin's Press. This memory researcher examines eight cases that centered on eyewitness identification disputes.

Loftus, E.F. (1996). Eyewitness Testimony. Cambridge, MA: Harvard University Press. Elizabeth Loftus makes the psychological case against the reliability of the eyewitness.

Suggested Audio-Visuals

Insight Media (1990). <u>Memory</u>. Biological and cognitive research is reviewed by memory researchers as well as application of memory research to witness recall in criminal trails.

CHAPTER 10

ANSWERS TO CHAPTER SUMMARY

1.   reconstructive
2.   anterograde
3.   flashbulb
4.   schemas
5.   explicit
6.   recognition
7.   implicit
8.   relearning
9.   priming
10.   information-processing
11.   encoding
12.   storage
13.   retrieval
14.   sensory
15.   short-term
16.   working
17.   long-term
18.   parallel distributed
19.   chunks
20.   procedural
21.   declarative
22.   semantic
23.   episodic
24.   serial position
25.   primacy
26.   recency
27.   rehearsal
28.   maintenance rehearsal
29.   elaborative rehearsal
30.   deep processing
31.   mnemonics
32.   metamemory
33.   overlearning
34.   decay
35.   interference
36.   retroactive
37.   proactive
38.   retrograde
39.   cue dependent

40. state dependent
41. childhood amnesia

ANSWERS TO MULTIPLE CHOICE SELF-TEST

1. B
2. B
3   C
4. B
5. A
6. C
7. C
8. A
9. A
10. A
11. B
12. A
13. C
14. A
15. C
16. A
17. A
18. D
19. C
20. B
21. B
22. D
23. D
24. B
25. B
26. D
27. D
28. D
29. C
30. D

ANSWERS TO TRUE FALSE SELF-TEST

1. F
2. T
3   F
4. F
5. T
6. F

7.   F
8.   F
9.   F
10.   F
11.   T
12.   F
13.   F
14.   F
15.   T
16.   T
17.   F
18.   T
19.   F
20.   T
21.   T
22.   T
23.   T
24.   F
25.   F
26.   F
27.   F
28.   F
29.   T
30.   F

CHAPTER 11

EVALUATING THE COGNITIVE PERSPECTIVE

LEARNING OBJECTIVES

After reading and studying this chapter, you should be able to:

1. Discuss the major contributions of the cognitive perspective.

2. Discuss misuses of the cognitive perspective, including cognitive reductionism, errors of cause and effect, and cognitive relativism.

3. Describe cognitive approaches to studying and understanding intelligence.

4. Discuss the contributions of the cognitive perspective to psychotherapy and the improvement of emotional well-being.

5. Discuss the controversy regarding childhood eyewitness testimony and the contribution of cognitive research to resolving the issues underlying this controversy.

CHAPTER 11 OUTLINE

I. Contributions and Misuses of The Cognitive Perspective.
   A. Contributions:
      1. Innovative methods for exploring the "black box" of the mind.
      2. An understanding of how cognition affects behavior.
      3. Strategies for improving mental abilities.
      4. Cognitive research has demonstrated that:
         a. humans are not always rational or capable of reflective judgement.
         b. strategies for effective thought can be learned.
         c. children have their own ways of reasoning.
         d. children's cognitive skills can improve through open-ended questions.
         e. there are measurable influences on mental abilities, such as the impact of technology.
   B. The cognitive perspective can be misused in various ways:
      1. cognitive reductionism is the tendency to reduce all behavior to mental processes.
      2. errors of cause and effect occur when people overlook the fact that the mind and body, and all thoughts and circumstances interact.
      3. cognitive relativism is the assumption that all thoughts, memories, and ideas should be taken equal seriously.

II. Issue #1: Becoming More Intelligent
   A. Traditional intelligence tests have focused on measuring abilities and have taken a psychometric approach.
   B. Newer, cognitive approaches emphasize problem solving strategies and how to help people use such strategies.
   C. Robert Sternberg's triarchic theory holds that there are three types of intelligence: componential, experiential, and contextual.
      1. Componential intelligence consists of information-processing strategies that occur during the thinking process.
      2. Experiential intelligence consists of the transfer of skills to new situations.
      3. Contextual intelligence consists of the practical application of intelligence, taking contexts into account.
   D. Most intelligence tests measure only componential intelligence, but the other two types are important in occupational and personal success.
   E. Together, experiential and contextual intelligence constitute practical intelligence. Practical intelligence allows you to pick up **tacit knowledge,** action-oriented strategies for success that usually are not formally taught but instead must be inferred.

244

F. **Metacognition** is the knowledge or awareness of one's own cognitive processes and plays an important role in intelligent behavior.

G. Howard Gardner's theory of multiple intelligences suggests that there are seven "intelligences" that are relatively independent, including:
   1. linguistic.
   2. logical-mathematical.
   3. spatial.
   4. musical.
   5. bodily-kinesthetic.
   6. interpersonal (understanding of others).
   7. intrapersonal (insight into yourself).

H. Some autistic and retarded individuals, known as savants (learned), have exceptional talents in one area, such as music, art or rapid mathematical computation, despite poor functioning in all others.

I. Interpersonal and intrapersonal intelligence correspond to what other theorists call emotional intelligence, the ability to know how to identify your own and other people's emotions, express your emotions clearly, and regulate emotions in yourself and others.

J. Cognitive research on "intelligences" has had practical benefits in improving school performance and also mental performance in older people.

III. Issue #2: Cognitive Psychotherapy and Emotional Well-Being
   A. Emotional reactions depend, in part, on the cognitive interpretation and explanation of events.
   B. Cognitive therapies help people identify and change cognitive appraisals that lead to negative emotional states and self-defeating behaviors.
      1. In Albert Ellis' rational emotive behavior therapy, the therapist challenges the client's irrational beliefs with rational arguments.
      2. Aaron Beck's approach encourages the person to see beliefs as hypotheses and test them.
      3. Donald Meichenbaum's self-instruction approach trains clients to substitute positive thoughts for self-defeating ones.
   C. Robert Fancher argues that cognitive therapy relies on commonsense views of cognition, does not actually incorporate many findings from cognition, and science, and ignores the objective difficulties of people with psychological problems.
   D. Cognitive therapy, especially when combined with behavior therapy, has been effective in the treatment of depression, physical pain, chronic fatigue syndrome, some anxiety disorders, and eating disorders.

IV.   Issue #3: Children's Eyewitness Testimony
    A.   There are two extreme views in the controversy about children's accuracy in reporting abuse.
        1.   Children never lie about abuse.
        2.   Children cannot be trusted.
    B.   Research studies indicate extremists on either side are wrong.
    C.   Cognitive research findings have demonstrated that children:
        1.   often need to be asked leading questions if they are to volunteer potentially embarrassing information, but can also be misled by leading questions.
        2.   often remember essential facts about events.
        3.   will sometimes say something happened when it did not.
        4.   will sometimes withhold information to protect someone or to keep a promise, or because an abuser has threatened to hurt them if they tell.
        5.   are influenced by stereotypes or perceptions about people.
        6.   may have trouble distinguishing reality from fantasy in emotionally intense situations.
        7.   will sometime give answers that they think adults want to hear, or may feel pressures to give certain answers.
        8.   are less accurate if they are very young.
    D.   Questioners are working on devising interview techniques that encourage accurate testimony from children without being coercive.
    E.   Overall, the findings of the cognitive perspective have consequences for intellectual development, emotional well-being, social problems, and legal policies.

CHAPTER 11 SUMMARY

The cognitive perspective shows that, although people are not always rational, there are techniques for improving learning, memory, and reasoning. At the same time, researchers warn that adults should use caution in trying to accelerate the pace of children's intellectual development.

Like all other viewpoints, the cognitive perspective has its critics. The cognitive perspective can also be misunderstood and misused. One of the greatest dangers is cognitive
1._____, the tendency to see all behavior as being caused only by cognitive factors. Because cognitive research has produced powerful findings, there is also a tendency to make errors about cause and effect by overlooking the interaction between thoughts and circumstances. And because cognitive research has demonstrated that emotional factors influence one's acceptance or rejection of arguments, there is the danger of cognitive
2._____, which involves the mistaken assumption that all thoughts, ideas, and memory have an equal claim to be taken seriously.

Cognitive findings have inspired new approaches to measuring intelligence. Traditional tests have focused on measuring individual differences in abilities and have used a 3._____ approach.

Sternberg's 4._____ theory of intelligence holds that there are three basic aspects to intelligence. The first is 5._____ intelligence, which includes information-processing strategies. 6._____ intelligence, the ability to transfer skills to new situations, is the second major type of intelligence in Sternberg's model. 7._____ intelligence, the ability to apply information practically, is the third. It includes the ability to acquire 8._____ knowledge, which is not formally taught. These three skills can be unequally distributed within a person. Traditional IQ tests mainly measure componential intelligence, but the other two types have been demonstrated to have a significant effect on personal and vocational success. Cognitive psychologists note that optimal functioning involves 9._____, awareness of one's own cognitive processes.

Gardner has also suggested that there are different kinds of independent "intelligences." He has labeled them linguistic, logical-mathematical, spatial, musical, body-kinesthetic, intrapersonal, and interpersonal. Intrapersonal and interpersonal intelligence correspond to what other theorists call 10._____. Sternberg and Gardner have developed an educational curriculum that reflects the new view that practical intelligence is as important as the kind of intelligence that has been traditionally emphasized.

The cognitive research on emotional well-being has contributed to the development of cognitive psychotherapy, which is based on the finding that a person's emotional reaction to an event is, in strong measure, the result of the person's 11._____ of the event.

Cognitive therapies are designed to help people change interpretations that lead to self-defeating behavior and negative emotional states. The 12._____ therapy approach of Ellis challenges irrational beliefs with rational argument. Beck's approach encourages clients to see their beliefs as hypotheses to be tested. Meichenbaum's approach trains people in techniques of 13._____, the substitution of positive thoughts for self-defeating ones. Most of these techniques require the client to monitor his or her reactions to various situations.

Critics of cognitive therapy argue that therapists always identify "wrong thinking." For instance, many depressed people have had significant failures, and their reactions are not merely due to faulty interpretations. Still, these therapies have been quite successful in the treatment of depression and other disorders.

Cognitive research has also been helpful in the controversial area of children's eyewitness testimony. Some people seem to believe that children's reports of having been abused could never be fabricated, while others believe that these reports can never be trusted. Research reveals that neither of these extreme views is supportable. While leading questions can influence children's reports, they are also necessary if the child is embarrassed or shy. While children can usually recall important events accurately, they sometimes do say something happened when it did not, and they may also withhold information out of loyalty or fear. Children's recollections are also influenced by stereotypes, strong emotion, and perceptions about what information is wanted by the adult.

MULTIPLE CHOICE SELF TEST

1. One of the ways in which cognitive psychologists have contributed to the field of psychology is by:

    a.   showing how reinforcement techniques can help mental patients.
    b.   developing innovative methods for exploring the mind.
    c.   demonstrating the differential effects of different reinforcement schedules.
    d.   helping our understanding of unconscious conflicts.

2. Cognitive psychologists would argue that if you want people to change their behavior, they need the opportunity to change their:

    a.   secondary reinforcers.
    b.   reinforcement schedules.
    c.   external environments.
    d.   attitudes and attributions.

3. Research on memory indicates that the best method of identifying a criminal perpetrator is to have victims:

    a.   pick out the offender in a lineup of people.
    b.   identify people from an array of pictures.
    c.   view lineup members one at a time.
    d.   compare lineup members to each other.

4. Cognitive psychologists would argue that one contributing factor to the increase in the inability of young people to use dialectical reasoning and reflective judgement is the:

    a.   gradual decline in average IQ in younger generations.
    b.   tendency for parents to ask mainly open-ended questions.
    c.   replacement of reading with television watching.
    d.   lack of behavior modification training by parents.

5. Harmful effects of excessive television watching can best be overcome by having children:

    a.   analyze and discuss with others what they are seeing.
    b.   watch mainly adult-oriented shows with greater verbal content.
    c.   concentrate on the visual images of television shows.
    d.   watch a good representative sample of television shows.

6. Ms. Jones is generally happy in her marriage to Mr. Jones, but sometimes they have marital problems. Research suggests she is most likely to attribute problems in her marriage to the fact that Mr. Jones:

    a. is sometimes thoughtless and stubborn.
    b. is experiencing stress from managing work and family obligations.
    c. has a mean streak that can be overcome with marital counseling.
    d. has never really learned to share his innermost feelings.

7. A behaviorist would argue that memory should best be studied as:

    a. an information processing phenomena.
    b. discrete "boxes."
    c. a way to explain behavior.
    d. another form of behavior.

8. A best selling self-help book states that the power of positive thinking can cure any illness, if only people would "think themselves well, since thinking patterns are related to wellness." This example of one of the common misuses of the cognitive approach is called:

    a. cognitive absolutism.
    b. cognitive relativism.
    c. the error of cause and effect.
    d. cognitive reductionism.

9. Ernestine reads an article presenting two opposing viewpoints on alien abductions. In the article, a popular author argues that alien abductions are real events, while a psychologist argues that alien abductions are merely the fabrications of highly suggestible people. The psychologist cites several research studies in support of her arguments, while the author cites case studies. Ernestine would be committing the error of cognitive relativism if she thought that:

    a. both persons have good arguments since everyone has a right to their opinion.
    b. the psychologist has to be correct, since scientists are always right.
    c. the popular author has to be correct, since psychologists are typically paid to give their opinion.
    d. both viewpoints are suspect because she would need to read the research studies and case histories herself before she made up her mind.

10. Mr. Grim is depressed and frequently voices negative and pessimistic thoughts. You conclude from observing his behavior that his depression is due to his negative and pessimistic attitude. This is an example of the error of:

    a.   cognitive absolutism.
    b.   cognitive relativism.
    c.   cause and effect.
    d.   cognitive reductionism.

11. Frank believes that the 1986 space shuttle disaster never really happened and that it was staged in order to deflect attention away from President Reagan. His position is absurd since a hoax of this magnitude could never be perpetrated, but Frank argues by proposing a large number of hypothetical events that are so unlikely as to be nearly impossible. His friend Ernest accepts Frank's position because he knows of other cases where a person who was telling the truth was not believed. Ernest has committed the error of:

    a.   cognitive absolutism.
    b.   cognitive relativism.
    c.   cause and effect.
    d.   cognitive reductionism.

12. Most traditional tests of intelligence focus on individual differences in how well people perform. This approach is based on _____ theory.

    a.   triarchic
    b.   psychometric
    c.   multiple intelligence
    d.   divergent thinking

13. According to Robert Sternberg's triarchic theory of intelligence, there are three aspects of intelligence including _____ intelligence.

    a.   componential, verbal, and contextual
    b.   quantitative, experiential, and tacit
    c.   componential, experiential, and contextual
    d.   verbal, quantitative, and musical

14. Joe gets straight A's in his accounting courses in college which involve a great deal of direction from professors about how to solve concrete problems. However, in his first job out of college, Joe has great difficulty transferring the skills and knowledge he learned in his classes to ambiguous, real-world, accounting problems. According to Sternberg's triarchic theory of intelligence, Joe lacks _____ intelligence.

     a.   quantitative
     b.   contextual
     c.   componential
     d.   experiential

15. Sheena directs the work activities of a large group of people. She is very successful in helping the people under her supervision to work effectively together as a team. Sheena was never formally taught these skills in college, but has intuitively developed good managerial abilities. Sheena can be described as high in the ability to pick up:

     a.   psychometric intelligence.
     b.   componential intelligence.
     c.   metacognition.
     d.   tacit knowledge.

16. Jorge is excellent at his job as an engineer. It requires him to recognize and solve problems and to evaluate the results of implementing a particular solution. According to Sternberg, Jorge has high _____ intelligence.

     a.   verbal.
     b.   contextual.
     c.   componential.
     d.   experiential.

17. According to research by Robert Sternberg, tacit knowledge about how to be a student predicts college success:

     a.   less well than standard scholastic aptitude tests.
     b.   better than academic tests.
     c.   less well than academic tests given by teachers.
     d.   as well as academic tests.

18. Alice always though she wanted to be a computer programmer. However, after taking a number of computer classes she found that she hated computers. In spite of this revelation, Alice still insists on becoming a computer programmer. Sternberg would say Alice has low _____ intelligence.

     a. verbal
     b. contextual
     c. componential
     d. experiential

19. According to Sterberg's triarchic theory of intelligence, practical intelligence consists of:

     a. experiential and contextual intelligence.
     b. experiential and componential intelligence.
     c. contextual and componential intelligence.
     d. verbal and componential intelligence.

20. Stewart reads "Hamlet" again and again and still can't understand what the characters in the play are saying. His friend Alisha also finds the material difficult, but decides to study some supplementary materials which explain some of the more difficult passages. She also discusses the material with her professor. Compared to Stewart's study methods, Alisha's study strategies reflect better _____ abilities.

     a. metacognitive
     b. componential
     c. verbal
     d. linguistic

21. Within the context of Gardner's theory of multiple intelligences, emotional intelligence corresponds to _____ intelligence.

     a. interpersonal and intrapersonal
     b. interpersonal and contextual
     c. intrapersonal and contextual
     d. contextual and bodily-kinesthetic

22. Suppose you are in the process of giving a long account of your vacation to one of your friends and you notice that she appears to be bored. In recognition of this observation, you change the subject to one which appears to interest her. According to Gardner you would be high in _____ intelligence.

   a. spatial
   b. linguistic
   c. interpersonal
   d. componential

23. Maria is a graceful and accomplished ballet dancer. Gardner would describe her as being high in _____ intelligence.

   a. spatial
   b. bodily-kinesthetic
   c. componential
   d. contextual

24. Studies indicate that low emotional intelligence is related to:

   a. low IQ as measured by standardized tests.
   b. low academic achievement.
   c. greater athletic ability.
   d. better math ability, but low verbal ability.

25. Research examining ways of increasing the mental abilities of older people indicates that efforts to assist the elderly can:

   a. improve inductive reasoning and spatial skills.
   b. improve verbal skills, but NOT spatial skills.
   c. do little to offset the inevitable natural decline in cognitive abilities.
   d. help a small minority of well-motivated elderly people.

26. Early experiments by Schachter and Singer seemed to indicate that emotion depended on:

   a. the person's reinforcement history and present behavior.
   b. physiological arousal and the person's reinforcement history.
   c. physiological arousal and the cognitive interpretation of the arousal.
   d. actual objective events.

27. Jaime does well on all his midterms because he believes he is having a "lucky streak." He is most likely to feel the emotion of:

    a.   pride.
    b.   satisfaction.
    c.   surprise.
    d.   arrogance.

28. Dr. Malinowsky is a cognitive therapist. He is trying to help a client overcome her feelings of unhappiness and depression. Dr. Malinoswky is most likely to suggest a treatment plan including:

    a.   an examination of the client's irrational beliefs and thoughts.
    b.   a consultation with a psychiatrist to recommend specific anti-depressant drugs.
    c.   an examination of the environmental factors causing behaviors that contribute to the client's depressed mood.
    d.   an examination of the client's unconscious dynamics and conflicts.

29. In children's eyewitness testimony, leading questions:

    a.   distort memory to the point where the testimony is useless.
    b.   are sometimes necessary to encourage a shy child.
    c.   are NOT permitted in legal proceedings.
    d.   rarely influence true memories at all.

30. Children are MOST likely to be suggestible when:

    a.   they are in grade school rather than in pre-school or high school.
    b.   the situation has minimal emotional intensity.
    c.   the child is allowed to free associate without pressure from adults.
    d.   when they want to cooperate with a trustworthy adult interviewer.

TRUE-FALSE SELF TEST

T   F   1.   Psychologists who take a cognitive perspective have produced convincing evidence that cognitions do explain the way that people act and feel.

T   F   2.   Happy spouses are more likely to attribute marital problems to their partner's disposition rather than the situation.

T   F   3.   Attributions about the causes of behavior can influence actions.

T   F   4.   The traditional lineup method of suspect identification is superior to viewing lineup members one at a time.

T   F   5.   Children's cognitive skills are more likely to develop rapidly when parents talk to them about many topics and describe things fully.

T   F   6.   Asking children to point out objects and answer yes-no questions is a superior method of encouraging language development as compared to asking open-ended questions.

T   F   7.   Mindful television watching, involving the analysis and discussion of the programs, can be intellectually enriching.

T   F   8.   Most complex personal problems can be quickly solved by thinking about the problem in a different way or new light.

T   F   9.   Cognitive relativism is consistent with the findings of cognitive research.

T   F   10.   Most intelligence tests are based on Robert Sternberg's Triarchic theory of intelligence.

T   F   11.   Componential intelligence refers to how well you transfer skills to new situations.

T   F   12.   Contextual intelligence refers to the practical application of intelligence by taking into account different situations you encounter.

T   F   13.   Tacit knowledge is knowledge that is typically explicitly and formally taught in school.

T   F   14.   Metacognition involves thinking about thinking.

T   F   15.   Intrapersonal intelligence refers to an understanding of other people's behavior.

T   F   16.   Howard Gardner suggests there is one general underlying factor responsible for intelligence.

T   F   17.   Emotional intelligence contributes to school achievement.

T   F   18.   Older people's verbal skills decline significantly between age 20 and age 80.

T   F   19. The physiology of emotion involves the simple activation of hormonal arousal alone.

T   F   20. A study of student reactions to succeeding or failing an exam found that their emotions were more closely related to their actual test performances, rather than their explanations for the test results.

T   F   21. Cognitive therapies usually involve helping clients to focus on self-defeating behaviors and to structure the environment to reinforce desired behaviors.

T   F   22. Cognitive therapy has been most effective in treating psychoses such as schizophrenia.

T   F   23. Most states permit authorities to ask children leading questions in sexual-abuse cases.

T   F   24. Children will generally never say something happened when it did not.

T   F   25. Younger children are more vulnerable to suggestion than older children.

T   F   26. Nonabused children will sometimes play with anatomically correct dolls in a sexual manner.

T   F   27. The recollections of children can be influenced by their stereotypes or beliefs about people.

T   F   28. Children are less vulnerable to suggestion when an adult repeatedly asks the same question.

T   F   29. The use of anatomically correct dolls to identify if a child has been abused is very reliable.

T   F   30. Human cognition is exactly like the "cognition" of a computer.

KEY TERMS

tacit knowledge - Strategies for success that are not explicitly taught but instead must be inferred.

metacognition - The knowledge or awareness of one's own cognitive processes.

Suggested Research Projects

1.   Brainstorm some examples of tacit knowledge regarding how to solve common problems encountered by college students.

2.   Evaluate your self-defeating thinking patterns using techniques from cognitive therapy.

Suggested Readings

Gardner, H. (1993). Frames of Mind: The Theory of Multiple Intelligences. NY: BasicBooks. Argues against the conception of intelligence as one general ability and in favor of the idea that intelligence consists of a variety of distinct competencies.

Gardner, H. (1993). Multiple Intelligences: The Theory in Practice. NY: BasicBooks. Reviews the practical implications of the theory of multiple intelligences for education.

Goleman, D. (1995). Emotional Intelligence. New York: Bantam. Research from psychology and neuroscience is examined and used to explain how emotional and rational intelligence work together.

CHAPTER 11

ANSWERS TO CHAPTER SUMMARY

1. reductionism
2. relativism
3. psychometric
4. triarchic
5. componential
6. experiential
7. contextual
8. tacit
9. metacognition
10. emotional intelligence
11. cognitive interpretation
12. rational emotive behavior
13. self-instruction

ANSWERS TO MULTIPLE CHOICE SELF-TEST

1. B
2. D
3. C
4. C
5. A
6. B
7. D
8. D
9. A
10. C
11. B
12. B
13. C
14. D
15. D
16. C
17. D
18. B
19. A
20. A
21. A
22. C
23. B

24.   A
25.   A
26.   C
27.   C
28.   A
29.   B
30.   D

ANSWERS TO TRUE FALSE SELF-TEST

1.   T
2.   F
3.   T
4.   F
5.   T
6.   F
7.   T
8.   F
9.   F
10.   F
11.   F
12.   T
13.   F
14.   T
15.   F
16.   F
17.   T
18.   F
19.   F
20.   F
21.   F
22.   F
23.   T
24.   F
25.   T
26.   T
27.   T
28.   F
29.   F
30.   F

CHAPTER 12

THE SOCIAL CONTEXT

LEARNING OBJECTIVES

After reading and studying this chapter, you should be able to:

1. Describe the fields of social psychology and industrial/organizational psychology.

2. Discuss classic research findings on the power of social roles.

3. Discuss the effects of power, resources, and gender roles on close relationships.

4. Describe the effects of social groups on conformity and groupthink.

5. Explain the social factors that decrease and individual's sense of responsibility.

6. Describe the conditions under which independent action is most likely to take place.

7. Explain some of the factors that influence attitude formation and change.

8. Summarize important research findings on work motivation.

9. Compare and contrast the effects of cooperative and competitive situations.

CHAPTER 12 OUTLINE

I.   Introduction
    A.   Systematic destruction of people defined as the enemy has been and continues to be a widespread practice. One aim of psychology is to try to understand why people act monstrously or with bravery and self-sacrifice.
    B.   Social and industrial/organizational psychologists focus on the situational and social forces that affect behavior and mental processes.

II.   Norms and Roles
    A.   **Norms** are rules and conventions of behavior that make our interactions with other people predictable and orderly.
    B.   **Roles** are positions in social groups.
        1.   Role behavior is regulated by norms - implicit cultural standards and sometimes explicit laws.
        2.   Role requirements can cause a person to behave in ways that violate personal standards.
    C.   Milgram's obedience study illustrates the power of roles.
        1.   Subjects were led to believe that they were inflicting painful and perhaps fatal electric shocks on another person.
        2.   At the urging of the experimenter, who was in the role of authority, about 2/3 of subjects delivered the highest shock level.
        3.   Subjects were more likely to disobey the experimenter when:
            a.   the experimenter left the room.
            b.   the victim was close at hand and the shocks had to be administered directly.
            c.   two experimenters issued conflicting demands.
            d.   the person who urged them on was not an authority figure.
            e.   peers refused to go further.
        4.   Milgram's experiment demonstrated that aggressive behavior may sometimes lie more in the role or the situation than the person.
        5.   Milgram's experiment has been criticized as unethical because of the use of deception and because the study caused many subjects emotional pain, but had great influence on public awareness of the dangers of uncritical obedience.
    D.   Zimbardo's prison experiment assigned the roles of prisoner and guard to ordinary college students.
        1.   The study was designed to be as true to life as possible.
        2.   "Prisoners" developed negative emotional and physical reactions.
        3.   Some "guards" (about a third of them) behaved in a cruel manner, some were "tough but fair," and some tried to be nice.
        4.   The study was discontinued after six days.

5. Zimbardo's experiment has been criticized as artificial and nonexperimental, but Zimbardo argues that real prisoners and guards also play "parts."

E. Demands for obedience, when accepted without question, can be dangerous. People follow orders because:
   1. they fear the consequences of disobedience.
   2. they want to be liked.
   3. they respect the legitimate authority.
   4. they hope to gain some advantage.
   5. they are mindless and define their actions in terms of routine duties and roles or fail to think critically.
   6. they do not want to appear rude.
   7. they lack a language of protest.
   8. they are victims of **entrapment**, the process in which people escalate their commitment in order to justify their investment in an activity.

F. The Role of Power
   1. The sociocultural view is that gendered behavior reflects differences in men's and women's power.
   2. Gender differences in communication styles reflect power and social norms for expressing it.
      a. People with higher levels of power use more direct strategies (asking, using persuasion and reason) and "hard" strategies (demanding, shouting, being assertive).
      b. People with lower levels use more indirect strategies (pouting, crying, manipulation, withdrawing) and "soft" strategies (acting nice, flattering the other person).
      c. Cross-cultural studies show that gender differences in communication styles are related less to the fact of being male or female than to power or social norms for expressing power.
      d. In Western countries direct strategies are used by the powerful and indirect strategies are used by the less powerful.
      e. Women tend to speak more tentatively and use more tag questions, rhetorical questions at the ends of statements, but only when speaking to men.
      f. People with higher levels of power are less sensitive to subordinates than subordinates are to them.

III. Conformity and Groupthink
   A. Conformity is taking action or adopting attitudes under real or perceived group pressure.
      1. Solomon Asch conducted experiments in which confederates made incorrect judgments about the lengths of lines.
         a. Only 20% of subjects were independent on every trial.

>
> b. 1/3 of subjects conformed over half the time to the group's incorrect decision.

2. Reasons for conformity include:
   a. identification with the group.
   b. desire to be accurate.
   c. desire for personal gain.
   d. a wish to be liked.

B. **Groupthink** is the tendency for group members to think alike and suppress dissent. Group members:
   1. avoid thinking about alternatives to the leader's suggestion.
   2. avoid examining the initial perspective for flaws.
   3. suppress private misgivings, creating an illusion of unanimity.
   4. avoid information from outside the group.

C. Groupthink can be counteracted by encouraging the expression of doubt and dissent by group members and by basing the group's decision on majority rule rather than unanimity.

D. Some researchers reject the term groupthink because it oversimplifies the complexities of group decision making through retrospective analysis and implies that conformity is always a bad thing.

E. Other factors affecting a group's decision include:
   1. its history.
   2. its cohesiveness and homogeneity.
   3. the nature of the decision.
   4. the leader's characteristics.
   5. the context of the decision.
   6. the temporary or permanent nature of the group.
   7. the amount of outside pressure.
   8. political agendas of the members.
   9. policies and politics of the organization.

F. Individual characteristics associated with susceptibility to group pressure include:
   1. a strong need for social approval.
   2. rigidity.
   3. low self-esteem.

G. Anonymity and Responsibility
   1. **Diffusion of responsibility** occurs when responsibility for the outcome of some event is spread out among many people. Individuals assume that someone else will take the responsibility.
      a. Bystander apathy occurs because of diffusion of responsibility.
      b. In work settings, such diffusion sometimes takes the form of social loafing, which occurs primarily when:
         1. individuals are not held accountable.
         2. people feel that hard work will duplicate another's efforts.

264

            3.   the work is uninteresting.
        c.   Social loafing is decreased when:
            1.   job challenge is increased.
            2.   workers have to evaluate their own performance.
            3.   group performance is evaluated against that of another group.
    2.   In extreme cases of diffusion of responsibility, people can experience **deindividuation**, in which they lose their sense of individuality and, as a result:
        a.   deny responsibility for their actions.
        b.   act mindlessly.
        c.   become disconnected from their values and attitudes.
    3.   Deindividuation increases when the situation provides anonymity
    4.   Experimental studies of deindividuation indicate that women are capable of acting aggressively and that deindividuation can overrule the influence of gender roles.
H.   The Conditions of Independent Action
    1.   <u>Altruism</u> is the willingness to take selfless or dangerous action on behalf of others and is, in part, a matter of personal belief or conscience.
    2.   People who refuse to conform or obey:
        a.   perceive a need for intervention or help.
        b.   make a conscious decision to take responsibility.
        c.   often have allies who support them.
        d.   consider the cost of doing nothing versus the cost of getting involved.
        e.   feel competent to do something positive.
        f.   may become committed to do more after an initial investment.

IV.   The Social Origins of Attitudes
    A.   An <u>attitude</u> is a relatively stable opinion that contains both cognitive elements and emotional elements.
    B.   Some attitudes are reasoned conclusions, but attitudes may also result from:
        1.   the <u>cohort</u> effect or the formation of a <u>generational identity</u>, a generation's shared identity, experiences, and economic concerns.
        2.   conformity.
        3.   habit.
        4.   rationalization.
        5.   other subtle influences.
    C.   Friendly persuasion
        1.   Acceptance of attitudes tends to increase when:
            a.   the **validity effect** occurs, that is people accept a statement as true or valid simply because it has been repeated many times.
            b.   the communicator is viewed as attractive or is admired.

   c. the message is linked with positive feelings.

  2. Fear increases acceptance only if it is moderate and accompanied by information about how to avoid danger; high fear messages can lead to resistance and/or denial.

 D. Coercive persuasion (sometimes called <u>brainwashing</u>) refers to techniques that suppress one's ability to reason and make choices in one's best interest. Techniques include:

  1. putting a person under physical or emotional distress.

  2. defining problems in simplistic terms and repeatedly offering simple answers.

  3. offering unconditional love, acceptance, attention, and solutions to personal problems by a leader.

  4. creating a strong group identity and hatred of "enemies."

  5. escalating commitment to the group (entrapment).

  6. controlling access to information.

  7. demanding conformity and groupthink.

V. The Social Origins of Motivation

 A. The Conditions of Work

  1. Motivation to work is affected by:

   a. certain aspects of the work situation, such as fringe benefits, pace, and pressure.

   b. degree of job flexibility.

   c. feedback and appreciation.

   d. opportunities for advancement, including the "glass ceiling" - a barrier to promotion that is subtle, yet strong enough to prevent advancement.

   e. the fit between the qualities of the person and the conditions of the work.

 B. Competition and Cooperation.

  1. Competition:

   a. often decreases work motivation.

   b. can cause insecurity and anxiety.

   c. can cause jealousy and hostility.

   d. can have a negative effect on achievement.

  2. Cooperation is built by promoting interdependence in reaching goals; it is associated with:

   a. liking others in the group and cooperating groups.

   b. higher motivation, achievement, and performance.

   c. better problem solving, satisfaction, and participation.

  3. Muzafer Sherif's classic "Robber's Cave" experiment found that competition enhanced negative and hostile interactions between two groups of boys at a camp, and cooperation through <u>interdependence in reaching mutual goals</u> enhanced positive interactions.

4. Motivation and reduced risk of groupthink are associated with:
   a. clarity of purpose.
   b. members' autonomy.
   c. prompt feedback on performance.
   d. a physical environment that allows for informal meetings.
   e. rewards to individuals for group or team performance.

V. The Question of Human Nature
   A. Some philosophers refer to the <u>banality</u> of evil, meaning that evil is commonplace and unoriginal.
   B. It is in our nature to behave both savagely and altruistically.

CHAPTER 12 SUMMARY

Whereas psychologists working in other perspectives usually generate explanations of human behavior based on qualities within the person, social and industrial/organizational psychologists stress social and situational influences, including the impact of the presence of others.

Social 1._____ are rules and conventions that guide social interactions. Social 2._____ are social positions governed by norms - sometimes including explicit laws, that prescribe proper behavior. These prescriptions can influence a person to behave in ways that contradict personal values or the person's sense of self.

The power of roles was demonstrated in two classic studies. In the 1960's, Milgram designed a study in which subjects were led to believe that they were giving painful electric shocks to others. Surprisingly, the proportion of over 3._____ of the subjects were willing to obey an experimenter who directed them to deliver even potentially fatal shocks. In subsequent experiments, Milgram manipulated several variables to investigate the conditions under which people were likely to disobey. He found that the physical closeness of both the experimenter and the 4._____ had an effect, as well as the conflict between different experimenters or within a group of subjects. When the person giving the orders was not placed in an authoritative role, the amount of obedience 5._____. Although Milgram convincingly demonstrated the power of authority, these experiments have been criticized as being 6._____.

Another major study, in the early 1970's, was Zimbardo's prison experiment, in which college students were given the roles of prisoners and guards. Zimbardo found that these subjects took on the characteristics of their assigned roles, with prisoners developing physical and emotional symptoms, and guards sometimes displaying sadistic behaviors. Critics of this study maintain that Zimbardo's setup was too 7._____ to be of value, but Zimbardo countered that these subjects were enacting roles just as real prisoners and guards do.

Social psychologists have pointed out several factors that promote obedience: fear of negative consequences, respect for authority, a wish to be liked, a desire for personal gain, and a failure to use 8._____ thinking in reacting to authority figures' demands. Norms of good manners can also facilitate obedience to authority. Many people also do not have the language skills to express disagreement. In addition, when a person complies with small requests, increasingly larger requests may be harder to resist because the person has already committed to a course of action and has become 9._____.

Power imbalance is a typical feature of role relationships, and the sociocultural approach provides unique insight into its effects. Power differences have characterized relationships between men and women, and these differences are reflected in communication differences. The person who has the greater power and status in a relationship tends to be relatively insensitive to the other person's nonverbal signals and tends to use 10._____ communication strategies. On the other hand, 11._____ strategies are more likely to be used by the less powerful person, who also tends to be sensitive to the other's nonverbal signals. Although it can be tempting to attribute male-female differences in communication styles to a biological difference, such disparities are due more to social roles and power than to gender, per se.

Groups can have significant effects on individual behavior. For example, the presence of others can result in social 12._____, the improvement of the individual's performance. This is likely to occur when skills are well mastered. When tasks are complex or difficult, it is more likely that the presence of others will result in social 13._____, a decrease in the individual's performance. The sociocultural perspective holds that group behavior is more a function of the nature of the group than of individual personalities.

14._____ occurs when people take action or adopt attitudes as a result of real or perceived group pressure. In a series of experiments by Asch, subjects were asked to match lines according to their length. Confederates in the experiments gave wrong answers. A proportion of 15._____ of the subjects conformed to the group's incorrect estimation over half the time. Conformity is affected by identification with the group, the wish to be accurate, the desire for personal gain, and the desire to be liked.

When groups are close, they tend to think alike and suppress dissent, a phenomenon called 16._____. The result may be risky decision making. Janis proposed that the following factors are involved: the desire to preserve harmony in the group and agree with the leader, the avoidance of disagreement and embarrassment, and the avoidance of outside information. These tendencies tend to work against critical thinking or expression of one's misgivings. Groupthink can be countered by encouraging these activities.

There are several other factors that influence group decision making, including the group's history and cohesiveness, the nature of the decision, the leader's characteristics, and group policies. Individual characteristics associated with people who have difficulty resisting group pressure include a high need for social approval, high rigidity, and low self-esteem.

There have been striking incidents in which large groups of people have failed to act to help a person in distress. 17._____ occurs when group members are inactive due to the belief that someone else will take responsibility. In work groups, the tendency to allow others to work harder is called 18.____; it is especially likely to occur when group members are not held accountable, when work is uninteresting, and when workers feel that their efforts will duplicate those of their coworkers. Work environments in which jobs are important and interesting, and in which individual and group performance is evaluated, are associated with greater motivation. In extreme instances, people lose themselves in situations and behave mindlessly, a phenomenon known as 19._____. This is especially likely to occur under conditions of 20.____.

Although there are often strong demands for obedience and conformity, people have sometimes been able to resist these pressures. Independent action is more likely when the person sees the need for action, decides to take responsibility, has an ally, weighs the costs of doing nothing, feels competent, and/or becomes entrapped into intervening. The willingness to take selfless or dangerous action on behalf of others, 21._____, is, in part, a matter of personal belief or conscience.

An 22._____ is a relatively stable opinion that contains both cognitive and emotional elements. A number of forces influence the formation of attitudes, including conformity, habit, rationalization, and cohort effects. Change in attitudes can be accomplished by mere repetition of a message. The existence of this 23._____ effect is the reason why advertisers repeat their messages over and over. Attitudes can also be affected by arguments from admired or attractive people, or by an association between a message and good feelings. Tactics that rely on extreme fear are not very effective in altering attitudes, but moderate fear can be useful if it is accompanied by information about how to avoid danger.

The term "brainwashing" is sometimes used to describe what social psychologists call 24. _____ persuasion. Several techniques can be used to strip an individual of his or her identity and suppress the ability to reason. These include the infliction of physical or emotional distress, the simplistic definition of personal problems and their solutions, unconditional acceptance by a leader, establishment of a new identity based on the group, entrapment, and restricted access to information.

Whereas some psychologists believe that motivation is internal, social psychologists tend to focus on situational forces that encourage or suppress motivation. In work settings, motivation has been demonstrated to be related to many aspects of the job itself, and also to job flexibility, feedback, appreciation, and chances for advancement. It is highly important that the qualities of the individual fit well with conditions of the work.

Competition in the workplace may undermine motivation and achievement, as it fosters feelings of insecurity, anxiety, jealousy, and hostility. On the other hand, an atmosphere of 25. _____ tends to increase performance and satisfaction. Work teams perform best when the group has a clear purpose, members have autonomy, feedback on performance is prompt, members can meet face-to-face, and individuals are rewarded for team performance.

MULTIPLE CHOICE SELF-TEST

1. Dr. Bennett is interested in studying the effect of involvement in work teams on job satisfaction. Dr. Bennett is most likely to be a(n) _____ psychologist.

    a. social
    b. industrial/organizational
    c. clinical
    d. counseling

2. The social constraints or rules that people are expected to follow are called:

    a. norms
    b. roles.
    c. social positions.
    d. cohorts.

3. Which of the following statements is an accurate interpretation of the research studies by Milgram and Zimbardo?

    a. the study shows that evil, sadistic people will harm others but good people won't.
    b. people who were categorized as having personality disorders were more likely to harm others.
    c. a strong situation is a very powerful determinant of human behavior.
    d. the research has very little relevance to real-life authority situations.

4. Approximately what percentage of persons in the Milgram obedience study obeyed the experimenter by shocking subjects at the highest shock level?

    a. 25
    b. 33
    c. 45
    d. 66

5. When Stanley Milgram asked a group of psychiatrists, students, and middle-class adults how many people they though would "go all the way" to the highest level on the shock generator, the group predicted that:

    a. most people would refuse to go beyond 150 volts and only sadists would administer the highest voltage.
    b. about half the people would go to the 450 volt level.
    c. two-thirds would go to the highest level on the shock generator.
    d. most people would refuse to participate in the experiment at all.

6. Obedience in the Milgram study declined significantly when:

    a. experimenters issued related and complementary demands on the subject.
    b. the subject worked with peers who refused to go further.
    c. the victim screamed in agony and it was clear he was in pain.
    d. the study was moved to an office in a nearby city.

7. The sociocultural perspective would indicate that one reason people obey authority is because:

    a. they pay more attention to what they are doing in the presence of an authority figure.
    b. they are too polite and smooth over conflict.
    c. they can avoid entrapment by listening to an authority figure.
    d. the authority figure provides moral courage and guidance.

8. The Zimbardo prison experiment study demonstrated that:

    a. subjects asked to play roles thought the entire study was a joke.
    b. having a power role corrupts and being powerless results in learned helplessness.
    c. only persons having a "sadistic personality profile" were abusive as guards.
    d. persons who lack power will stand together as a group to overturn authority.

9. Subjects were assigned a "prisoner" or "guard" role in the Zimbardo prison study based on:

    a. each subject volunteering to play a particular role.
    b. how they scored on a personality test.
    c. random assignment to each role.
    d. how they scored on an intelligence test.

10. The reason why women are more intuitive than men is because they generally have:

    a. less power and therefore must learn to "read" the signals of the powerful.
    b. brain hemispheres that communicate more successfully as compared to men.
    c. greater perceptive thinking abilities as compared to men.
    d. learned to use direct communication to gain information.

11. Research on gender differences and power shows that women who speak tentatively are:

    a. more influential with men and less influential with women.
    b. less influential with men and more influential with women.
    c. more influential with both sexes.
    d. less influential with both sexes.

12. In general, in order to get what they want, North American women are more likely to use the technique of:

    a. demanding.
    b. shouting.
    c. being assertive.
    d. acting nice.

13. S.C. Chen's study found that an ant would work the hardest when it was:

    a. by itself.
    b. in a very crowded environment.
    c. prodded by light electrical stimulation.
    d. in the presence of two or three other ants.

14. The conformity study by Asch found that when people made line comparisons in a group of confederates who gave an incorrect response:

    a. less than one percent of the students remained completely independent of the group on every trial.
    b. very few students ever conformed to the incorrect response of the confederates.
    c. about one third of subjects conformed to the group's incorrect response more than half the time.
    d. almost all subjects conformed consistently to the incorrect response on every experimental trial.

15. You are performing a well-learned dance routine in front of the entire campus. Psychologists would predict that the presence of a crowd would _____ your performance.

    a. obstruct
    b. inhibit
    c. have no effect on
    d. enhance

16. The Bay of Pigs incident in which Kennedy approved a failed plan to invade Cuba illustrates the psychological concept of:

    a. social loafing.
    b. mindlessness.
    c. groupthink.
    d. deindividuation.

17. Groupthink is characterized by:

    a. a full explanation of possible alternatives.
    b. soliciting outside information.
    c. encouraging doubt and dissent.
    d. preserving harmony and the leader's preferences.

18. Not long ago in Detroit, Deletha Ward was pulled from her car and beaten. To escape her attackers, she jumped from a bridge to her death. Forty people witnessed the event and did nothing. Social psychologists would explain this bystander effect as being due to:

    a. the bystanders being immoral and sadistic people.
    b. the fact that there were many people present instead of just one or a few.
    c. poor critical thinking among group members because of groupthink.
    d. the cohort effect.

19. After the Rodney King verdict in Los Angeles, large numbers of people rioted and looted. This behavior best illustrates the concept of:

    a.   social dispersement.
    b.   groupthink.
    c.   deindividuation.
    d.   social loafing.

20. People believed that Ronald Reagan was much more popular than he really was because this "fact" was repeated by the media many times. This example illustrates the _____ effect.

    a.   conditioning
    b.   confirmation
    c.   reliability
    d.   validity

21. Studies indicate that people are most likely to be altruistic and take independent action when they:

    a.   are in a large group of people.
    b.   become entrapped into helping someone.
    c.   find that costs to help are very high.
    d.   have powerful pressures to conform.

22. A generational identity is most likely to form during the age range of:

    a.   10-15.
    b.   16-24.
    c.   25-35.
    d.   35-40.

23. David Koresh successfully persuaded the Branch Davidian cult members to follow his lead by:

    a. giving them complex philosophical arguments for joining the cult.

    b. offering them love, acceptance, attention, and answers to their personal problems in exchange for adoration and idealization.

    c. ensuring that they maintained a close relationship with their non-cult member friends and relatives.

    d. allowing them to gain knowledge about various religious philosophies.

24. Militia groups dress in khaki uniforms or camouflage to promote a state of mind that leads people to feel more anonymous and less accountable for their own actions. Social psychologists would refer to this state of mind as:

    a. the validity effect.

    b. social facilitation.

    c. groupthink.

    d. deindividuation.

25. In the Robber's Cave experiment, the researchers were successful in eliminating the hatred between the rival Eagles and Rattlers by:

    a. subjecting the boys to extensive psychotherapy to explore their conflict.

    b. helping the boys to work together.

    c. lecturing them on the evils of fighting.

    d. eliminating the boys with the "troublemaker" personalities.

26. A psychologist wants to create an advertising campaign to convince people to practice safe sex in order to avoid contracting AIDS. The most effective campaign would:

    a. create an overwhelmingly strong emotion of fear.

    b. provide graphic portrayals of the medical effects of AIDS.

    c. induce moderate anxiety and provide information about AIDS prevention.

    d. provide informative statistics about AIDS deaths and the causes of AIDS.

27. Coercive persuasion is most likely to occur when the person being persuaded is:

   a. convinced to eat and sleep as much as they want in order to put them into a relaxed state.
   b. provided with complex explanations for his or her problems.
   c. given information discrepant from the philosophy imposed by the group and asked to provide counterarguments to confirm their new beliefs.
   d. convinced to make a greater and greater commitment to the group.

28. Current research on the motivation of women to succeed in work settings indicates that:

   a. a drive for success is related to opportunities for advancement in work situations.
   b. women have a strong "fear of success" that prevents them from breaking into top management positions.
   c. the women that have the strongest enduring self-motivation triumph even if there is a severe lack of opportunity.
   d. women who don't "make it" in the work world have only themselves to blame.

29. People who fall outside the dominant culture of corporate life encounter subtle barriers to promotion including not being "in the network" or an inability to find a mentor. This barrier is referred to as:

   a. illegal discrimination.
   b. the "glass ceiling".
   c. reverse affirmative action.
   d. the "corporate wall".

30. Organizational psychologists who have compared the effects of working in cohesive teams rather than competitive environments have found that:

   a. competition between workers is uniformly the best strategy for improving worker productivity.
   b. cooperation inevitably produces groupthink as compared to competition.
   c. cooperation can lead to better problem solving and job satisfaction than competition.
   d. competition promotes more interdependence in reaching mutual goals than cooperation.

TRUE FALSE SELF-TEST

T F 1. Adolph Eichmann, a Nazi SS officer responsible for the murder of missions of Jews during World War II, was an average middle-class man with a normal upbringing and no readily identifiable criminal tendencies.

T F 2. In modern life, most people generally play only one major societal role.

T F 3. In Stanley Milgram's obedience study, only about 1 percent of the subjects consented to shock another person at the highest voltage level.

T F 4. Replications of Milgram's research find that men are much more likely than women to inflict a dangerous shock to another person.

T F 5. Protests of pain by the victim in the Milgram study resulted in an immediate refusal of subjects to continue the experiment.

T F 6. In the Milgram study, when the person ordering the shocks to continue was an ordinary person rather than an authority figure, subjects were more likely to refuse to go on.

T F 7. When the experimenter left the room in the Milgram experiment, obedience decreased.

T F 8. In the Milgram study, when the teacher had to administer shocks directly to the victim's body, compliance decreased.

T F 9. The Milgram study has been criticized as being unethical.

T F 10. In the Zimbardo study, most "guards" were fair and tried to be nice to the "prisoners."

T F 11. In the Zimbardo study, many of the college men participating were found to have mental disorders.

T F 12. Some guards in the Zimbardo study were willing to work extra hours for no additional pay.

T F 13. The Zimbardo experiment continued for about one month.

T   F   14.   People who watch videotapes of the Milgram experiment are more favorably inclined towards dissenters who get morally indignant and furiously "riled up" as compared to dissenters who politely disobey.

T   F   15.   Women are more likely to use "hard" persuasive strategies.

T   F   16.   In Malagasy society, men are more likely to display their power by speaking in a misleading and vague manner.

T   F   17.   Communication styles are related more to the fact of being male or female than to social norms for expressing power.

T   F   18.   Women use more tag questions when speaking with men.

T   F   19.   The mere presence of another member of the same species can enhance performance on a task.

T   F   20.   In the Solomon Asch study, 70 percent of the students remained completely independent on every judgement trial.

T   F   21.   Groupthink occurs when groups encourage the expression of doubt and dissent.

T   F   22.   People are more likely to take action to help another person when they are entrapped into doing so.

T   F   23.   Social loafing increases when individual performance on a task is identifiable.

T   F   24.   Social loafing occurs more frequently when work is interesting.

T   F   25.   Deindividuation increases under conditions of anonymity.

T   F   26.   Deindividuated women are typically less aggressive than men.

T   F   27.   Altruism is based on personal convictions and social and situational influences.

T   F   28.   Population size rather than density increases the sensory overload on people and makes them more deindividuated.

T   F   29.   A generational identity is most likely to form during the age range of 12-16.

T   F   30.   Good arguments rather than mere repetition are essential to increase the rated validity of a statement or assertion.

KEY TERMS

norms - Social conventions that regulate human life, including explicit laws and implicit cultural standards.

role - A given social position that is governed by a set of norms for proper behavior.

entrapment - A gradual process in which individuals escalate their commitment to a course of action to justify their investment of time, money, or effort.

groupthink - In close-knit groups, the tendency for all members to think alike for the sake of harmony and conformity and to suppress dissent.

diffusion of responsibility - In organized or anonymous groups, the tendency of members to avoid taking responsibility for actions or decisions, assuming that others will do so.

deindividuation - In groups or crowds, the loss of awareness of one's own individuality and the abdication of mindful action.

validity effect - The tendency of people to believe that a statement is true or valid simply because it has been repeated many times.

Suggested Research Projects

1.   Together, with a group of students, discuss the relevance of the research on the power of roles to historical and current tragedies such as the Holocaust or the "ethnic cleansing" in Bosnia. How can psychological research findings contribute to ways of preventing such events and promoting more altruistic and cooperative behavior between people and nations?

2.   Construct a questionnaire of work conditions such as pay, flexibility, appreciation, etc. and ask a group of college students of different majors to rank these aspects of work from most to least important. Are there differences between groups? What are some of the individual and situational factors that might influence these differences?

Suggested Readings

Aronson, E. (1995). <u>The Social Animal</u>. (7th ed.). New York: Freeman. An interesting presentation of a variety of topics in social psychology.

Kohn, A. (1990). <u>The Brighter Side of Human Nature: Altruism and Empathy in Everyday Life</u>. NY: BasicBooks. Examines arguments in favor of the view that altruistic behavior is more natural than selfish and aggressive behavior.

Milgram, S. (1974). <u>Obedience to Authority: An Experimental View</u>. New York: Harper & Row. Milgram's account of his classic studies on obedience to authority.

Suggested Audio-Visuals

Obedience. (1965). The original Milgram studies presented by Stanley Milgram.

Quiet rage: The Standford Prison Experiment (1990). This video documents the classic study on the power of social roles. The footage includes commentary by Dr. Phillip Zimbardo and updates the status of the original prisoner and guards study participants.

CHAPTER 12

ANSWERS TO CHAPTER SUMMARY

1. norms
2. roles
3. 2/3
4. victim (confederate)
5. decreased
6. unethical
7. artificial
8. critical
9. entrapped
10. direct
11. indirect
12. facilitation
13. inhibition
14. conformity
15. 1/3
16. groupthink
17. diffusion of responsibility
18. social loafing
19. deindividuation
20. anonymity
21. altruism
22. attitude
23. validity
24. coercive
25. cooperation

ANSWERS TO MULTIPLE CHOICE SELF-TEST

1. A
2. A
3. C
4. D
5. A
6. B
7. B
8. B
9. C
10. A
11. A
12. D

13.	D
14.	C
15.	D
16.	C
17.	D
18.	B
19.	C
20.	D
21.	B
22.	B
23.	B
24.	D
25.	B
26.	C
27.	D
28.	A
29.	B
30.	C

ANSWERS TO TRUE FALSE SELF-TEST

1.	T
2.	F
3.	F
4.	F
5.	F
6.	T
7.	T
8.	T
9.	T
10.	F
11.	F
12.	T
13.	F
14.	F
15.	F
16.	T
17.	F
18.	T
19.	T
20.	F
21.	F
22.	T
23.	F

24.   F
25.   T
26.   F
27.   T
28.   F
29.   F
30.   F

CHAPTER 13

THE CULTURAL CONTEXT

LEARNING OBJECTIVES

After reading and studying this chapter, you should be able to:

1. Describe the fields of cultural and cross-cultural psychology.

2. Discuss the methodological difficulties inherent in studying culture.

3. Describe some general cultural differences in communication styles, time organization, and the concept of self.

4. Compare and contrast four possible outcomes of the ethnic identity and acculturation process.

5. Describe research on cultural conceptions of intelligence.

6. Define social constructionism.

7. Discuss cultural variations in gender roles.

8. Discuss the functions and dangers of ethnocentrism and stereotyping.

9. Describe the sources of prejudice and bigotry.

CHAPTER 13 OUTLINE

I. Introduction
    A. **Culture** is a program of shared rules that govern the behavior of members of a community or society, and a set of values, beliefs, and attitudes shared by most members of that community.
        1. The system of rules is passed from one generation to another.
        2. The system of rules concerns almost everything in the human-made environment.
        3. An example of the influence of culture is eating behavior. Culture can influence what you eat, who you eat with, and how much you are obsessed with your weight, as in the eating disorders of <u>anorexia nervosa</u> (self-starvation) or <u>bulimia</u> (bingeing and vomiting).
    B. <u>Cultural psychologists</u> study the effects of culture on behavior.
    C. <u>Cross-cultural psychologists</u> compare members of different societies.
    D. <u>Cultural anthropology</u> overlaps with cultural psychology and is the cross-cultural study of human groups.
    E. However, anthropologists tend to study the economy and customs of a cultural unit as a whole, while cultural psychologists are more interested in how cultural affects individual psychological and physiological processes.

II. The Study of Culture
    A. There are numerous research difficulties and issues in the study of culture.
        1. There are many criteria that must be considered in selecting samples (societal, community, individual, and behavioral) and designing studies (the problem of cultural and linguistic equivalence).
        2. Some cultural differences can be measured <u>indirectly</u> by drawing inferences from data about collective behavior, but indirect measurements permit different interpretations.
        3. Many psychologists prefer <u>direct</u> measures, such as questionnaires or observations of <u>matched samples</u> of respondents from different countries. Matching means that an effort is made to study samples of individuals who are similar in all aspects of their lives except their nationality, including age, economic status, and education.
        4. One matched sample study performed by Michael Bond and Geert Hofstede found that IBM employees from around the world differed on four key dimensions:
            a. the extent to which they accept and expect an unequal distribution of power in organizations and families.
            b. the extent to which they are integrated into groups or are expected to be "individualistic."
            c. the extent to which they endorse "masculine" values of assertiveness or "feminine" values of nurturance.
            d. the extent to which they can tolerate uncertainty.

1. Cultures that minimize or avoid uncertainty tend to adhere to strict laws, religious and philosophical beliefs, rules, and safety and security measures.
2. People in cultures that are more tolerant of uncertainty are more accepting of differing behavior, opinions, and religious views.

5. There is the problem of interpreting results because of difficulty in ensuring linguistic and functional equivalence on questionnaires and tests.
6. A custom in one culture might not have the same meaning or purpose as the same practice elsewhere.
7. There is a risk of stereotyping; however, the study of culture does not rest on the assumption, implicit in stereotypes, that all members of a culture behave the same way.
8. There is the temptation to reify (to regard an intangible process as if it were a literal object) culture or use culture as an explanation for behavior, without identifying specific mechanisms within the culture.
9. Many findings are politically sensitive.

III. The Rules of Culture
   A. Context and Communication
      1. Most aspects of body language, the nonverbal signals of body movement, posture, gesture and gaze, are specific to a particular culture, but some signals of body language, like facial expressions, seem to be "spoken" universally.
         a. Conversational distance (how close to stand to another when talking) is one example illustrating cultural differences.
         b. In **high-context cultures**, people attend closely to nonverbal signals and assume a shared context.
         c. In **low-context cultures**, people emphasize directly stated verbal communication and do not take shared context for granted.
   B. The Organization of Time
      1. **Monochronic cultures** see time as organized into linear segments. People in monochronic cultures:
         a. are low-context.
         b. do one thing at a time.
         c. take time commitments seriously.
         d. place high value on jobs, plans, privacy, and promptness.
         e. develop many short-term relationships.
      2. **Polychronic cultures** see time as parallel and schedules as flexible. People in polychronic cultures:
         a. are high-context.
         b. do many things at a time.

        c.   give people priority over jobs.

        d.   are more concerned with relationships that privacy.

        e.   change plans often and easily.

        f.   build lifetime relationships.

C.   The Self and Self-identity

    1.   <u>Individual-centered</u> cultures emphasize the self as more important than the group.

        a.   The self is defined as a collection of personality traits.

        b.   Independence and self-reliance are highly valued.

        c.   Friendships develop quickly.

    2.   <u>Collectivist</u> cultures emphasize the group over the individual.

        a.   The self is seen and defined as embedded in the community.

        b.   Family and group are emphasized.

        c.   Friendships develop slowly.

D.   People develop a **social identity** based on their ethnicity, religion, nationality, and social roles as well as a <u>personal identity</u>, a sense of who one is based on individual traits and unique history.

    1.   **Ethnic identity** is an identification with one's racial, religious, or ethnic group.

    2.   **Acculturation** is the process by which members of minority groups come to identify with and feel part of the dominant culture.

    3.   Ethnic identity and acculturation are relatively independent processes.

    4.   For any individual, there are four possible outcomes:

        a.   <u>bicultural</u>: strong ethnic identity, strong acculturation.

        b.   <u>assimilated</u>: weak ethnic identity, strong acculturation.

        c.   <u>separatist</u>: strong ethnic identity, weak acculturation.

        d.   <u>marginal</u>: weak ethnic identity, weak acculturation.

    5.   Because of different ideas about the relative benefits of acculturation versus ethnic identity, ethnic labels have great symbolic and emotional significance.

E.   Mental Abilities

    1.   Cross-cultural research on Jean Piaget's theory supports the hierarchical sequence of cognitive stages, but cultural differences may occur in the <u>rate</u> of development of these stages.

    2.   People in all cultures can reason deductively, but differ in the areas in which they are apt to apply this reasoning.

    3.   Cultures differ in their definition of intelligence.

    4.   Cultures differ in their encouragement of the development of various human capacities.

    5.   Cultural beliefs and attitudes of teachers and parents about the origins of intelligence and the reasons for achievement affect skill development.

        a.   Americans, who score on average much lower in mathematics than do Asians, are more likely than Asians to believe that mathematical ability is innate.

        b.   Americans tend to have lower standards for performance than Asians.

        c.   American students have more stressful, conflicting demands on their time than do their Asian counterparts.

        d.   Americans are more ambivalent about the value of education.

    6.   Some abilities that are highly developed in minority cultures are not valued by the mainstream culture or taken advantage of by schools.

    7.   Ethnic groups differ in social support for achievement found in children's and teenager's peer groups, which in turn is affected by actual opportunities for success.

IV.   The Origins of Culture

    A.   Cultural attitudes and traditions reflect a group's history, physical environment, and survival needs.

    B.   **Social constructionism** is the view that there are no universal truths about human nature because people construct reality differently depending on their culture, the historical moment, and power arrangements within their society.

    C.   With regard to gender differences, cross-cultural psychologists have found the following common themes:

        1.   men have had more status and power then women, especially in public affairs.

        2.   men typically handle making weapons and traveling a long way from home and women have responsibility for home and child care if the society's economy is based on hunting large game.

        3.   males must prove their self-reliance and courage in initiation rites.

        4.   femininity corresponds with responsibility, obedience, and child care.

    D.   In the social constructionist view, a distinction should be made between biological sex and learned gender. Gender roles differ cross-culturally with regard to:

        1.   the status of women -- it is not uniformly low.

        2.   work roles of males and females.

        3.   personality traits attributed to men and women.

        4.   the amount of daily contact permitted between the sexes.

        5.   the value placed on female chastity.

        6.   the degree of emphasis on assumed gender differences.

    E.   Gender roles depend on <u>production</u> (matters pertaining to the economy) and <u>reproduction</u> (matters pertaining to the bearing, raising, and nurturing of children) needs in the culture.

1. Rigid ideas about masculinity and male aggressiveness tend to exist where:
   a. there is competition for scarce resources.
   b. enemies must be fought.
   c. community resources must be protected.
2. Two conditions are operating to erode male supremacy and promote gender equality:
   a. the availability of reliable contraception.
   b. changing modes of production in industrialized societies, with an emphasis on service skills and mental work.

IV. Cross-cultural Relations
   A. Ethnocentrism and Stereotypes
      1. **Ethnocentrism** is the belief that one's ethnic group, nation, or religion is superior to all others.
         a. Ethnocentric thinking is especially common in war or other competition.
         b. Such "us-them" thinking encourages **stereotypes**, summary expressions of groups and a belief that all members of those groups share common traits.
            1. Stereotypes are cognitive schemas that make information processing more efficient. However, they distort reality by:
               a. accentuating group differences and overlooking commonalities
               b. producing selective perception
               c. underestimating differences within a group.
         c. The same trait can be stereotypically positive or negative, depending on whether the group is liked or disliked.
         d. People from different cultures will evaluate the same event differently, and thus positive and negative stereotypes depend on the cultural norms of the observer.
   B. Prejudice
      1. A prejudice is an unreasonable negative feeling toward a group or cultural practice; it includes emotional discomfort with and dislike of the group in question.
      2. A prejudice allows a person to:
         a. deal with negative feelings by scapegoating (warding off feelings of inadequacy, doubt, and fear by projecting them onto a target) a group.
         b. bolster vulnerable self-esteem.
      3. The social and economic roots of prejudice include:
         a. socialization.
         b. social support for expressing prejudice.

      c.   economic benefits and justification of discrimination.

4.   As with any attitude, prejudice has cognitive, emotional, and behavioral components.

5.   Not all prejudiced people are prejudiced in the same way or to the same extent, but researchers are divided about when such labels as "bigoted" and "racist" should be applied and whether racial animosity is declining; reducing prejudice is a process rather than an "all-or-none event."

6.   Some scientists believe that racial animosity and sexism are undiminished because people hide behind a mask of <u>symbolic racism</u>, a focus on issues rather than people.

7.   There are two types of sexism that are empirically distinct:

      a.   <u>hostile sexism</u> involves strongly negative feelings about women.

      b.   <u>benevolent sexism</u> involves positive feelings about women along with paternalistic and stereotyped attitudes towards them.

V.   Can Cultures get Along?

    A.   Cross-cultural psychology has identified the reasons for cultural conflict and has given us some ideas about reducing such conflict.

    B.   Ways to reduce cross-cultural conflict include educating people about cultural differences and reducing inequities between groups.

CHAPTER 13 SUMMARY

1._____ is a program of shared rules, values, and beliefs that govern the behavior of members of a community or society. Cultural psychologists study the effects of culture on behavior, whereas 2._____ psychologists compare members of different societies. The latter field is similar to the field of 3._____. Researchers in these areas have demonstrated that culture has powerful influences, even on biological processes.

The task of designing adequate research methods is especially difficult when one is making cultural comparisons. For example, the researcher needs to consider how many different cultures to study and how many groups or individuals to use as samples. A custom or term in one culture may not always have the same meaning in another culture; thus there is a problem of cultural and linguistic 4._____. There is a temptation, in cultural research, to 5._____ by assuming that all members of a culture are alike. Further, if the specific mechanisms that influence behavior are not identified, then appealing to "culture" as an explanation is simply an instance of 6._____ reasoning. Finally, cross-cultural psychologists must be aware of the political sensitivity of many studies.

People learn many cultural rules automatically and conform to them without awareness. Communication by 7._____, the nonverbal signals of body movement, gesture, and gaze, provides information beyond that of language. Cultures differ in their norms for 8._____, which regulate how close or how far apart people normally stand to one another while they are talking. Cultures also differ in how much attention is paid to nonverbal forms of communication. In 9._____ cultures, people attend closely to posture and distance between speakers, whereas in 10._____ cultures, people attend more to verbal communications.

Cultural factors affect how people think about and react to time. In 11._____ cultures, people tend to do one thing at a time, emphasize promptness, and adhere to plans. This tendency is associated with an economic history in which work efforts had to be coordinated. In 12._____ cultures, people do many things at once, and they often change plans spontaneously. These cultures usually have economies based more on natural rhythms than on coordinated work.

While many Western peoples tend to emphasize individualism, other cultures are more group-centered, or 13._____. They define the "self" as embedded in the community. This basic difference in self definition has important implications. Individualist cultures emphasize independence, whereas group-oriented peoples are more likely to emphasize family cohesiveness and interdependence. Child rearing is seen as a task for the community, and "privacy" for children is considered unimportant. Americans tend to make friends quickly and socialize at a surface level, but friendships develop much more slowly in collectivist cultures.

People develop 14._____ identities based on their ethnic, national, religious, and other affiliations. Many people struggle with a tension between 15._____ identity, the identification with their racial group or culture of origin, and 16._____, joining and feeling part of the dominant culture. Research suggests that these two processes are relatively independent. Thus there are four possible outcomes for an individual. When people have strong identifications with both the dominant culture and their ethnicity, they are 17._____. Some people opt for 18._____, in which ethnic identity is not strong, but cultural identification is. In contrast, 19._____ have a strong ethnic identification and weak identification with the dominant culture. Finally, some people feel 20._____, without strong connections to either culture.

Researchers are interested in the development, definition, and measurement of mental abilities cross-culturally. One interesting finding is that most people in every culture are able to reason 21._____, but that they apply this reasoning in different areas, depending on their needs and experiences. Cultures differ in the meaning of "intelligence", and they tend to encourage the development of some intellectual skills, but not others.

The set of skills a culture nurtures probably has an affect on the rate of development of a particular skill. Beliefs about the origins of intelligence, standards for performance, and values about education also appear to be important factors in skill development. For example, Americans are more likely than Asians to believe that mathematical ability is 22. _____, and they set lower standards for their children's school performance. Specific interactions between parents and children, and the support by peers for school achievement, may differ across cultures and ethnic groups. Schools do not always recognize and take advantage of the strengths of minority children.

Although many people assume that there are natural roles and characteristics for males and females, in reality gender arrangements vary considerably across cultures. This fact supports the social 23. _____ view that people create different notions of reality depending on their culture, the historical moment, and power arrangements. Thus, although masculinity is associated with power and achievement in many parts of the world, women's status varies across cultures, as do ideas of gender appropriate work, gender differences in emotional expression, and the amount of social contact permitted between the sexes. Gender role arrangements appear to be related to a society's reproduction needs, its economy, and its need to defend itself from other groups. Because production and reproduction have been changing throughout this century, gender roles also are changing.

People get attached to their cultural groups, and therefore tend toward 24. _____, the belief that one's own group is superior to all others. People also tend to see members of other groups as being all the same. While such 25. _____ helps in information processing, it also leads to distortions in judgment, such as an overattention to differences among groups, underattention to similarities within other groups, and 26. _____, which causes people to see only those behaviors that fit their stereotypes. The same characteristic can be viewed in a positive or negative light depending on whether or not a group is liked.

When feelings about other groups are unreasonably negative, a person is 27. _____. This cognitive and emotional state allows a person to defend against feelings of inadequacy, fear, and insecurity. Prejudice is learned through socialization and reinforcement. The greatest prejudice usually occurs when there are 28. _____ benefits to discriminating against some group. One psychological benefit is 29. _____, which is warding off feelings of inadequacy, doubt, and fear by projecting them onto a target group. Other benefits include bolstering vulnerable self-esteem. Like any attitude, prejudice has cognitive, emotional, and behavioral components, but researchers have historically focused on only the cognitive components. Some researchers have argued that many people are not overtly racist, but instead hide behind a mask of 30. _____, a focus on issues rather than people. Knowledge of how cultures differ can help in resolving conflicts and preventing misunderstandings.

MULTIPLE CHOICE SELF-TEST

1. In the study of cross-cultural psychology, reification refers to the tendency to:

    a. regard culture itself as an explanatory concept.
    b. assume that a concept in one culture is the same as in another culture.
    c. employ stereotyping when studying another culture.
    d. being politically insensitive to the findings of one's research.

2. A field of study concerned with examining the economy and customs of a cultural unit as a whole is termed:

    a. cultural psychology.
    b. cross-cultural psychology.
    c. cultural anthropology.
    d. comparative psychology.

3. Abdul is an exchange student from Iran. If you are meeting him for the first time and he is speaking to you he is most likely to stand at a distance:

    a. very close to you and uncomfortable for you.
    b. which is comfortable for you and is what you usually experience.
    c. slightly closer than what you usually experience, but still comfortable for you.
    d. very far away from you, across the room.

4. You are visiting Japan and meet the Japanese family you are staying with for the first time. You bow politely and look at them "straight in the eye." They are likely to think that your eye contact is:

    a. rude
    b. indicative of character.
    c. respectful.
    d. indicative of ambivalence.

5. The Japanese family you are staying with would be likely to react to your direct eye contact by:

    a. looking frightened.
    b. scowling.
    c. maintaining a neutral expression.
    d. smiling.

6. In Germany and America, people pay more attention to what is said rather than nonverbal signals. This is characteristic of _____ cultures.

    a.   monochronic
    b.   high-context
    c.   low-context
    d.   ethnocentric

7. Which of the following characteristics best describes people from monochronic cultures?

    a.   they do many things at once.
    b.   they develop many long-term relationships.
    c.   they emphasize promptness.
    d.   they give people first priority.

8. You are visiting your friend Maria in South America. You ask her to meet you at a local cafe in one hour. When she arrives one hour late you are very upset but she acts as if her behavior is quite normal. Maria is from a _____ culture.

    a.   polychrnoic
    b.   monochronic
    c.   ethnocentric
    d.   low-context

9. Wendy is extremely upset that her roommate borrowed her CD player without asking her. Wendy is likely to be from a _____ culture.

    a.   high-context
    b.   polychronic
    c.   monochronic
    d.   marginal

10. Sarah is a young college student from Kuwait. She finds it difficult to understand why American students are always worried about getting appointments to see their professors immediately. She sees nothing wrong with waiting even a week to see a professor. Sarah's attitudes reflect those of a _____ culture.

    a.   low-context
    b.   polychronic
    c.   monochronic
    d.   ethnocentric

11. Monochronic ways of organizing time are more likely to occur in societies that are:

    a. hunter-gatherer.
    b. agriculturally-based.
    c. suburban.
    d. industrialized.

12. In collectivistic societies, people tend to complete the phrase, "I am a..." as follows:

    a. part of my religious group.
    b. star athlete.
    c. good student.
    d. nice person.

13. Japanese people are more likely to report that their sense of self:

    a. is based mainly on their occupation and personality.
    b. is based on a stable, core identity.
    c. changes depending on the situation.
    d. is highly distinguishable from that of family members.

14. A sense of who one is, based on nationality, ethnicity, religion, and social roles is referred to as a _____ identity.

    a. personal
    b. acculturated
    c. social
    d. ethnocentric

15. Patrick wears a "Kiss me I'm Irish" button, attends Irish folk festivals, maintains some Irish traditions in his family, and is generally proud of his cultural heritage. He also loves being American. Patrick's ethnic identity is best described as:

    a. bicultural.
    b. assimilated.
    c. separatist.
    d. marginal.

16. Ivan has lived in the United States for many years, but yet still only speaks Russian. He follows the customs of his country of origin and does not vote or participate in local community events. Ivan's ethnic identity can be best described as:

    a. bicultural.
    b. assimilated.
    c. separatist.
    d. marginal.

17. Tristan's ethnic background is German, but has no awareness of German customs, language, or culture. On the other hand, Tristan is proud to be an American and is heavily involved in his community and local politics. Tristan's ethnic identity is best described as:

    a. bicultural.
    b. assimilated.
    c. separatist.
    d. marginal.

18. John feels that he is an individualist who wants to live peacefully in his own cabin in the woods without interference from or ties to anyone or any group. John's ethnic identity is best described as:

    a. bicultural.
    b. assimilated.
    c. separatist.
    d. marginal.

19. Cross-cultural research on Jean Piaget's theory has generally found:

    a. a lack of support for the entire theory.
    b. support for the hierarchical sequence at different rates.
    c. support for the hierarchical sequence of cognitive stages at the same rate.
    d. a lack of support for the first stage.

20. Harold Stevenson's cross-cultural study of American and Asian attitudes towards achievement found that:

    a.   Americans and Asians both believe math ability is innate.
    b.   Asian students valued education and were more devoted to study than Americans.
    c.   Americans parents had higher standards for their children's performance than Asian parents.
    d.   Americans were less likely to find school stressful than Asians.

21. Shirley Brice Heath's study of African-American child and parent verbal interactions in a southern city in the United States found that parents are more likely to ask _____ questions.

    a.   "What?"
    b.   "Where?"
    c.   "Who?"
    d.   "What's that like?"

22. Studies of African-American high-school students indicate that academic achievement is often correlated with:

    a.   high feelings of self-efficacy, and feelings of anxiety and depression.
    b.   strong peer group support and high feelings of self-efficacy.
    c.   a strong ethnic identity and harmony with one's peers.
    d.   high feelings of self-efficacy and tranquility.

23. Until the late 1800s, in many Plains Indians tribes, if a boy wanted to live the life of a woman he was:

    a.   ostracized from the tribe and sent away.
    b.   given honored status as a spiritual healer.
    c.   shamed into changing his ambition and becoming a warrior.
    d.   thought of as "crazy" and tolerated as a low status person.

24. In the Sambian society of Papua New Guinea, if a parent discovered his/her adolescent boy engaged in oral sex with an older male, they would probably react by:

    a.   calling the police.
    b.   being happy that he demonstrated his manhood.
    c.   realizing he wants to live as a woman.
    d.   sending him to a shaman for healing.

25. The belief that one's own culture and ethnic group is superior to all others is termed:

    a.   scapegoating.
    b.   prejudice.
    c.   stereotyping.
    d.   ethnocentrism.

26. Cross-cultural studies examining commonalities in gender behavior have found that:

    a.   the status of women is uniformly low.
    b.   in all cultures men are less emotional than women.
    c.   men and women universally regard each other as different.
    d.   "men's" and "women's" work can vary across cultures.

27. Southern regions of the United States have higher rates of white homicide than the rest of the country because of:

    a.   poverty.
    b.   cultural beliefs.
    c.   racial tensions.
    d.   the tradition of slavery.

28. Psychologists who have studied prejudice have found that:

    a.   prejudice toward other groups is simply part of human nature and is inevitable.
    b.   the greatest prejudice occurs when groups must cooperate with each other.
    c.   there is little relationship between economic conditions and prejudice.
    d.   prejudice is an unconscious defense mechanism that reduces anxiety.

29. Surveys find that African-Americans as compared to white Americans are more likely to place the highest value on:

    a.   individualism.
    b.   self-reliance.
    c.   justice.
    d.   legalism.

30. Prejudice in a culture will vary in degree over time. Under what conditions is prejudice within a culture likely to increase?

    a.   poor economic conditions.
    b.   increase in leisure time.
    c.   integration of political leadership.
    d.   efforts to eliminate stereotypes in the media.

TRUE FALSE SELF-TEST

T   F   1.   Culture can affect biological processes such as eating habits.

T   F   2.   Cultural pressures can conflict directly with biological dispositions.

T   F   3.   Anorexia nervosa involves bingeing on food and then purging it.

T   F   4.   Some cultural differences can be measured indirectly, by drawing data from collective behavior.

T   F   5.   The study of culture rests on the assumption that all members of a culture behave in the same way.

T   F   6.   Reification of the concept of culture involves the use of circular reasoning.

T   F   7.   Americans smile more than Japanese in order to disguise negative emotions.

T   F   8.   Most aspects of body language are specific to particular verbal languages and cultures.

T   F   9.   In many Asian cultures, "looking someone in the eye" is a sign of disrespect.

T   F   10.   High-context cultures are generally heterogeneous and individualistic.

T   F   11.   Low-context cultures pay more attention to nonverbal signals than words.

T   F   12.   Polychronic cultures usually have industrially based economies.

T   F   13.   Monochronic people are typically low-context.

T   F   14.   Polychronic cultures tend to give the job rather than people the first priority.

T   F   15.   Monochronic cultures tend to emphasize promptness.

T   F   16.   Americans are more likely to change their sense of self in different situations as compared to Japanese.

T   F   17.   In some collectivist cultures, the strongest human bond is between parent and child rather than husband and wife.

T   F   18.   Friendships develop slowly in collectivistic cultures.

T   F   19.   Bicultural people typically have weak ethnic identities.

T   F   20.   Cultures differ in terms of which human intellectual capacities are emphasized.

T   F   21.   Asians are more likely than Americans to believe that mathematical skills are the result of hard work.

T   F   22.   Chinese students typically perform better than American students do on tests of mathematical achievement because the Chinese have better facilities and smaller class sizes than Americans do.

T   F   23.   American students have more stressful, conflicting demands on their time as compared to Asian students.

T   F   24.   In general, studies have demonstrated that while African-American students who have attained high academic achievement have a high sense of self-efficacy, they also have feelings of anxiety and depression.

T   F   25.   Social constructionism is the view that there are universal truths about human nature.

T   F   26.   The status of women worldwide is uniformly low.

T   F   27.   The content of "men's work" and "women's work" varies from culture to culture.

T   F   28.   In some cultures, men are considered the "emotional" sex.

T   F   29.   In some cultures, women are expected to have sex before marriage.

T   F   30.   Stereotypes often contain a "grain of truth."

KEY TERMS

culture - A program of shared rules that govern the behavior of members of a community or society, and a set of values, beliefs, and attitudes shared by most members of that community.

high-context cultures - Cultures in which people pay close attention to nonverbal forms of communication and assume a shared context for their interactions -- a common history and set of attitudes.

low-context cultures - Cultures in which people do not take a shred context for granted and instead emphasize direct verbal communication.

monochronic cultures - Cultures in which time is organized sequentially; schedules and deadlines are valued over people.

polychronic cultures - Cultures in which time is organized horizontally; people tend to do several things at once and value relationships over schedules.

social identity - The part of a person's self-concept that is based on his or her identification with a nation, culture, or ethnic group or with gender or other roles in society.

ethnic identity - Having a close identification with one's own racial, religious, or ethnic group.

acculturation - The process by which members of groups that are minorities in a given society come to identify with and feel part of the mainstream culture.

social constructionism - The view that there are no universal truths about human nature, because people construct reality differently depending on their culture, the historical moment, and degree of power within their society.

ethnocentrism - The belief that one's own ethnic group, nation, or religion is superior to all others.

stereotype - A cognitive schema or a summary impression of a group, in which a person believes that all members of the group share a common trait or traits positive, negative, or neutral.

Suggested Research Projects

1. If you live in a large, culturally diverse city, visit several ethnic restaurants and observe the variations in gendered work roles. Do men, women, or both wait on tables, work in the kitchen, seat customers, clean up, etc. How many people who appear to be from outside of the ethnic group work at the restaurant? What conclusions can you tentatively draw from your observations?

2. Construct some scenarios about specific behaviors and ask people to judge the behaviors you describe. For example, you might describe a person's behavior in a certain situation and ask people to estimate the person's level of mental health, intelligence, morality, responsibility for his or her actions. Vary the race, ethnicity, or sex of the person in the story. Do you get different judgements, for instance, about an Asian who does poorly in math compared to a Latino who has the same problem, or about a woman who cries as the result of work pressure compared with a man who reacts the same way?

Suggested Readings

Gilmore, D.D. (1990). Manhood in the Making: Cultural Concepts of Masculinity. New Haven, CT: Yale University Press. In an anthropological study of the social construction of masculinity in several different cultures, Gilmore concludes that masculinity is associated with a culture's experience of war and competition for scarce resources.

Hochschild, A. (1989). The Second Shift. New York: Avon. The author summarizes research on the sharing of domestic tasks in dual-earner households, and concludes that wives still do significantly more domestic work than their husbands.

Matsumoto, D. (1996). Culture and Psychology. Pacific Grove, California: Brooks/Cole Publishing Company. The author examines cross-cultural psychological research and provides readers with the knowledge and skills necessary to interact in a multicultural world.

Suggested Audio-Visuals

In My Country: An International Perspective on Gender. (1993). This two volume series examines diverse cultural attitudes related to gender.

CHAPTER 13

ANSWERS TO CHAPTER SUMMARY

1. culture
2. cross-cultural
3. anthropology
4. equivalence
5. stereotype
6. circular
7. body language
8. conversational distance
9. high-context
10. low-context
11. monochronic
12. polychronic
13. collectivist
14. social
15. ethnic
16. acculturation
17. bicultural
18. assimilation
19. ethnic separatists
20. marginal
21. deductively
22. innate
23. constructist
24. ethnocentrism
25. stereotyping
26. selective perception
27. prejudiced
28. economic
29. scapegoating
30. symbolic racism

ANSWERS TO MULTIPLE CHOICE SELF-TEST

1. A
2. C
3. A
4. A
5. D
6. C

7.	C
8.	A
9.	C
10.	B
11.	D
12.	A
13.	C
14.	C
15.	A
16.	C
17.	B
18.	D
19.	B
20.	B
21.	D
22.	A
23.	A
24.	B
25.	D
26.	D
27.	B
28.	D
29.	B
30.	A

ANSWER TO TRUE FALSE SELF-TEST

1.	T
2.	T
3.	F
4.	T
5.	F
6.	T
7.	F
8.	T
9.	T
10.	F
11.	F
12.	F
13.	T
14.	F
15.	T
16.	F
17.	T

18. T
19. F
20. T
21. T
22. F
23. T
24. T
25. F
26. F
27. T
28. T
29. T
30. T

CHAPTER 14

EVALUATING THE SOCIOCULTURAL PERSPECTIVE

LEARNING OBJECTIVES

After reading and studying this chapter, you should be able to:

1. Discuss the impact of the sociocultural perspective on the field of psychology, as well as misinterpretations and misuses of the perspective, including sociocultural reductionism, stereotyping, extreme cultural relativism, and heightened ethnocentrism.

2. Discuss the implications of the sociocultural perspective for the issue of IQ testing.

3. Discuss contributions of the sociocultural perspective to the practice of psychotherapy.

4. Discuss insights from the sociocultural perspective on the factors necessary for reducing prejudice.

CHAPTER 14 OUTLINE

I. Contributions and Misuses of The Sociocultural Perspective.
    A. Major contributions of this perspective include:
        1. the recognition of the importance of social and cultural context, which poses a challenge to the absolutist position that there are universal laws of behavior that apply to human beings everywhere.
        2. findings that make psychology more scientific, encompassing, and relevant to the problems of social life and that emphasize the importance of culture in every domain of psychological research.
    B. The sociocultural perspective can be misused in a number of ways:
        1. Sociocultural reductionism is the tendency to reduce all the complexities of human behavior to the single factor of culture or society.
        2. Stereotyping may occur when people exaggerate differences between groups and overlook variation within them.
        3. Extreme cultural relativism may occur when people misread the sociocultural perspective and excuse cultural practices that are abusive and cause suffering.
        4. Heightened ethnocentrism may occur if old biases are merely replaced with new ones, or if sociocultural findings are used to argue for ethnic, societal, or gender separatism.

II. Issue #1: IQ Testing
    A. Sociocultural findings have enormous implications for educational policy and the intelligence test industry.
    B. Traditional intelligence tests favored urban, middle-class, white children.
    C. Culture affects test-taking attitude and approach.
    D. Schools reflect mainstream values, and so IQ tests measure skills useful in school.
        1. Assimilated people value the tests.
        2. People with strong ethnic identity want schools to accommodate their children.
    E. The sociocultural perspective has encouraged researchers to abandon a "deficit" model for a difference model of intelligence.
    F. The resolution of the IQ-test debate may depend on whether the tests are used more intelligently than in the past.

III. Issue #2: Social and Cultural Factors in Psychology
    A. Sociocultural approaches to psychotherapy treat the individual as embedded in a social and cultural context.
    B. Therapists working in a family-systems perspective view an individual's problems in the context of family relationships and focus on producing change by bringing about changes in the family system.

C.   Culture influences which behaviors therapists and others regard as normal and abnormal.
D.   Cultural differences can lead to misunderstandings between therapist and client.
E.   Therapists need to distinguish normal cultural patterns from individual psychological problems.
F.   American cultural beliefs about people include three myths that increase dissatisfaction:
    1.   people should always be happy.
    2.   change is always possible.
    3.   change is easy.

IV.   Issue #3: Reducing Prejudice
    A.   Traditionally proposed solutions include:
        1.   educating and building self-esteem in prejudiced persons.
        2.   bringing members of different groups together (the "contact hypothesis").
    B.   Approaches based on the individual have not been very successful.
    C.   Necessary conditions for reduction of prejudice (all must be present) include:
        1.   a cooperative environment.
        2.   equal status and economic standing among groups.
        3.   support of people in authority.
        4.   opportunities to work and socialize together.

CHAPTER 14 SUMMARY

The sociocultural perspective teaches us that behavior occurs in a social, historical, and cultural context. This lesson is affecting every domain of psychological research. For example, sociocultural findings have persuaded many developmental psychologists that certain "milestones" of infant development are culture-specific. Likewise, because of sociocultural studies, most developmental psychologists have abandoned the attempt to identify universal stages of adult development.

However, there are some concerns about the potential misinterpretation and misuse of sociocultural findings. First, there is the danger of sociocultural 1._____, the tendency to view behaviors as caused only by sociocultural and situational forces and to lose sight of the part played by the individual. A second concern is that this kind of research may encourage 2._____, the tendency to see all members of a culture as being alike. Sociocultural researchers must be especially careful to avoid this trap, as their expectations can affect their own perceptions. Third, there is the danger of extreme cultural 3._____, the view that all culturally influenced behaviors must be viewed nonjudgmentally, even when they are harmful and cause suffering. Finally, sociocultural discourse may unintentionally encourage heightened 4._____, the view that one's cultural group is better than others.

Despite these concerns, it is clear that the sociocultural perspective has provided valuable insights in many important areas. IQ testing is one. Historically, these tests have favored urban, middle-class people of ethnic majorities. Sociocultural research has demonstrated that cultural values have an important impact on test-taking approaches and on the kinds of skills that are considered valuable within a community. For example, the degree of acculturation has an effect on the approach to learning and testing. Highly 5._____ people want to join the system, and therefore they are more likely to value traditional IQ tests and the abilities they measure. On the other hand, groups with strong ethnic identities want educational systems to accommodate their cultural learning styles. The sociocultural perspective has encouraged people to abandon the 6._____ model of intelligence and see people as different, but not necessarily deficient.

Sociocultural work has also had important effects on the world of psychotherapy. It has encouraged therapists to consider social and cultural contexts when treating individuals. From the 7._____ systems perspective, a person's family situation has as much to do with behavior as does the person's individual personality, and therefore therapeutic approaches should address this system. It is important for therapists to understand clients' cultures in order to avoid misunderstandings, and distinguish cultural differences from psychopathology. American values, which emphasize individual happiness and promote the idea that behavior change is easy, are not necessarily those of other cultures.

A third issue illuminated by sociocultural research is the reduction of prejudice. In the past, a number of solutions to the problem of prejudice have been attempted, with varying degrees of success. Solutions that are individually focused and those involving desegregation or cooperative learning as the only intervention have not been highly successful. Changes in laws have been helpful in reducing injustices but not necessarily in changing attitudes.

Sociocultural research has, however, identified a group of conditions that together have an effect in reducing prejudice. These include cooperation among groups, equal status and economic standing among groups, opportunities for members of different groups to work and socialize with one another, and the support of people in authority. Some employment and educational organizations are now attempting to create these conditions.

MULTIPLE CHOICE SELF-TEST

1. The sociocultural perspective has contributed to psychology by showing that:

    a. reinforcement history is the most important determinant of human behavior.
    b. biology is the most important determinant of human behavior.
    c. there may be fewer than anticipated laws of behavior that apply to all human beings.
    d. the idea of cultural absolutism is essentially a correct one.

2. The assumption of traditional psychology is that fundamental laws of behavior apply to all people everywhere at all times. This assumption can be categorized as:

    a. relativistic.
    b. overcontextual.
    c. absolutist.
    d. diversified.

3. The separation of adolescents from their parents takes on greater importance in societies that value:

    a. extended families.
    b. male independence.
    c. filial piety.
    d. polychronic time structures.

4. Contemporary research on adult development indicates that:

    a. people generally follow consistent and predictable stages for most life events.
    b. many people change careers or jobs, and the timing of marriage and family are less predictable.
    c. there are inevitable "passages" from adolescence to adulthood for marriage and family, but NOT for career or job choice.
    d. a consideration of generational effects or differences is inappropriate.

5. The milestone of infant development in which babies sleep eight uninterrupted hours at night is most likely to occur in cultures where:

    a. babies sleep apart from parents in their own crib.
    b. mothers nurse their children throughout the night.
    c. there are many extended family members living in the same dwelling.
    d. there are polychronic time arrangements.

6. Contemporary research on adolescence indicates that:

    a. an adolescent's failure to separate from parents is psychologically unhealthy.

    b. turmoil between parents and children is inevitable.

    c. an adolescent's quarrels with parents often signify a change to a more reciprocal adult relationship.

    d. close attachment can happen between adolescent and parent, but it is rare.

7. Ellen is an unwed teenage mother of two, who blames all her problems on society. Her thinking reflects:

    a. sociocultural reductionism.

    b. biological reductionism.

    c. cultural relativism.

    d. cultural absolutism.

8. In some cultures, pubescent males must undergo painful circumcision as a passage to manhood. Debra reads about this practice and views it as acceptable since it is culturally based. Her thinking reflects:

    a. cultural absolutism.

    b. biological reductionism.

    c. stereotyping.

    d. sociocultural relativism.

9. Research on gender differences indicates that:

    a. men are more likely than women to regard attachment as a source of danger and threat.

    b. both men and women can be nurturant and aggressive.

    c. masculinity is universally equated with a need for power and toughness.

    d. average gender differences are good indicators of individual behavior.

10. In some African and Middle Eastern countries, girls are subjected to removal of the clitoris and all or part of the labia. This practice is termed:

    a. circumcision.

    b. excision.

    c. infibulation.

    d. psychosurgery.

11. A professor teaches that Asians are the naturally "reflective, spiritual" people while, whites are the "impulsive, decadent" people. This thinking reflects:

    a.   ethnocentrism.
    b.   dialectical reasoning.
    c.   cultural relativism.
    d.   biculturalism.

12. Traditional IQ tests favored children who were:

    a.   urban, middle-class, and white.
    b.   rural, middle-class, and white.
    c.   urban and minority.
    d.   rural and minority.

13. Suppose you meet a psychologist who believes that cultures are so different from one another that they can only be judged on their own terms. This person would be called a(n):

    a.   minimalist.
    b.   relativist.
    c.   reductionist.
    d.   absolutist.

14. Intelligence tests that attempt to incorporate knowledge and skills that are common to many cultures are characterized as being:

    a.   culture fair.
    b.   culture free.
    c.   culture saturated.
    d.   culture dominant.

15. The sociocultural approach has influenced researchers to question the:

    a.   deficit model of intelligence testing.
    b.   use of intelligence testing for research purposes.
    c.   triarchic theory of intelligence.
    d.   multiple theory of intelligence.

16. The first intelligence test was developed by Alfred Binet in order to:

    a.   identify fast learners so they could benefit from an enriched environment.
    b.   sort and track people according to natural ability.
    c.   identify slow learners who could benefit from remedial attention.
    d.   help teachers make subjective judgements of student potential.

17. When Americans first used Binet's intelligence test, they used it mainly to:

    a.   provide special assistance for disadvantaged children.
    b.   track people according to natural ability.
    c.   identify high ability minority students.
    d.   identify individual strengths and weaknesses.

18. People from many non-Western cultures, or people who are unschooled, tend to classify objects according to:

    a.   category.
    b.   function.
    c.   size.
    d.   appearance.

19. Family therapists believe most individual problems originate from:

    a.   within the individual.
    b.   genetic predispositions.
    c.   irrational beliefs.
    d.   the individual's social setting.

20. Family therapists are most likely to attempt to help individuals with their problems by:

    a.   focusing their investigation on the individual's internal conflicts.
    b.   determining each family member's reinforcement histories.
    c.   observing the family to discover imbalances in power and communication.
    d.   focusing on the one "problem" family member.

21. In the Chinese and Hopi culture, during the grieving process, hallucinations are regarded as:

    a.   a sign of a serious psychotic breakdown.
    b.   indicative of a personality disorder.
    c.   normal and acceptable.
    d.   indicative of neurosis.

22. In Latino cultures, a normal response to a catastrophic stress may include an episode of screaming, crying, fainting, and agitation. This is termed:

    a.   el triste.
    b.   el cuento.
    c.   los locos.
    d.   ataque de nervios.

23. Toan comes from a culture that believes that the parent-child bond is the most important relationship. Toan expresses the idea to her therapist that she will live with her parents until they die. This response can be considered:

    a.   culturally determined.
    b.   the result of irrational belief.
    c.   abnormal.
    d.   biologically determined.

24. One early theory proposed that the way to reduce prejudice is to bring members of two groups together to discover their shared humanity. This approach is based on the _____ hypothesis.

    a.   cooperation
    b.   similarity
    c.   acculturation
    d.   contact

25. Devine and her associates suggest that prejudice can be overcome by:

    a.   mere social contact.
    b.   legal restrictions against prejudice and discrimination.
    c.   providing prejudiced individuals with cooperative tasks.
    d.   understanding and breaking the cycle of mistrust between individuals.

TRUE FALSE SELF-TEST

T   F   1.   The sociocultural perspective assumes that it is possible to find universal laws of behavior that apply to all people everywhere.

T   F   2.   In some cultures the time span between puberty and adulthood is only a few months.

T   F   3.   Children who maintain close bonds with parents as adolescents are immature and dependent.

T   F   4.   Culture is the one best single explanation of human behavior.

T   F   5.   Research has confirmed that men are more likely than women to regard attachment as a sign of danger and threat.

T   F   6.   Men are more likely to behave aggressively than women.

T   F   7.   Research supports the idea that the vast majority of men are aggressive and very few women are aggressive.

T   F   8.   The relativist position concludes that there are universal truths and a common human nature.

T   F   9.   In more than 25 countries throughout Africa, the Middle East, and Indonesia, girls are subjected to genital mutilation to ensure chastity and marital fidelity.

T   F   10. The African slave trade was developed by Arab traders with the collaboration of black African traders.

T   F   11. Intelligence tests, developed between World War I and the 1960s, favor rural children over city children.

T   F   12. Test scores derived from tests that are considered to be "culture-free" are still affected by culture.

T   F   13. In early versions of IQ tests, girls scored higher than boys at every age.

T   F   14. IQ tests are poor predictors of success in school.

T   F   15. Alfred Binet, the developer of the first IQ test, aimed to develop an impartial test so that poor children would not be unfairly judged.

T   F   16.   Family therapists believe that most adjustment problems originate in an individual's biological makeup.

T   F   17.   In some cultures, experiencing hallucinations of deceased loved ones are thought to be normal expressions of grief.

T   F   18.   Latino and Asian psychotherapy clients are more likely to react to a formal therapy interview with passivity, deference, and silence.

T   F   19.   Susto, or "loss of the soul," as a response to extreme grief or fright is a sign of pathology in Latin American culture.

T   F   20.   A person will do poorly in therapy unless the therapist and client are matched according to ethnicity.

T   F   21.   Eastern cultures tend to believe that change is easy and almost any change is possible.

T   F   22.   In the Japanese practice of Morita therapy, clients are taught how to eradicate their most troubling emotions.

T   F   23.   Solutions to prejudice that focus on individual change have been very successful.

T   F   24.   People who lack prejudiced feelings may behave in discriminatory and prejudiced ways.

T   F   25.   In the "jigsaw method," students compete against each other in the classroom.

T   F   26.   Research indicates that improving relations between minority and majority group members is mainly a "majority group problem."

T   F   27.   Reduction in power differences and greater economic equality tends to reduce prejudice.

T   F   28.   Informal socialization is important in reducing prejudice.

T   F   29.   Improving social contact alone has been a universally successful way of reducing prejudice.

T   F   30.   Even with legal reforms, de facto segregation of schools and neighborhoods is still common in the United States.

Suggested Research Projects

1.   Discuss your own unique family culture with your siblings (if you have any). What is coinsidered "normal" and "abnormal" within your own family? How would an outsider evaluate the "normal" and "abnormal" behavior?

Suggested Readings

Gilman, S. L. (1985). <u>Difference and Pathology: Stereotypes of Sexuality, Race, and Madness</u>. Ithaca, NY: Cornell University Press. Presents the view that human beings create sterotypes as a means of dealing with anxiety and lack of control over the environment.

Sternberg, R. (1996). <u>Successful Intelligence: How Practical and Creative Intelligence Determine Success in Life</u>. NewYork: Simon & Schuster. One of the foremost experts on intelligence examines why creative and practical intelligence rather than IQ are the best predictors of success in life.

CHAPTER 14

ANSWERS TO CHAPTER SUMMARY

1.   reductionism
2.   stereotyping
3.   relativism
4.   ethnocentrism
5.   assimilated
6.   deficit
7.   family

ANSWERS TO MULTIPLE CHOICE SELF-TEST
1.   C
2.   C
3.   B
4.   B
5.   A
6.   C
7.   A
8.   D
9.   B
10.   B
11.   A
12.   A
13.   B

14. A
15. A
16. C
17. B
18. B
19. D
20. C
21. C
22. D
23. A
24. D
25. D

ANSWERS TO TRUE-FALSE SELF-TEST

1. F
2. T
3. F
4. F
5. F
6. T
7. F
8. F
9. T
10. T
11. F
12. T
13. T
14. F
15. T
16. F
17. T
18. T
19. F
20. F
21. F
22. F
23. F
24. T
25. F
26. F
27. T
28. T
29. F
30. T

CHAPTER 15

THE INNER LIFE

LEARNING OBJECTIVES

After reading and studying this chapter, you should be able to:

1. Describe the main elements of psychodynamic psychology.

2. Summarize Freud's theory of psychoanalysis, including his ideas about the structure of personality, defense mechanisms, and stages in the development of personality.

3. Explain similarities and differences in the theories of Freud, Horney, Adler, Jung, Erikson, the object-relations school, and existential psychology.

4. Describe the goals, methods, and processes of psychoanalytic psychotherapy.

5. Discuss the controversies surrounding psychodynamic psychology and criticisms by researchers from other perspectives.

CHAPTER 15 OUTLINE

I.   Introduction
      A.   This perspective attempts to account for the emotional pain and longing that are part of the human experience.
      B.   More than any other psychological perspective, the psychodynamic perspective is embedded in popular culture.
      C.   The first psychodynamic theory of personality was Sigmund Freud's theory of **psychoanalysis**; it had worldwide influence.
      D.   The major psychodynamic theories share five elements:
            1.   an emphasis on unconscious **intrapsychic** dynamics, the movement of psychic forces within the mind.
            2.   an assumption that adult behavior and ongoing problems are determined primarily by experiences in early childhood.
            3.   a belief that psychological development occurs in fixed stages.
            4.   a focus on fantasies and the symbolic meaning of events; a person's <u>psychic reality</u>.
            5.   a reliance on subjective rather than objective methods of getting at the truth.

II.   Freud and Psychoanalysis
      A.   There are differing viewpoints regarding the significance of Freud's work:
            1.   some believe Freud was one of the great intellectual geniuses of history.
            2.   the most common view among psychiatrists and clinical psychologists is that some of Freud's ideas have lasting value and others are incorrect.
            3.   Others, including most scientists and psychologists in other perspectives, believe Freud was a poor scientist and an unethical therapist.
      B.   In Freud's theory, the prime motives affecting behavior are unconscious and instinctual, and the most important of these are sexual and aggressive.
      C.   The Structure of Personality
            1.   The personality is a system of three components, which a person must constantly struggle to keep in balance:
                  a.   the **id** is the reservoir of instinctual drives.
                        1.   The id operates according to the **pleasure principle**, which seeks to avoid pain and obtain pleasure.
                        2.   The id is not concerned with objective reality and is not affected by environment, culture, or learning.
                        3.   The id is fueled by the **libido**, psychic energy.
                        4.   The id contains two competing instincts:
                              a.   life, sexual.
                              b.   death, aggressive.

b. The **ego** represents reason and good sense and is the mediator between instinct and social demands.
    1. The ego obeys the **reality principle**, which takes into account objective reality and delays the gratification of the id until a suitable outlet can be found.

c. The **superego** represents internalized social rules and demands. It consists of the:
    1. ego ideal, moral and social standards.
    2. conscience, the inner voice responsible for guilt.

2. **Defense mechanisms** have the following characteristics:
  a. they reduce the anxiety that accompanies threats to the ego
  b. they also distort reality.
  c. they operate unconsciously.

3. Defense mechanisms include:
  a. repression - blocking of threatening material from consciousness.
  b. projection - attribution of one's unacceptable feelings to someone else.
    1. A familiar target of projection is the scapegoat - a powerless person or group that is blamed for a problem by individuals who feel insecure or threatened.
  c. reaction formation - transformation of an uncomfortable feeling into its opposite.
  d. regression - a return to a less mature level of emotional functioning.
  e. denial - refusal to admit that an unpleasant feeling or experience is occurring.
  f. intellectualization - the control of emotions by overdependence on rational or philosophical explanations.
  g. displacement - redirection of emotion to other targets (or in sublimation, to culturally or socially useful purposes).
  h. acting out - behaving impulsively in reaction to unconscious feelings.
  I. humor - used to defend against fear or other uncomfortable feelings.

3. Neurosis is the result of unhealthy attempts to defend against anxiety.

D. The Development of Personality
1. According to Freud, personality development occurs in predictable stages, which are the result of the changing expression of sexual energy in different parts of the body. Each stage (except for latency) involves a conflict, and poorly resolved conflicts result in fixation, which causes neurosis.

a. The <u>oral stage</u> occurs in the first 12 to 18 months of life, when the mouth is the focus of sensation. Problems occurring in this stage later result in the adult's constant seeking of oral gratification.

b. The <u>anal stage</u> occurs at about ages to 3, when the major issue is the control of bodily waste and the child must first respond to demands of reality. Fixation in this stage may result in obsessive neatness and cleanliness (and <u>anal retentiveness</u>) or messiness and disorganization (<u>anal expulsiveness</u>).

c. The <u>Oedipal (or phallic) stage</u> lasts from ages 3 to 6, when sexual energy is concentrated in the penis for boys and the clitoris for girls. Development in this stage involves:

1. the **Oedipus complex**, a desire for the other-sex parent and rivalry with the same sex parent.

2. **castration anxiety** in boys which occurs from the unconscious sense that females are males who have been castrated, and the consequent fear that their fathers will castrate them. Castration anxiety causes the boy to repress his desire for his mother and identify with his father. This is the beginning of superego development. (Note: Freud used the term <u>castration</u> to refer to loss of the penis; in modern medical terms it means removal of the testes).

3. <u>penis envy</u> in girls, which is expressed in adulthood as a desire for children.

d. The <u>latency stage</u> lasts from about age 6 until puberty. In this stage the child concentrates on learning skills and social rules. Memories from earlier stages have been repressed.

e. The <u>genital stage</u> starts at puberty, when mature sexual identity begins to develop.

E. The Talking Cure

1. Psychoanalysis as an approach to psychotherapy is aimed at inducing <u>insight</u> (the conscious awareness of unconscious conflicts) in order to cure neuroses. Techniques of psychoanalysis include:

a. **Free association** - saying whatever comes to mind.

b. **Transference** - the displacement of emotional elements of the patient's life, usually feelings about the parents, outward onto the therapist.

2. Freud's psychoanalysis established two key assumptions that still guide psychodynamic therapists today:

a. that conscious memories and perceptions are not as important in affecting behavior as unconscious dynamics.

        b.   that what actually happened in a person's past is not as important as that person's "psychic reality," how the unconscious has interpreted that experience.

    3.   Freud's development of psychoanalysis emerged from his work with relatively few patients, and these cases are still a source of controversy, as is Freud himself.

    4.   Freud rejected the idea that patients were reporting real events of sexual molestation, and instead considered them "fantasies".

III. Early Dissenters

A. Karen Horney

1. Horney challenged Freud's ideas about women. She argued that:
   a. when women feel inferior to men, it is because it is because they are socially subordinated to men, not because of some perceived anatomical defect.
   b. men suffer from "womb envy," jealousy of women's ability to bear children.
   c. men may unconsciously fear women's sexual power over them, and castration anxiety may be an expression of this fear.
2. According to Horney, the driving force in personality is **basic anxiety**, the feeling of being helpless and isolated in a hostile world. People cope with basic anxiety by:
   a. moving toward others
   b. moving against others
   c. moving away from others.
3. Images of the <u>ideal self</u>, an image of what a person would like to be affects a person's aspirations and actions. Modern researchers have expanded this concept to include <u>possible selves</u>, images of what you believe you could become and would like to be.

B. Alfred Adler

1. Adler had a more positive view of human nature than Freud. He believed that:
   a. the prime motive in human behavior is a <u>drive for superiority</u> (self-improvement and perfection).
   b. some people develop an **inferiority complex**, an inability to accept one's natural limitations, when their parents fail to encourage their abilities.
   c. a person's personality structure is expressed in a unique style of life.
2. According to Adler, the healthy personality is characterized by <u>social interest</u> (i.e., empathy and concern for others). This notion has been supported by modern research.

3.   Adler believed that the essence of human personality is the <u>creative self</u>, the personality each person creates from heredity and experience. The resulting personality is expressed in a unique <u>style of life</u>.

C.   Carl Jung

1.   Jung emphasized the strengths of the ego.

2.   He believed that the prime motive in behavior is the desire to fulfill oneself.

3.   Jung argued that in addition to a personal unconscious, there is a **collective unconscious**, containing the universal memories and experiences of humankind.

    a.   The collective unconscious can be understood by analyzing universal **archetypes**, symbolic images that appear in myths, dreams, art, and folklore.

    b.   Important archetypes include the <u>persona</u> or the public personality, the <u>anima</u> (for men) and <u>animus</u> (for women), the unconscious subpersonality, and the <u>shadow</u> which represents the animal part of human nature.

    c.   Like Freud, Jung was rather disdainful of women but recognized that "masculine" and "feminine" qualities are to be found in both sexes.

IV.   Later Descendants

A.   Erikson's Psychosocial Theory

1.   Erik Erikson believed that psychosocial events are the most important influences on personality development, and that this development continues in stages throughout one's life, each marked by a different crisis. Erikson's 8 stages are:

    a.   <u>trust vs. mistrust</u>, when an infant develops faith that his or her needs can be met.

    b.   <u>autonomy vs. shame and doubt</u>, when a toddler learns to believe in his or her abilities without feeling ashamed.

    c.   <u>initiative vs. guilt</u>, when a child learns to acquire new skills and enjoy new talents while controlling impulses and energies.

    d.   <u>competence vs. inferiority</u>, when a school-age child learns mastery and competence.

    e.   <u>identity vs. role confusion</u>, when an adolescent defines the self and plans for the future.

    f.   <u>intimacy vs. isolation</u>, when young adults learn to commit to others in relationships.

    g.   <u>generativity vs. stagnation</u>, when adults share their work or relationships with younger generations.

    h.   <u>ego integrity vs. despair</u>, when older adults strive to accept their lives and deal with their fear of death.

2. Erikson showed that development is an ongoing process and identified the essential concerns of adulthood, but modern research suggests that his developmental sequence of stages is far from universal.

B. The Object-Relations School

1. The **object-relations school** emphasizes relationships during the first two years of life as the most important determinants of personality.

   a. The child introjects, or internalizes, a perception or representation of the primary caregiver, usually the mother.

   b. The central issue in life is the constantly changing balance between independence and connection to others.

   c. Early development involves **splitting** of the caregiver's qualities into positive and negative opposites, because of an inability to understand that people are made up of good and bad qualities.

      1. Healthy development requires the acceptance of ambivalence about oneself and others.

      2. However, even emotionally healthy people may resort to splitting when threatened or overwhelmed.

   d. In object-relations theory, male identity is more precarious and insecure than female identity because it is based on separating from the mother and being different from women.

      1. Men develop more rigid ego boundaries than women do.

      2. Men's distance from women affects their moral development.

      3. Later in life, the typical problem for women is how to increase their autonomy and independence, whereas the typical problem for men is how to develop attachment.

2. Heinz Kohut, the founder of **self psychology**, believed that the most important parental task is to act as a mirror for the child and help the child develop a cohesive sense of self and protect self-esteem.

V. Existential and Humanistic Psychology

A. Humanistic and existential psychologists approach the study of the individual based on **phenomenology,** which focuses on the persons' subjective interpretation of what is happening right now.

B. Abraham Maslow, Rollo May, and Carl Rogers rejected the psychoanalytic emphasis on hostility and unconscious conflicts.

C. Human nature included peak experiences, rare moments of fulfillment caused by the attainment of excellence of drive towards higher values.

D. Carl Rogers' theory of personality is based on:
  1. the relationship between the <u>self</u> (your conscious view of yourself) and the <u>organism</u> (the sum of all your experiences).
  2. the belief that we need <u>unconditional positive regard</u>, love and support for who we are without conditions to be a fully functioning person. Many children are raised with <u>conditional</u> positive regard.
E. **Existentialists** emphasize:
  1. free will.
  2. individual responsibility for moral decisions.
  3. the struggle to find meaning in life.

VI. The Psychodynamic Paradox
  A. Psychodynamic theorists rely on inference and subjective interpretation, and most psychodynamic assumptions are untestable by the usual methods of research.
  B. However, the psychodynamic perspective is able to provide a coherent framework for describing personality and behavior, and confronts the depths of emotional experience.

CHAPTER 15 SUMMARY

Psychodynamic psychology has several unique features: an emphasis on the study of unconscious intrapsychic dynamics, a focus on the effects of 1._____ experiences in the formation of adult personality, and a concentration on the individual's symbolic and subjective interpretations of events. 2._____ is widely regarded as the father of psychoanalysis. He is thought by some to have been the ultimate psychological thinker, but others view him as misguided or even fraudulent.

Freud believed that humans, like other animals, are driven by sexual and aggressive 3.____, but humans are also raised to be social. As a result, primitive urges are experienced as threatening. They are often hidden from the conscious mind, but they are expressed in symbolic form.

Freud thought of the personality as a system with three components. The 4._____ is the instinctual component; it seeks primitive pleasure. The 5._____ attempts to mediate between the id and social demands, which are represented by the third component, the 6._____. Freud saw human beings as inevitably in the midst of internal conflict, with the ego always trying to stay in control by balancing the opposing demands of the id and superego.

When the ego feels threatened that the id or the superego will overwhelm it, it employs 7. _____, which distort reality and allow the ego to avoid psychological discomfort. These defenses operate unconsciously and function to keep the ego in control, but they can cause emotional problems and self-defeating behavior if they are overused. People tend to develop characteristic styles of defense. When these styles are unhealthy, the person is termed 8. _____. Freud believed that the unconscious was the prime mover in personality. Freud's view was that civilized people and cultures are able to exert control over the demands of the id. Thus, they are able to control primitive, often destructive, forces in healthy ways.

The personality, according to Freud, develops in a sequence of predictable stages, each with its own critical psychological issue. If the characteristic problem of each stage is handled well, the child grows up to be a healthy adult. However, if the crisis is not resolved, 9. _____ occurs, and 10. _____ is the outcome. Freud named these stages 11. _____, 12. _____, 13. _____, and 14. _____, with a period of 15. _____ occurring between the phallic and genital stages. The 16. _____, which occurs during the 17. _____ stage, is one of the most controversial aspects of Freud's theory, as he believed that children experience primitive sexual attractions toward their other-sex parent during this stage. He also thought that males and females progress through this stage differently, a claim that has frequently been contested.

Freud developed this theory of the mind through his interactions with his psychotherapy patients. He invented and developed several psychoanalytic techniques to explore the 18. _____ life of his patients and cure them of their neuroses, including 19. _____ (in which the patient says whatever comes to mind), and 20. _____ (in which the patient displaces emotions onto the therapist). The goal of psychoanalysis is 21. _____, a heightened emotional awareness of childhood conflicts and unconscious dynamics.

Freud came to his conclusions about the Oedipus conflict through analyses of several female patients who reported childhood sexual abuse at the hands of their fathers or male family members and friends. Early in his career he believed their stories, but later he concluded that these accounts of sexual abuse were actually 22. _____. Many historians have pointed out that such abuse was rampant during Freud's time, and that his patients were probably recounting real incidents.

Freud's influence on later psychodynamic thinkers is far-reaching. He established two cornerstones of psychoanalysis: that the unconscious is the prime motivator of behavior, and that a person's subjective interpretations of events are more important than the events themselves. The psychoanalyst learns to read between the lines and to analyze defense mechanisms in order to discover the patient's unconscious motives.

23. _____ was one of the first to challenge Freud's ideas about women. Whereas Freud suggested that females suffer from 24. _____, she argued that it was men's social status that women envied, not their penises. In contrast to Freud, she suggested that men suffer from 25. _____, a feeling of inferiority that results from an inability to give birth. Thus, men unconsciously fear women because of their power.

Horney's theory centers around the person's continuing quest to cope with 26. _____, a feeling of being alone and vulnerable. In order to deal with the discomfort of this anxiety, people adopt strategies such as aggression, dependence, or isolation. Horney termed these strategies 27. _____, 28. _____, and 29. _____, respectively. The healthy person is able to balance all three orientations, whereas the 30. _____ compulsively uses only one style. Horney also believed that, in addition to being affected by the past, we are also influenced by our fantasies of ourselves in the future, as represented by the 31. _____.

32. _____ believed that the prime motivator of behavior is the 33. _____, a desire for self-improvement. This drive is a compensation for the childhood 34. _____, which occurs because children are small and weak compared to adults. Adler thought that the development of 35. _____, that is empathy and concern for others, both reflects and strengthens the healthy personality, and there is a good deal of research to support this notion. According to Adler, a person actively constructs a creative self and develops a unique 36. _____ that allows the person to strive for superiority.

One of the most important aspects of 37. _____'s theory was his conception of the 38. _____, a repository of the universal experiences of the human race. This part of the mind contains 39. _____ (such as the Hero, the Powerful Father, the Shadow, the Persona, and the Nurturing Mother), which predispose people to react in certain ways. Personality development involves experiencing, developing, and integrating the various archetypes.

40. _____ expanded Freud's theory to encompass the development of the personality throughout the entire life span. Unlike Freud, Erikson believed that 41. _____ events, not psychosexual events, were the most important influences on personality. Among these events are the development of childhood independence and achievement, as well as adult identity formation and relationship development. Erikson recognized that cultures function to inhibit or facilitate movement from one psychosocial stage to the next. However, his rigid sequence has been shown to be far from universal.

The 42. _____ school is made up of theorists who emphasize relationships as the central issue in personality development. The most important of these relationships involves the child's emotional attachments and reactions to his or her primary caregiver, usually the mother. During infancy, the child 43. _____, or internalizes, a representation of the parent, and develops a characteristic style of interacting with others and experiencing the self. Early development involves 44. _____, the separation of the mother's qualities into positive and negative opposites. During later development, a person must learn to accept and deal with conflicting and ambivalent feelings about others in order to be psychologically healthy.

Object-relations theorists have been influential in psychodynamic thinking about gender roles. In their view, the fact that the primary caregivers of children are usually mothers results in the development of 45. _____ in girls and the formation of rigid 46. _____, a sense of separateness, in boys. This leads to later conflicts with dependence, independence, and connectedness in adult relationships. Many theorists believe that these conflicts can be eased if fathers became more involved with their children.

47. _____ developed an object-relations theory called 48. _____. He believed that the most important parental task is to appropriately 49. _____ the child. Parents do so by communicating their love, acceptance, and approval to the child. The child is then able to develop self-approval based on this parental approval. The child grows up aware of his or her own power, competence, and value, and solid basis for self-esteem is formed. The unhealthy person must continue to seek approval from others, as he or she has not developed the capacity to provide it for the self.

50. _____ emphasizes the free will that comes with being human. Freedom of choice, however, entails absolute responsibility for one's actions, and loneliness, anxiety, and alienation are experienced along with a full appreciation of freedom. Each person, faced with the realities of death, loss, and ultimate aloneness, must create his or her own meaning in life.

Psychodynamic psychologists differ a great deal with regard to many issues, including human motivation, personality differences between the sexes, moral development, and the amount of personal control each individual has over his or her life. Theorists from other perspectives often criticize psychodynamic theories for their reliance on 51. _____ data and inference. Since structures such as the unconscious and the human spirit are unobservable, much of psychodynamic theory is not directly testable. At the same time, these theories make some intuitive sense and create a deeper sense of understanding of human personality than learning theory and biological research seem to provide.

MULTIPLE CHOICE SELF-TEST

1.   Psychoanalysis differs from other approaches to personality by:

   a.   focusing on a person's psychic reality.
   b.   emphasizing the importance of external environmental events.
   c.   relying on objective tests and inventories.
   d.   examining the challenges of adult adaptation.

2.   You want to go to a rock concert instead of studying for your psychology final. That part of your personality that would go to the concert regardless of the consequences would be the:

   a.   id.
   b.   ego.
   c.   alter ego.
   d.   superego.

3.   That structure of personality that operates on the morality principle is the:

   a.   id.
   b.   ego.
   c.   alter ego.
   d.   superego.

4.   If you think of Freud's notion of the personality as a furnace, the fuel that produces the heat or dynamism of the personality is the:

   a.   ego.
   b.   superego.
   c.   libido.
   d.   preconscious.

5.   Billy overeats, drinks too much alcohol, bites his nails, and talks incessantly. A Freudian could interpret this behavior as:

   a.   an example of rationalization.
   b.   an overdeveloped superego.
   c.   a reaction formation.
   d.   a regressed fixation at the oral stage.

6. Psychoanalytic ideas about the personality development of normal individuals were based on:

    a. scientific laboratory experimentation.
    b. disturbed individuals seeking therapy.
    c. observation and testing of representative individuals.
    d. longitudinal studies of children as they grew and developed.

7. Garth frequently seeks out and discovers pornographic pictures on the Internet, explaining that he wants to see the type of Cyberspace perverts who look at this "porno filth". Garth is exhibiting the defense mechanism of:

    a. repression.
    b. sublimation.
    c. projection.
    d. rationalization.

8. Freud would say Madonna is channelling her sexual impulses into a socially acceptable outlet (being a pop musician and dancer). This is an example of:

    a. denial.
    b. reaction formation.
    c. sublimation.
    d. repression.

9. John is a little afraid of flying and says to the stewardess on the plane, "Well at least if we crash I'll have had a good meal and a few free drinks!" This is an example of:

    a. intellectualization.
    b. humor.
    c. projection.
    d. reaction formation.

10. A man who says that his recurrent chest pains are probably "only heartburn" is probably experiencing the defense mechanism of:

    a. repression.
    b. denial.
    c. displacement.
    d. regression.

11. Wilma told her parents she got a C in her psychology course because all the As and Bs went to students who cheated on tests and had professionals write their papers. This is an example of:

    a.   displacement.
    b.   acting out.
    c.   rationalization.
    d.   reaction formation.

12. A person who is fixated in the anal stage would probably be:

    a.   a compulsive smoker or overeater.
    b.   excessively sloppy or excessively neat.
    c.   sexually dysfunctional or prudish.
    d.   self-absorbed.

13. According to Freud, the "man on horseback" structure of our personality who has to carry out but hold "in check" our sexual and aggressive impulses is the:

    a.   id
    b.   ego
    c.   superego
    d.   conscience.

14. A powerless person or group that is blamed for a problem by individuals who feel insecure or threatened is termed a(n):

    a.   persona.
    b.   animus.
    c.   misogynist.
    d.   scapegoat.

15. The psychoanalytic theorist who developed the concept of "womb envy" is:

    a.   John Bowlby.
    b.   Carl Jung.
    c.   Karen Horney.
    d.   Melanie Klein.

16. Freud's famous phrase "anatomy is destiny" is best interpreted to mean that:

     a.   gender roles are fixed and predetermined by our genes.
     b.   biology dictates the kind of person we will become.
     c.   masculinity and femininity are totally opposite concepts.
     d.   children's gender development is based on unconscious reactions to anatomical differences.

17. The Oedipal complex is resolved at approximately the age of:

     a.   five.
     b.   eight.
     c.   ten.
     d.   twelve.

18. According to Freud, during the Oedipal stage girls develop a sense of:

     a.   penis envy and a desire to bear children.
     b.   "clitoral anxiety" similar to castration anxiety in boys.
     c.   "womb egotism" and a sense that they are nurturers.
     d.   strong identification with their parent's standards of conscience.

19. A woman who failed to resolve her Oedipal love for her father falls in love with her therapist. According to Freud this is an example of:

     a.   transference.
     b.   free association.
     c.   intellectualization.
     d.   sublimation.

20. According to Carl Jung, the concept of "Mother Nature" is an example of a(n):

     a.   persona.
     b.   shadow.
     c.   mandela.
     d.   archetype.

21. According to Erik Erikson, the psychosocial stage in which you experience creativity and renewal either through parenthood or work is called:

     a.   ego integrity versus despair.
     b.   generativity versus stagnation.
     c.   identity versus role confusion.
     d.   competence versus inferiority.

22. Lisa's boyfriend is generally kind and considerate. However, when he forgets her birthday she says, "What a selfish jerk. What did I ever see in that idiot!" According to the object-relations school, Lisa is engaging in:

    a. rationalization.
    b. projection.
    c. splitting
    d. acting out.

23. Wendall is afraid to confront his boss at work. When he comes home he yells at his wife and their two children. This is an example of the defense mechanism of:

    a. acting out.
    b. sublimation.
    c. reaction formation.
    d. displacement.

24. Karen is constantly afraid of getting sick, and frequently has headaches and stomachaches. When she is examined by a physician, she is found to be quite healthy. Freud would say Karen is suffering from a:

    a. fixation.
    b. reaction formation.
    c. psychosis.
    d. neurosis.

25. The psychosexual stage in which the child settles down, goes to school and learns social rules for appropriate behavior is the _____ stage:

    a. latency
    b. genital
    c. phallic
    d. anal

26. A person who feels isolated in a hostile world can be described as having:

    a. ambivalence.
    b. an identity crisis.
    c. an inferiority complex.
    d. basic anxiety.

27. With regard to the expression of masculine and feminine qualities in a relationship, both Freud and Jung would say that men and women should:

    a.   express both their anima and animus, respectively.
    b.   repress the internal archetype of the Other.
    c.   project archetypes acquired in childhood onto our partner.
    d.   focus on only one archetype.

28. Psychodynamic individuals who study the universal struggle to find meaning in life are termed _____ psychologists:

    a.   analytic
    b.   self
    c.   object-relations
    d.   existential

29. The part of personality that is responsible for the defense mechanisms is the:

    a.   id.
    b.   ego.
    c.   superego.
    d.   preconscious.

30. You are worried about your best friend because he won't admit he has a serious drug problem. When you speak to your friend about his problem, you suggest that he is in denial about the effects that drugs have on his life. Which of the following psychological perspectives seems to have the greatest influence on your understanding of your friend's problem?

    a.   the biological perspective.
    b.   the cognitive perspective.
    c.   the psychodynamic perspective.
    d.   the sociocultural perspective.

TRUE FALSE SELF-TEST

T   F   1.   The psychodynamic approach to human behavior is often reflected in popular culture.

T   F   2.   Psychodynamic theories involve speculations about intrapsychic events.

T   F   3.   To Freud, jokes and dreams often have hidden psychic meaning.

T   F   4.   The ego operates on the pleasure principle.

T   F   5.   The id contains instincts towards both life and death.

T   F   6.   The superego represents the moral part of personality.

T   F   7.   Defense mechanisms operate consciously.

T   F   8.   Reaction formation occurs when one's own unacceptable feelings are repressed and then attributed to someone else.

T   F   9.   Regression occurs when a person reverts to a previous phase of psychic development.

T   F   10.   The phallic stage begins at puberty.

T   F   11.   Freud conducted many carefully controlled experiments.

T   F   12.   Feminists view Freud as something of a hero.

T   F   13.   Humor can be a defense mechanism.

T   F   14.   People who are fixated at the anal stage develop an Oedipus complex.

T   F   15.   Freud believed that gender roles are fixed and predetermined by our genes.

T   F   16.   To a Freudian, "psychic reality" is more important than objective reality.

T   F   17.   Freud's theory was readily accepted by the medical establishment of his day.

T   F   18.   Freud readily accepted dissent by his followers and incorporated their suggestions into his theory.

T   F   19.   Karen Horney coined the term "inferiority complex."

T   F   20.   According to Karen Horney, people are driven by basic anxiety.

T   F   21.   Alfred Adler's concept of a "drive for superiority", means that people desire to dominate other people.

T   F   22.   According to Carl Jung, there is a collective unconscious containing the universal memories and history of mankind.

T   F   23.   Carl Jung believed men should concentrate on developing their masculine side and eliminating their feminine side or "anima."

T   F   24.   Freud believed homosexuality was immoral and unnatural.

T   F   25.   Erikson emphasized the importance of psychosexual rather than psychosocial forces in the development of personality.

T   F   26.   People in the middle years of life are most concerned with Erikson's crisis of competence versus inferiority.

T   F   27.   Erikson was the first psychodynamic theorist to examine changes in the functioning of the ego throughout the life cycle.

T   F   28.   Object-relations theory holds that the first two years of life are the most critical for personality development.

T   F   29.   The object-relations theory agrees with classic Freudian notions on the nature of male and female psychological development.

T   F   30.   Phenomenology seeks to predict behavior and uncover hidden motivations.

KEY TERMS

psychoanalysis - A theory of personality and a method of psychotherapy developed by Sigmund Freud; it emphasizes unconscious motives and conflicts.

intrapsychic - Within the mind (psyche) or self.

id - In psychoanalysis, the part of the mind containing sexual and aggressive impulses; from the Latin for "it."

pleasure principle - The principle guiding the operation of the id as it seeks to reduce tension, avoid pain, and enhance pleasure.

libido - In psychoanalysis, the psychic energy that fuels the sexual instincts of the id.

ego - In psychanalysis, the part of the mind that represents reason, good sense, and rational self-control; it mediates between id and superego.

reality principle - The principle guiding the operation of the ego as it seeks to find socially acceptable outlets for instinctual energies.

superego - In psychoanalysis, the part of the mind that represents conscience, morality, and social standards.

defense mechanisms - Strategies used by the ego to prevent unconscious anxiety from reaching consciousness.

Oedipus complex - In psychoanalysis, a conflict in which a child desires the parent of the other sex and views the same-sex parent as a rival; the key issue in the phallic stage of development.

castration anxiety - In psychoanalysis, the boy's unconscious fear of castration by the powerful father that motivates the resolution of the Oedipus complex.

free association - In psychoanalytic therapy, a method of uncovering unconscious conflicts by saying freely whatever comes to mind.

transference - In psychoanalysis, a critical step in which the patient transfers unconscious emotions or reactions, such as emotional responses to his or her parents, onto the therapist.

basic anxiety - To Karen Horney, the feeling of being isolated and helpless in a hostile world; it is the motivating emotion in social relations.

inferiority complex - To Alfred Adler, an inability to accept one's natural limitations; it occurs when the need for self-improvement is blocked or inhibited.

collective unconscious - To Carl Jung, the universal memories and experiences of humankind, represented in the symbols, stories, and images (archetypes) that occur across all cultures.

archetypes - To Carl Jung, the universal, symbolic images that appear in myths, dreams, art, folklore, and other expressions of the collective unconscious.

object-relations school - A psychodynamic approach that emphasizes the importance of the infant's first two years of life and the baby's formative relationships.

splitting - In object-relations theory, the division of qualities into their opposites, as in the Good Mother versus the Bad Mother; it reflects an inability to understand that people are made up of good and bad qualities.

self psychology - A psychodynamic theory that emphasizes the importance of having a cohesive sense of self and self-esteem throughout life.

phenomenology - The study of events and situations as individuals experience them; in personality, the study of an individual's qualities from the person's own point of view.

humanistic psychology - An approach to psychology that emphasizes personal growth and the achievement of human potential rather than the scientific understanding, prediction, and control of behavior.

unconditional positive regard - To Carl Rodgers, love or support given to another person with no conditions attached.

existential psychology - An approach to psychology that emphasizes free will and responsibility for one's actions, and the importance of struggling with the anxieties of existence such as the need to find meaning in life and to accept suffering and death.

Suggested Research Projects

1.   Describe a character in a television show, movie, or novel using psychoanalytic concepts and terms. Summarize the character's behavior, then try to explain why the person acted as he or she did, using a psychodynamic theory that interests you.

Suggested Readings

Gay, P. (Ed.). (1989). <u>The Freud Reader</u>. New York: Norton. A large collection of Freud's most important writings.

Gay, P. (1988). <u>Freud: A Life For Our Time</u>. A biography of Freud which reveals the man behind the theory. New York: W.W. Norton & Company.

Horney, K. (1967). <u>Feminine Psychology</u>. New York: Norton. A collection of essays by one of the most influential women psychanalyses.

Jung, C.G. (1964). <u>Man and His Symbols</u>. New York: Doubleday. An illustrated description of the important of art and religion to psychology.

May, R. (Ed.). (1961). <u>Existential Psychology</u>. New York: Random House. A description of the application of existential philosophy to psychological functioning.

Robertson, R. (1992). <u>Beginner's Guide to Jungian Psychology</u>. YorkBeach, Maine: Nicholas-Hays. Readable introduction to the basic concepts of Jungian psychology.

Suggested Audio-Visuals

NOVA: Freud Under Analysis (1987). PBS Video.

CHAPTER 15

ANSWERS TO CHAPTER SUMMARY

1. childhood
2. Freud
3. instincts
4. id
5. ego
6. superego
7. defense mechanisms
8. neurotic
9. fixation
10. neurosis
11. oral
12. anal
13. Oedipal (phallic)
14. genital
15. latency
16. Oedipus conflict
17. phallic
18. unconscious
19. free association
20. transference
21. insight
22. fantasies
23. Karen Horney
24. penis envy
25. womb envy
30. neurotic
31. ideal self
32. Alfred Adler
33. drive for superiority
34. inferiority complex
35. social interest
36. style of life
37. Carl Jung
38. collective unconscious
39. archetypes
40. Erik Erikson
41. psychosocial
42. object-relations
43. introjects

44. splitting
45. attachment
46. ego boundaries
47. Heinz Kohut
48. self psychology
49. mirror
50. existential
51. mirror

ANSWERS TO MULTIPLE CHOICE SELF-TEST

1. A
2. A
3. D
4. C
5. D
6. B
7. C
8. C
9. B
10. B
11. C
12. B
13. B
14. D
15. C
16. D
17. A
18. A
19. A
20. D
21. B
22. C
23. D
24. D
25. A
26. D
27. A
28. D
29. B
30. C

ANSWERS TO TRUE FALSE SELF-TEST

1. T
2. T
3. T
4. F
5. T
6. T
7. F
8. F
9. T
10. F
11. F
12. F
13. T
14. F
15. F
16. T
17. F
18. F
19. F
20. T
21. F
22. T
23. F
24. F
25. F
26. F
27. T
28. T
29. F
30. F

CHAPTER 16

EVALUATING THE PSYCHODYNAMIC PERSPECTIVE

LEARNING OBJECTIVES

After reading and studying this chapter, you should be able to:

1. Explain the main contributions of the psychodynamic perspective, including its willingness to address "big picture" questions and the role of unconscious motives in seemingly irrational behavior.

2. Discuss misuses of and problems with this perspective, including psychodynamic reductionism, violations of the principle of falsifiability, overgeneralization from selected case studies, reliance on subjective projective methods, and reliance on the retrospective memories of patients.

3. Discuss the evidence regarding the efficacy of psychotherapy, and summarize the research on this issue.

4. Discuss the scientist-practitioner gap as reflected in the controversies regarding recovered memories of childhood abuse and multiple personality disorder and summarize the research on these issues.

CHAPTER 16 OUTLINE

I.   Researchers from other perspectives criticize psychodynamic psychology as unscientific.

II.   Contributions of this Perspective
      A.   The psychodynamic perspective addresses "big picture" questions ignored by other perspectives.
      B.   Psychodynamic psychologists use a variety of methods, including projective tests, and are willing to look everywhere for qualitative evidence to explore questions that are difficult to study by the usual methods of science.
      C.   The most important contribution of this perspective is in showing us that people are often the last to know the reasons for their own behavior.

III.   Misuses and Limitations of this Perspective
      A.   However, critics have raised several concerns:
            1.   psychodynamic reductionism is the tendency to reduce all behavior to unconscious processes and overlook the effects of biology, learning, and culture.
            2.   psychodynamic theories often violate the principle of falsifiability.
            3.   reliance on a limited number of case studies to illustrate universal principles results in overgeneralization.
            4.   retrospective analysis creates the illusion of causality. <u>Retrospective</u> studies, in which people tell interviewers or therapists about their pasts, often find what seem to be consistent patterns of development. <u>Longitudinal</u> studies, in which people are followed from childhood to adulthood, find more gradual and fluctuating development.
            5.   Some psychologists use subjective methods that are often unvalidated and unreliable, such as **projective tests** which are based on the psychodynamic assumption that when people are asked to make up a story about a neutral picture or statement, they will project their own unconscious feelings and beliefs onto it.
                  1.   One famous projective test is the **Thematic Apperception Test (TAT)**, which consists of a set of ambiguous pictures for which subjects are asked to speculate about what is happening.
                  2.   The TAT is useful in research on the **achievement motive**; people who have more internal motives to achieve as measured by the TAT are indeed more likely to actually do so.
                  3.   A criticism is that projective tests are used for clinical rather than research purposes, and when used this way may not be reliable or valid.

          4.   Another projective test is the **Rorschach Inkblot Test**, which consists of ten cards with symmetrical abstract "inkblot" patterns; many hypothesized relationships of the Rorschach with behavior have never been empirically validated.

          5.   Clinicians believe projectives are useful in establishing rapport and a good source of information because they are hard to fake; however, some clinicians rely exclusively on projective tests.

  B.   The "scientist-practitioner gap" has important implications for people's lives, such that some practitioners ignore findings of scientific research.

IV.   Issue #1: Assessing Psychotherapy

  A.   Hundreds of evaluation studies have found mixed results for the effectiveness of psychotherapy.

  B.   Psychotherapy is better than doing nothing at all.

  C.   The people who do the best in psychotherapy have treatable problems and are motivated to improve.

  D.   For many common mild disorders and everyday problems, paraprofessionals may be as effective as professional therapists.

  E.   In a significant minority of cases, psychotherapy is harmful because of the therapist's incompetence, bias against the client, or unethical behavior.

  F.   Psychodynamic approaches may be as helpful as other types of therapies except for major depression, anxiety, fears, panic, behavior problems, and family conflicts.

  G.   About half of all clients obtain the maximum benefits of therapy within 8 to 11 sessions, and another fourth benefit from treatment lasting up to a year in psychodynamic approaches; therefore, many use <u>time-limited analysis</u> offering 15, 20, or 25 sessions.

  H.   Serious mental problems require continued therapy.

  I.   Many psychotherapists are <u>eclectic</u>, avoiding strong allegiances to narrow therapies or schools of thought and borrowing from different approaches.

  J.   Therapy is a relationship which involves the therapist and client forming and effective bond called the **therapeutic alliance**.

  K.   For many problems, short-term therapy is as good as long-term therapy.

V.   Issue #2: The Mystery of Multiple Personality

  A.   **Multiple personality disorder (MPD)** involves the appearance, within one person, of two or more distinct identities, sometimes called "alters;" each identity appears to have its own memories, preferences, handwriting, and medical problems. MPD is now officially called **dissociative identity disorder**.

  B.   There are two totally incompatible views of what MPD is and what causes it.

          1.   Some believe it is an unwitting collusion between therapists and suggestible patients, and that if it exists at all, it is very rare.

2.   Others believe that MPD originates in childhood as a way of coping with terrible traumas.

C.   Studies comparing MPD patients with control subjects who are merely role-playing have not found any reliable differences in EEG activity.

D.   A sociocognitive view of MPD is that it is an extreme form of a normal human process: the ability we all have to present different aspects of ourself.

VI.   Issue #3: The Case of Recovered Memories

A.   Recovered memories of childhood events, such as abuse, are controversial. There are two schools of thought on this issue.

1.   Proponents of the <u>recovered memory school</u> believe that some of these memories are accurate.

2.   Proponents of the <u>pseudomemory school</u> believe that some of these memories are manufactured.

3.   Mental-health practitioners are overrepresented in the first group and research psychologists are overrepresented in the second.

B.   One disagreement between the two schools is over the basic question of whether traumatic events can be repressed and later recovered in accurate form.

1.   Some survivors of childhood sexual abuse report having repressed their memories for many years.

2.   However, the scientific study of memory has shown that memories are subject to distortion and the research on repression is ambiguous as is a definition of repression.

C.   Another disagreement concerns whether clients can be influenced by the therapist's explanations and leading questions.

1.   The recovered memory school believes this is unlikely when it comes to something as horrible as sexual abuse.

2.   The pseudomemory school argues that there is a risk of this happening, especially when practitioners are unaware of the findings on memory and hypnosis, as many are.

3.   Research suggests that traumatic pseudomemories can be induced by suggestion.

D.   Many psychodynamic therapists are less concerned about verifying a patient's perceptions and memories than validating the person's psychic reality; the pseudomemory school argues that this view is misguided, and that it matters if a person's beliefs are mistaken and can cause harm.

E.   The two schools of thought also disagree on the aftermath of abuse.

F.   In a landmark court case, the judge ruled that repressed memory evidence is not admissible in court because it is not scientifically reliable.

G.   In general, childhood memories are more reliable if they occur spontaneously and if there is other corroborating evidence.

348

CHAPTER 16 SUMMARY

The psychodynamic perspective is not afraid to address the "big picture" questions relatively ignored by other perspectives. However, critics have raised several concerns about psychodynamic theories and methods.

Critics of the psychodynamic approach cite its tendency to reduce all behavior to unconscious processes and neglect the importance of biology, learning, culture, and other factors known to affect behavior. Critics also point out that the construction of psychodynamic theories makes them impossible to either confirm or disprove, thus violating the principle of 1._____. Thus, they represent ideologies more than scientific theories, with their appeal based more on popularity than on research evidence.

Psychodynamic psychologists often rely on 2._____ studies, in which people tell interviewers or therapists about their pasts, to illustrate their theories. The findings from these cases are then 3._____ to the rest of the population and tend to find what seem to be consistent patterns of development. However, 4._____ studies, in which people are followed from childhood to adulthood, find more gradual and fluctuating development. They also base their theories on patients' memories, which have a great capacity for distortion. The tendency to draw causal inferences from events that occur together in time is unscientific.

Many psychodynamic practitioners have also relied on subjective methods such as 5._____ tests, which are based on the psychodynamic assumption that when people are asked to make up a story about a neutral picture or statement, they will project their own 6.____ feelings and beliefs onto it. One such famous test is the 7._____, which consists of a set of ambiguous pictures for which subjects are asked to speculate about what is happening. This test is useful in research on the 8._____ motive; people who have more internal motives to achieve as measured by this test are indeed more likely to actually achieve. However, the use of this test in clinical practice is suspect because it may not be reliable or valid. Another projective test is the 9._____ test, which consists of ten cards with symmetrical abstract "inkblot" patterns. However, many hypothesized relationships of the Rorschach with behavior have never been empirically validated. Clinicians believe projectives are useful in establishing rapport with clients, and they are a good source of information because they are difficult to 10._____.

Many psychodynamic practitioners consider what they do to be an art, and there exists in psychology a gap between 11._____ and 12._____. In recent years, empirical psychologists have tried to bridge this gap by using innovative research methods to measure the effectiveness of psychotherapy. Hundreds of evaluation studies have found mixed results for the effectiveness of psychotherapy. However, psychotherapy is often better than doing nothing at all. For many common mild disorders and everyday problems, 13._____ may be as effective as professional therapists. In a small minority of cases, psychotherapy may actually be harmful.

In response to research findings on and criticisms of the length of psychodynamic therapies, many newer psychodynamic approaches emphasize a smaller number of sessions, known as 14._____, which may be as effective as longer sessions for many disorders. On the other hand, serious mental problems typically require continuous therapy. Psychodynamic approaches may be as helpful as other types of therapies for certain problems with the exception of major depression, anxiety, fears, behavior problems, and family conflicts. However, many psychotherapists are 15._____, avoiding strong allegiances to narrow therapies or schools of thought and borrowing from different approaches. In any case, therapy is a relationship which involves the therapist and client forming an effective bond called the 16._____.

Tensions between scientists and practitioners are evident in debates about the nature of 17._____, which involves the appearance, within one person, of two or more distinct identities, and recovered memories of childhood sexual abuse. The two sides in this debate disagree about the reality of repression, the role of the therapist in influencing such memories, the results of emphasizing psychic reality during the psychotherapy process, and the aftermath of abuse. Those individuals, mainly mental-health practitioners, who are proponents of the 18._____ school, believe that some of these recovered memories are accurate. On the other hand, those individuals, mainly research scientists, who are proponents of the 19._____, believe that some of these memories are manufactured. These controversies show how important it is to try bridge the distance between clinical practice and scientific psychology by subjecting clinical assumptions to empirical tests.

MULTIPLE CHOICE SELF-TEST

1. Joe's therapeutic perspective is based on his assumption that his own interpretations of clients, people's everyday behavior, and society's myths are all that is necessary to construct a science of the mind. Joe would best be categorized as a _____ therapist:

   a. learning therapist
   b. sociocultural therapist
   c. cognitive therapist
   d. psychoanalytic

2. According to psychodynamic theories, an individual's current problems are most likely to be due to:

   a. learned patterns of behavior.
   b. unconscious dynamics.
   c. problems with family relationships.
   d. biological deficits.

3. In the early years of the nineteenth century, slaves were thought to suffer from "mental illness" if they wanted to escape from slavery. This "disorder" was known as:

   a. drapetomania.
   b. kleptomania.
   c. agoraphobia.
   d. nymphomania.

4. One of the major criticisms of psychodynamic theory is that it:

   a. is not falsifiable.
   b. is based on large samples.
   c. does not overgeneralize.
   d. does not use retrospective analysis.

5. In the psychoanalytic perspective causality is assessed through:

   a. meta-analysis.
   b. cross-sectional research.
   c. retrospective analysis.
   d. longitudinal research.

6. Many clinicians may score the same projective test differently. This is a problem which calls into question the test's:

    a.   fakeability.
    b.   subjectivity.
    c.   reliability.
    d.   standardization.

7. A subject in a research experiment is asked to look at a series of pictures and tell a story about each one of them. This subject is most likely being given the:

    a.   Thematic Apperception Test.
    b.   Rorschach Inkblot Test.
    c.   Projective Personality Inventory.
    d.   Psychodynamic Picture Test.

8. Studies which follow people from childhood to adulthood often find that psychological development fits a pattern of:

    a.   lockstep and consistent change.
    b.   randomness.
    c.   gradual and fluctuating changes.
    d.   precipitous stages.

9. Research on the Rorschach Inkblot test indicates that the test:

    a.   has repeatedly failed as a prediction of practical criteria.
    b.   is of great value as many of the relationships between personality dynamics and behavior have been empirically validated.
    c.   is easily fakeable and is useless in clinical practice.
    d.   is very reliable as clinicians often interpret the test in the same way, but is not valid.

10. One limitation of psychodynamic theory is:

    a.   that it looks at the "big picture."
    b.   its imaginative use of folklore and symbols.
    c.   its emphasis on self-knowledge.
    d.   its use of subjective methods and tests.

11. Psychodynamic theory will most likely be successful with:

    a.   mild emotional disorders.
    b.   long-standing personality disorders.
    c.   schizophrenia.
    d.   manic-depressive psychosis.

12. With respect to mild disorders and everyday problems, the success rates of paraprofessionals when compared to professional therapists is:

    a.   better.
    b.   the same.
    c.   worse.
    d.   uncertain.

13. According to surveys, most therapists use the _____ approach to therapy.

    a.   cognitive
    b.   psychodynamic
    c.   eclectic
    d.   learning

14. Therapeutic qualities such as empathy, warmth, and genuineness help to establish:

    a.   the therapeutic alliance.
    b.   transference.
    c.   projection of emotion.
    d.   overdependence.

15. Eve shifts from a shy, retiring, and "mousy" personality, to a flamboyant, talkative, and sexy personality, and then to a more even-tempered personality. Eve is likely to have the mental disorder of:

    a.   manic-depressive psychosis.
    b.   antisocial personality disorder.
    c.   schizophrenia.
    d.   dissociative identity disorder.

16.   Some practitioners view multiple personality disorder as a real disorder that has been largely undiagnosed. Most of these practitioners adhere to the:

    a.   scientist side of the scientist-practitioner model.
    b.   psychodynamic perspective.
    c.   clinical research perspective.
    d.   sociocultural perspective.

17.   According to psychodynamic theorists, multiple personality disorder is a mental splitting of the personality due to:

    a.   genetic defects.
    b.   hormonal imbalances.
    c.   ongoing childhood trauma.
    d.   ongoing patterns of reinforcement.

18.   Clinicians who support the multiple personality disorder claim it can be more accurately diagnosed because the physiological changes that occur within each personality, such as EEG activity, can't be faked. Research results on EEG activity indicate:

    a.   normal people can NOT create EEG changes.
    b.   support for the multiple personality disorder.
    c.   that EEG differences between different personalities are greater in the MPD patient.
    d.   EEG changes can be induced by MPD "personalities" and normal individuals who role-played different personalities.

19.   Many clinicians and researchers who are doubtful of the MPD diagnosis believe clinicians who believe in the existence of MPD create the disorder through:

    a.   exploration of childhood trauma.
    b.   their reliance on counterconditioning.
    c.   the power of suggestions.
    d.   conscious falsification of data.

20. Through therapy, an individual recovers memories of sexual abuse by her father that occurred when she was a child. Prior to therapy, these memories were considered to be:

    a. repressed.
    b. projected.
    c. sublimated.
    b. suppressed.

21. Most individuals who believe in the validity of recovered memories are:

    a. clinical researchers.
    b. academic scientists.
    c. psychological researchers.
    d. mental-health practitioners.

22. According to the psychodynamic perspective, repressed material is stored in the brain and can be retrieved when:

    a. counterconditioning occurs.
    b. anxiety associated with the memory is removed.
    c. countertransference takes place.
    d. memory displacement is removed.

23. When it comes to remembering traumatic experiences, most academic researchers believe people:

    a. remember all aspects of the experience.
    b. confabulate the entire experience.
    c. remember they experienced trauma but forget details.
    d. forget the event until the memory is recovered in therapy.

24. In general, childhood memories of abuse are most reliable if they occur:

    a. when recovered by a psychotherapist.
    b. spontaneously and if there is corroborating evidence.
    c. after extensive questioning by a police officer.
    d. when recovered by a medical doctor rather than a psychologist.

25. Tavris and Wade state that "if you agree with them, fine; but if you don't agree with them you are being defensive." This criticism of psychodynamic theory refers to:

    a.   psychodynamic reductionism.
    b.   drawing universal principles from case studies.
    c.   basing theories on retrospective accounts.
    d.   violating the principle of falsifiability.

TRUE FALSE SELF-TEST

T   F   1.   Psychodynamic psychologists are the most willing to use myths, cultural rituals, jokes, and stories as evidence for their theories.

T   F   2.   Psychodynamic psychologists believe a person's unconscious psychic reality is more important than biology, culture, and conscious thought processes.

T   F   3.   Culture affects psychological diagnoses, explanations, and labels for behavior considered to be abnormal.

T   F   4.   Psychoanalytic theory has been proven to be correct.

T   F   5.   Psychoanalysis is based on rigorous, scientifically reliable methods.

T   F   6.   Freud's theory was based on experiences with large, representative samples of people.

T   F   7.   Research supports the idea that gay men and lesbians are more emotionally disturbed than heterosexuals.

T   F   8.   Contemporary research on penis envy confirms Freud's notion.

T   F   9.   Psychoanalytic theories are typically based on adult recollections.

T   F   10. Most psychodynamic theorists have observed random samples of children at different ages to construct their theories of development.

T   F   11. Retrospective analysis is a scientifically sound method for determining causality between events.

356

T   F   12.   Longitudinal studies find consistent, lockstep patterns of developmental events.

T   F   13.   Freud's notion of a latency stage during which children lack sexual feelings has been confirmed by modern research.

T   F   14.   Projective tests rely on the assumption that people can express their unconscious feelings and beliefs by making up stories about a neutral picture or statement.

T   F   15.   When validated empirically, the TAT can be a useful research method.

T   F   16.   The majority of the relationships between personality dynamics as measured by the Rorschach Inkblot Test and behavior have been empirically validated.

T   F   17.   Psychotherapy is better than doing nothing at all.

T   F   18.   Professional psychologists are vastly more effective than paraprofessionals in treating many common mild disorders and everyday problems.

T   F   19.   In some cases psychotherapy can be harmful.

T   F   20.   Long-term therapy is more likely to be effective than short-term therapy.

T   F   21.   Most modern psychotherapists are psychodynamic in orientation.

T   F   22.   Multiple personality disorder is very common.

T   F   23.   Regarding multiple personality disorder, research suggests that physiological changes that occur within each personality can be faked.

T   F   24.   A recovered memory for abuse that allegedly took place in infancy should be regarded as doubtful.

T   F   25.   Research on memory supports the view that all forgetting of early memories is motivated by anxiety.

T   F   26.   It is very likely that a person can forget they experienced a trauma <u>at all</u>.

T   F   27.   Hypnosis is a useful technique in uncovering repressed memories.

T	F	28.	Most users of hypnosis are up-to-date on the empirical research on it.
T	F	29.	Traumatic pseudomemories can be induced by suggestion.
T	F	30.	Childhood sexual abuse inevitably causes long-term trauma and predictable symptoms.

KEY TERMS

projective tests - Psychological tests used to infer a person's motives, conflicts, and unconscious dynamics on the basis of the person's interpretations of ambiguous or unstructured stimuli.

achievement motive - A learned motive to meet personal standards of success and excellence in a chosen area.

Thematic Apperception Test (TAT) - A projective personality test that asks respondents to interpret a series of drawings showing ambiguous scenes of people.

Rorschach Inkblot Test - A projective personality test that asks respondents to interpret abstract, symmetrical inkblots.

therapeutic alliance - The bond of confidence and mutual understanding established between therapist and client that allows them to work together to solve the client's problems.

multiple personality disorder (dissociative identity disorder) - A controversial disorder marked by the appearance within one person of two or more distinct personalities, each with its own name and traits.

Suggested Readings

Amada, G. (1983, 1995). <u>A Guide to Psychotherapy</u>. NY: Ballatine Books. Answers common questions about psychotherapy including whether or not psychotherapy is effective, what happens during psychotherapy, and how to select a therapist.

Ceci, S.J., & Bruck, M. (1996). <u>Jeopardy in the Courtroom: A Scientific Analysis of Children's Testimony</u>. American Psychological Association. A comprehensive review of research on children's testimony. The book also discusses applied techniques used to evaluate children as witnesses.

Dawes, R. (1984). <u>House of Cards: Psychology and Psychotherapy</u>. New York: The Free Press. Critically examines the scientific validity of psychotherapy.

Loftus, E., & Ketcham, K. (1994). <u>The Myth of Repressed Memory: False Memories and Allegations of Sexual Abuse</u>. Prominent memory researcher argues against the notion of recovered memories.

Spanos, N.P. (1996). <u>Multiple Identities and False Memories: A Sociocognitive Perspective</u>. American Psychological Association. Spanos critically examines the proliferation of cases of multiple personality disorder (MPD) from a sociohistorical perspective and in light of scientific research relevant to the subject of MPD.

Suggested Audio-Visuals

PBS video (1995). <u>Frontline: Repressed Memories</u>. This video explores memory and how it works, techniques therapists use to access repressed memories, and the impact of accusations of abuse on the families of the accused.

CHAPTER 16

ANSWERS TO CHAPTER SUMMARY

1.   falsifiability
2.   retrospective
3.   generalize
4.   longitudinal
5.   projective
6.   unconscious
7.   Thematic Apperception Test
8.   achievement
9.   Rorschach Inkblot
10. fake
11. scientists
12. practitioners
13. paraprofessionals
14. time-limited analysis
15. eclectic
16. therapeutic alliance
17. multiple personality disorder
18. recovered
19. pseudomemory

ANSWERS TO MULTIPLE CHOICE SELF-TEST

1.   D
2.   B
3.   A
4.   A
5.   C
6.   C
7.   A
8.   C
9.   A
10. D
11. A
12. B
13. C
14. A
15. D
16. B
17. C
18. D

19.	C
20.	A
21.	D
22.	B
23.	C
24.	B
25.	D

ANSWERS TO TRUE-FALSE SELF-TEST

1.	T
2.	T
3.	T
4.	F
5.	F
6.	F
7.	F
8.	F
9.	T
10.	F
11.	F
12.	F
13.	F
14.	T
15.	T
16.	F
17.	T
18.	F
19.	T
20.	F
21.	F
22.	F
23.	T
24.	T
25.	F
26.	F
27	F
28.	F
29.	T
30.	F

CHAPTER 17

PUTTING THE PERSPECTIVES TOGETHER

LEARNING OBJECTIVES

After reading and studying this chapter, you should be able to:

1.   Summarize and discuss how the five psychological perspectives contribute to the understanding of musical appreciation and talent.

2.   Summarize and discuss how each of the five psychological perspectives contributes to our understanding of drug use and abuse.

3.   Define the four major classes of drugs.

4.   Compare and contrast the disease model with the learning model of addiction.

5.   Describe the contributions of each of the five perspectives to psychology in general and discuss how they can be used to analyze personal and social problems.

CHAPTER 17 OUTLINE

I.   The Whole Elephant
     A.   Musical talent and the appreciation of music can be examined from each of the five perspectives.
          1.   Everyone shares core musical abilities according to Howard Gardner, including the ability to recognize and appreciate the basic structure of music, which indicates that is a biologically based phenomena.
          2.   The biological perspective indicates musical <u>genius</u> is partly heritable.
          3.   Some persons, <u>idiot savants</u>, may have one stunning musical ability but be impaired in all other areas.
          4.   Musical ability is localized in the right hemisphere.
          5.   The sociocultural perspective indicates cultures differ regarding whether or not they emphasize <u>pitch</u> (melody), <u>rhythm</u> (sounds grouped according to a prescribed system), or <u>timbre</u> (the qualities of a tone that distinguish different sounds).
          6.   The cognitive perspective indicates that schemas for music are formed at a young age and that learning influences musical talent.

II. Drug Use and Abuse
     A.   A **psychoactive drug** is a substance that alters perception, mood, cognition, or behavior.
          1.   There are four major drug classifications.
               a.   <u>Stimulants</u> speed up central nervous system activity, and include cocaine, amphetamines, nicotine, and caffeine.
               b   <u>Depressants</u> (sedatives) slow down central nervous system activity and include alcohol, tranquilizers, and barbiturates.
               c.   <u>Opiates</u> mimic the action of endorphins, and include opium, heroine, morphine, and methadone.
               e.   <u>Psychedelics</u> produce alterations of consciousness, and include LSD, mescaline, and psilocybin.
          2.   <u>Marijuana</u> is probably the most widely used illegal drug in the United States and is not readily classifiable; it has properties of several of the other classes.
               a.   Danger of lung damage is less than smoking tobacco, but marijuana can cause lung damage.
               b.   THC is found in marijuana in greater concentrations, but people may adjust their intake to compensate.
               c.   Marijuana may have medical benefits by reducing nausea and vomiting for chemotherapy, reducing some symptoms of multiple sclerosis, alleviating some seizures in epileptic patients, and alleviating retinal swelling caused by glaucoma.

3. Drugs are an emotional subject for many people, who have difficulty separating moderate and occasional use from the dangers and costs of drug misuse.
    a. Moderate use is often relatively harmless.
        1. A longitudinal study revealed that moderate experimentation with drugs in adolescence was associated with better adjustment than either abstinence or abuse.
        2. Moderate use of alcohol may have some health benefits.
    b. The legal status and the dangerousness of a drug are relatively unconnected.
4. <u>Substance abuse</u> refers to a maladaptive pattern of substance use leading to clinically significant impairment or distress.

B. The Biological Perspective
    1. This perspective has focused on the physiology of drug effects and the biology of addiction.
    2. Psychoactive drugs act on brain neurotransmitters.
        a. **Tolerance** occurs when more and more of a drug is needed for a similar effect.
        b. **Withdrawal** symptoms are negative physical and psychological effects that occur when someone addicted to a drug stops taking it.
    3. Biological views of addiction are based on the <u>disease model</u>, which describes addiction as a biochemical process.
        a. There may be an inherited predisposition for alcoholism.
            1. Some studies have found a gene that affects the function of key dopamine receptors to be disproportionately present in alcoholics.
            2. Other studies have found either no difference or mixed findings.
            3. At this time, it cannot be concluded that a single gene causes alcoholism.
            4. Several genes may interact to affect the response to alcohol.
            5. Genes that affect temperament, personality, and liver functioning may have an indirect effect.
            6. Alcohol alters physiological functioning long-term, which may then cause alcoholism.
    3. Biological researchers seek medical solutions to drug addiction.

C. The Learning Perspective
    1. Researchers in this perspective hold a learning model of addiction.
        a. Drug effects depend partly on one's motivation for taking the drug.
        b. People get "addicted" to things other than drugs.

        c.   Reactions change when a user becomes familiar with the effects of a drug.

        d.   Drug use functions to allow escape or avoidance of problems.

2.   Drug use involves classical conditioning.

        a.   The drug's effect is the unconditioned stimulus for compensatory physiological responses.

        b.   Environmental cues are the conditioned stimuli.

        c.   The body reacts to conditioned stimuli with conditioned compensatory responses, which promotes tolerance to the drug.

        d.   Overdose is more likely to occur when conditioned stimuli are not present, because the usual conditioned compensatory response does not occur.

3.   These findings suggest that addicts can overcome dependence by changing environments and dealing with the problems to which drug use is a response.

4.   In contrast to the disease model, the learning model sees controlled drinking as a possibility for some former alcoholics.

D.   The Cognitive Perspective

1.   Cognitive research finds that responses to drugs depend heavily on expectations, beliefs, and motivations (mental set).

2.   People learn how to interpret the effects of a drug.

3.   Thinking that a drug is being taken will affect behavior.

        a.   Alcohol increases the likelihood of aggression only when people are aware that they are consuming it.

        b.   Alcohol provides a social excuse for behaving violently.

E.   The Sociocultural Perspective

1.   Drug use and abuse are affected by external conditions such as:

        a.   peer pressure.

        b.   environmental setting.

        c.   cultural practices.

2.   Research done from this perspective finds that:

        a.   many people go through a period of heavy drinking but become social drinkers when their environments change.

        b.   alcoholism rates are higher in cultures where children are forbidden to drink but drunkenness is condoned in adults.

        c.   alcoholism rates are lower in cultures where children are taught to drink responsibly and drunkenness in adults is disapproved.

        d.   alcoholism rates are higher in cultures that use alcohol as a rite of passage into adulthood and/or associate alcohol use with masculinity and power.

        e.   policies of total abstinence tend to increase rates of alcoholism rather than reduce them.

F.   The Psychodynamic Perspective
    1.   According to this perspective, alcohol and other drugs are used for internal, unconscious reasons; drug use allows one to protect the self from awareness of negative feelings.
        a.   In this view, maladjusted people are more likely to abuse drugs.
        b.   However, not every study has supported this idea; maladjustment can also be the result of drug or alcohol use.
    2.   This perspective offers useful descriptions of people who have already become addicted and the defense mechanisms they use.
G.   Integrating Insights from the five perspectives gives us a fuller understanding of the causes of drug abuse.
    1.   Drug abuse and addiction are most likely to occur in a person who:
        a.   has a biological vulnerability.
        b.   is in psychological pain.
        c.   is in an environment that supports drug abuse.
        d.   is reinforced for abusing drugs.
        e.   holds beliefs conducive to abuse and addiction.
    2.   Research findings suggest that reduction of drug abuse and addiction depends on changes in mental sets, environments, and cultural attitudes, and that total elimination of drug use is not realistic.

III.   Reflections on Psychology
A.   No single perspective can explain all psychological phenomena. Behavior is affected by:
    1.   biological factors such as physiology, heredity, and hormonal activity.
    2.   environmental factors that encourage certain kinds of learning.
    3.   the style and content of explanations for events.
    4.   the expectations and demands of others.
    5.   unconscious intrapsychic forces.
B.   Seeing a situation from all five points of view can inoculate laypeople and professionals alike against the temptations of psychobabble.

CHAPTER 17 SUMMARY

A 1._____ drug alters perception, mood, cognitions, or behavior. Drugs can be grouped into several classes. 2._____ speed up central nervous system activity, whereas 3._____slow this activity. 4._____ have pain-killing and euphoria-producing properties, and 5._____ are consciousness-altering drugs. 6._____ is difficult to classify, as its effects do not fit neatly into any of these groups.

While drug misuse presents considerable social problems, the effects of moderate use of some drugs are harmless or may even be beneficial. In all cultures, certain drugs are considered "good' and are legal, while others are considered "bad" and are illegal, but this distinction is usually drawn without any medical or biological basis. Psychologists from every perspective are interested in learning why some people use drugs responsibly whereas others 7._____ drugs by using them compulsively to the point where the person experiences serious negative effects.

Researchers from the biological perspective study the physiology of drug effects. They are interested in 8._____, which occurs when more and more of a drug is needed to achieve the same effect, and 9._____, which involves unpleasant or dangerous physical symptoms resulting from an abrupt cessation of drug use.

Biological views of addiction are based on the 10._____ model, which holds that biochemical processes are responsible for drug use. Some studies have located genes that might affect alcoholism, but the research evidence is far from conclusive. It is possible that several genes in interaction set the stage for a biological readiness, or 11._____, for alcoholism. Heavy drinking also alters physiological functioning over time.   Biological researchers are searching for medical solutions to the addiction problem.

The 12._____ model of addiction stands in contrast to the disease model. Theorists from this perspective point out that people become "addicted" to nonchemical stimuli, and that experience with a drug influences the drug's psychological effects. Principles of 13._____ conditioning have been used to explain tolerance, withdrawal, and overdose. In this model, the drug is the 14._____ stimulus and environmental cues act as conditioned stimuli for a 15._____ response by the body. The learning perspective implies that a cure for addiction must involve the alteration of environmental cues. In contrast with advocates of the disease model, advocates of the learning model believe that 16._____ drinking is possible for some former alcoholics.

The cognitive perspective has demonstrated the impact of 17._____ (expectations and motivations for using drugs) on responses to a drug. People behave differently when they believe they are taking a drug, even if they are not actually taking one. Expectations about drug effects are formed from observation and affected by culture.

The sociocultural perspective emphasizes the influence of 18._____ factors such as peer pressure and cultural tradition, on drug abuse. Longitudinal research has demonstrated that changes in drinking behavior occur with changes in environment, and cultures differ in rates of alcoholism, which is more likely to occur when children are forbidden to drink but adult 19._____ is condoned. Alcoholism is also more prevalent when 20._____ and power associated with alcohol.

The psychodynamic perspective holds that addictive behaviors are caused by internal, 21._____ forces. From this viewpoint, people abuse drugs because they are maladjusted and the drug acts as a 22._____ against unpleasant feelings.

In summary, people are vulnerable to drug abuse when they have biological predispositions and personal problems, especially when these occur in a social and cultural environment that supports abusive behavior.

No one psychological perspective can account for all behavior. Together, the five perspectives show us that people are affected by physiology, environmental forces, their interpretations of events, social and cultural factors, and unconscious dynamics.

MULTIPLE CHOICE SELF-TEST

1.   In the human brain, linguistic abilities are located in the:

        a.   left hemisphere.
        b.   right hemisphere.
        c.   cerebellum.
        d.   medulla.

2.   In the human brain, musical abilities are located in the:

        a.   left hemisphere.
        b.   right hemisphere.
        c.   cerebellum.
        d.   limbic system.

3.   Gardner's research suggests that the ability to recognize the basic structure of music is:

        a.   the result of an imitative process.
        b.   a biologically based phenomenon.
        c.   the result of one's reinforcement history.
        d.   due to the collective unconscious.

4.   Amphetamines are classified as:

        a.   depressants.
        b.   stimulants.
        c.   opiates.
        d.   psychedelics.

5.   Drugs that slow down the activity of the nervous system are called:

        a.   depressants.
        b.   stimulants.
        c.   opiates.
        d.   psychedelics.

6.   Cocaine is classified as a(n):

        a.   psychedelic.
        b.   depressant.
        c.   opiate.
        d.   stimulant.

7. Barbiturates are classified as:

   a. stimulants.
   b. depressants.
   c. opiates.
   d. psychedelics.

8. Another term for sedatives are:

   a. stimulants.
   b. depressants.
   c. opiates.
   d. psychedelics.

9. Heroin and morphine are examples of:

   a. stimulants.
   b. depressants.
   c. opiates.
   d. psychedelics.

10. Opiates relieve pain by mimicking the action of:

   a. acetylcholine.
   b. serotonin.
   c. adrenaline.
   d. endorphins.

11. Bill recently took a drug and is seeing brilliant colors and having distortions of perception. Bill most likely took a(n):

   a. depressant.
   b. stimulant.
   c. opiate
   d. psychedelic.

12. One type of drug that is difficult to classify is:

   a. heroin.
   b. mescaline.
   c. marijuana.
   d. caffeine.

13. With respect to drugs, many extremists make the error that:

    a. legal drugs are harmless and illegal drugs are equally dangerous.
    b. there are gradations of drug abuse and abuse.
    c. legal drugs are harmless and only some illegal drugs are dangerous.
    d. only lower class individuals use drugs.

14. Studies of hospital patients who are prescribed narcotics indicate that such patients:

    a. develop severe withdrawal symptoms and require special hospitalization prior to release.
    b. rarely, if ever, develop addictions to these drugs.
    c. are more likely in the future to use "hard drugs" once released from the hospital.
    d. are more likely to use marijuana and alcohol to get "high."

15. Current psychological research suggests that with most psychoactive drugs, detrimental effects are most directly related to:

    a. gender or race of user.
    b. age of user.
    c. body weight of user.
    d. frequency of usage.

16. Hank believes that alcohol increases aggression. If he is given alcohol without his knowledge, what is likely to happen to his level of aggressive behavior?

    a. It will increase.
    b. It will decrease.
    c. It will not change.
    d. It will increase, and he will not recognize he is more aggressive.

17. Some recent research suggests that adolescents who experimented with moderate amounts of alcohol and marijuana were:

    a. alienated and impulsive.
    b. well-adjusted.
    c. anxious and lacked social skills.
    d. emotionally constrictive.

18. Moderate drinking can have beneficial effects for:

   a. men who drink up to three drinks a day and women who drink one or at most two drinks per day.
   b. both women and men who drink about three drinks a day.
   c. no one at all.
   d. a very small proportion of men who are at high risk of cancer.

19. The second most important cause of cancer deaths and overall mortality in the United States is:

   a. heavy drinking.
   b. overeating.
   c. marijuana use.
   d. smoking tobacco.

20. One of the illegal drugs that can reduce the effects of multiple sclerosis, the number of seizures due to epilepsy, and the swelling caused by glaucoma is:

   a. opium.
   b. LSD.
   c. heroin.
   d. marijuana.

21. Psychoactive drugs work by affecting:

   a. cerebral-spinal fluid production.
   b. brain neurotransmitters.
   c. glial cells.
   d. the reabsorption of nutrients.

22. When habitual users of drugs such as heroin and tranquilizers suddenly stop taking the drug they experience:

   a. flashbacks.
   b. euphoria.
   c. withdrawal symptoms.
   d. tolerance.

23. One important assumption of the disease model of addiction is that:

    a.   addiction is a way of coping.
    b.   most problem drinkers can learn to drink in moderation.
    c.   treatment in group support lasts only as long as necessary.
    d.   a person must accept his or her identity as an addict.

24. With respect to alcohol addiction, researchers in the biological perspective would all agree that alcoholism is:

    a.   caused by a single gene.
    b.   a medical problem with a medical cause.
    c.   the result of alcohol altering brain function.
    d.   caused by a gene regulating dopamine production.

25. Theorists who believe that an individual's responses to psychoactive drugs depend on his or her expectations of the drug's effects would be best categorized as being of the _____ perspective.

    a.   biological
    b.   learning
    c.   cognitive
    d.   psychodynamic

26. Research indicates that the most important predictors of whether a problem drinker can learn to control excessive drinking are:

    a.   previous severity of dependence on the drug, social stability, and beliefs about the necessity of abstinence.
    b.   gender, social stability, and economic status.
    c.   previous severity of dependence on the drug, economic status, and race.
    d.   social stability, economic status, and beliefs about the necessity of abstinence.

27. Dawn went from an environment in which her entire family smoked cigarettes to one in which her roomates and co-workers do not smoke and disdain smoking. She was subsequently able to quit smoking after many previous repeated failures. Her success can be best explained by the _____ perspective.

   a. biological
   b. cognitive
   c. sociocultural
   d. psychodynamic

28. Numerous studies indicate that alcoholism is much <u>more</u> likely to occur in societies that:

   a. allow children to drink responsibly but disapprove of adult drunkenness.
   b. have more relaxed liquor laws as opposed to prohibition.
   c. forbid children to drink and condone adult drunkenness.
   d. teach children to drink alcohol in social settings at a young age.

29. Rodney's therapist believes that the reason why he takes drugs is to compensate for parental rejection. Rodney's therapist can be best categorized as being from the _____ perspective.

   a. cognitive
   b. learning
   c. biological
   d. psychodynamic

30. Research on low self-esteem indicates that it is a major cause of:

   a. violent behavior.
   b. poor school performance.
   c. teenage pregnancy.
   d. none of the above.

TRUE FALSE SELF-TEST

T   F   1.   Musical genius seems to be partly heritable.

T   F   2.   It is possible for someone to have severe overall intellectual impairment but have the ability to flawlessly imitate any musical piece.

T   F   3.   Musical abilities are located in the left hemisphere.

T   F   4.   Cultures are very similar in which of the fundamental components of music they emphasize.

T   F   5.   The majority of young children in some cultures are expected to be musically proficient.

T   F   6.   Most adults, anywhere in the world, have taken a psychoactive drug.

T   F   7.   Stimulants speed up activity in the central nervous system.

T   F   8.   Cocaine is a synthetic drug.

T   F   9.   Alcohol is a central nervous system depressant.

T   F   10.   Morphine and heroin mimic the effects of natural endorphins.

T   F   11.   Emotional reactions to psychedelics vary from person to person and from time to time for any individual.

T   F   12.   Marijuana is probably the most widely used illicit drug in the United States.

T   F   13.   All legal drugs are harmless.

T   F   14.   Adolescents who experiment moderately with alcohol and marijuana are at high risk for emotional problems.

T   F   15.   Moderate drinking can reduce the risk of heart attacks and strokes and increase longevity for men.

T   F   16.   Women should drink less than men.

T   F   17.   A weekly drinking "binge" is less harmful than a consistent daily drink.

T   F   18.   There are more deaths from cocaine than from tobacco.

T   F   19.   Research has demonstrated that marijuana has medical benefits.

T   F   20.   A single gene causes alcoholism in a direct way.

T   F   21.   When people take opiates to relieve pain, they usually get "high."

T   F   22.   All drug addicts go through physiological withdrawal symptoms when they stop taking addictive drugs.

T   F   23.   According to the learning model, "once an alcoholic, always an alcoholic."

T   F   24.   People will act intoxicated when they believe they are drinking liquor even if they are drinking plain tonic water.

T   F   25.   Many people who go through a period of heavy drinking can become moderate, social drinkers due to a change in environmental circumstances.

T   F   26.   Alcoholism is more likely to occur in cultures that teach children to drink in family settings.

T   F   27.   Policies or laws mandating total abstinence tend to increase rates of alcoholism.

T   F   28.   Some research indicates that personality factors thought to cause alcoholism are instead a result of alcoholism.

T   F   29.   Low-self esteem is strongly related to poor academic achievement and violence.

T   F   30.   Consumers of psychological information and services should have a cautious, open, and questioning attitude, rather than accepting information and services at face value.

KEY TERMS

psychoactive drug - A drug capable of influencing perception, mood, cognition, or behavior.

tolerance - The increasing resistance to a drug's effects with continued use; as tolerance develops, larger doses are required to produce effects once brought on by smaller ones.

withdrawal symptoms - Physical and psychological symptoms that occur when someone addicted to a drug stops taking it.

Suggested Research Project

1.   Survey your friends about how their attitudes and behaviors towards alcohol and drug use were formed. How were your own attitudes and behaviors formed? Is there any relationship between how you or your friend's attitudes and behaviors were shaped and actual drug/alcohol use?

2.   Examine another complex problem or topic that you have read about in newspapers and magazines, or have seen on television from all five perspectives.

Suggested Readings

Hunt, M. (1993). The Story of Psychology. NY: Anchor Books. An entertaining broad overview of the history of psychology and its attempts to understand the mind and causes of behavior.

CHAPTER 17

ANSWERS TO CHAPTER SUMMARY

1. psychoactive
2. stimulants
3. depressants
4. opiates
5. psychedelics
6. marijuana
7. abuse (misuse)
8. tolerance
9. withdrawal
10. disease
11. predisposition
12. learning
13. classical
14. unconditioned
15. compensatory
16. controlled
17. mental set
18. environmental (social)
19. drunkenness
20. masculinity
21. unconscious
22. defense

ANSWERS TO MULTIPLE CHOICE SELF-TEST

1. A
2. B
3. B
4. B
5. A
6. D
7. B
8. B
9. C
10. D
11. D
12. C

13.	A
14.	B
15.	D
16.	C
17.	B
18.	A
19.	A
20.	D
21.	B
22.	C
23.	D
24.	B
25.	C
26.	A
27.	C
28.	C
29.	D
30.	D

ANSWERS TO TRUE-FALSE SELF-TEST

1.	T
2.	T
3.	F
4.	F
5.	T
6.	T
7.	T
8.	F
9.	T
10.	T
11.	T
12.	T
13.	F
14.	F
15.	T
16.	T
17.	F
18.	F
19.	T
20.	F
21.	F
22.	F
23.	F

24. T
25. T
26. F
27. T
28. T
29. F
30. T